INTERNATIONAL DEVELOPMENT IN FOCUS

Back to School
Pathways for Reengagement of
Out-of-School Youth in Education

Subhashini Rajasekaran and Joel Reyes

© 2019 International Bank for Reconstruction and Development / The World Bank
1818 H Street NW, Washington, DC 20433
Telephone: 202-473-1000; Internet: www.worldbank.org

Some rights reserved

1 2 3 4   22 21 20 19

Books in this series are published to communicate the results of Bank research, analysis, and operational experience with the least possible delay. The extent of language editing varies from book to book.

This work is a product of the staff of The World Bank with external contributions. The findings, interpretations, and conclusions expressed in this work do not necessarily reflect the views of The World Bank, its Board of Executive Directors, or the governments they represent. The World Bank does not guarantee the accuracy of the data included in this work. The boundaries, colors, denominations, and other information shown on any map in this work do not imply any judgment on the part of The World Bank concerning the legal status of any territory or the endorsement or acceptance of such boundaries.

Nothing herein shall constitute or be considered to be a limitation upon or waiver of the privileges and immunities of The World Bank, all of which are specifically reserved.

Rights and Permissions

This work is available under the Creative Commons Attribution 3.0 IGO license (CC BY 3.0 IGO) http://creativecommons.org/licenses/by/3.0/igo. Under the Creative Commons Attribution license, you are free to copy, distribute, transmit, and adapt this work, including for commercial purposes, under the following conditions:

Attribution—Please cite the work as follows: Rajasekaran, Subhashini, and Joel Reyes. 2019. *Back to School: Pathways for Reengagement of Out-of-School Youth in Education*. International Development in Focus. Washington, DC: World Bank. doi: 10.1596/978-1-4648-1404-4 License: Creative Commons Attribution CC BY 3.0 IGO

Translations—If you create a translation of this work, please add the following disclaimer along with the attribution: This translation was not created by The World Bank and should not be considered an official World Bank translation. The World Bank shall not be liable for any content or error in this translation.

Adaptations—If you create an adaptation of this work, please add the following disclaimer along with the attribution: This is an adaptation of an original work by The World Bank. Views and opinions expressed in the adaptation are the sole responsibility of the author or authors of the adaptation and are not endorsed by The World Bank.

Third-party content—The World Bank does not necessarily own each component of the content contained within the work. The World Bank therefore does not warrant that the use of any third-party-owned individual component or part contained in the work will not infringe on the rights of those third parties. The risk of claims resulting from such infringement rests solely with you. If you wish to re-use a component of the work, it is your responsibility to determine whether permission is needed for that re-use and to obtain permission from the copyright owner. Examples of components can include, but are not limited to, tables, figures, or images.

All queries on rights and licenses should be addressed to World Bank Publications, The World Bank Group, 1818 H Street NW, Washington, DC 20433, USA; e-mail: pubrights@worldbank.org.

ISBN: 978-1-4648-1404-4
DOI: 10.1596/978-1-4648-1404-4

Cover photo: Saadetalkan/iStock by Getty Images. Used with the permission of iStock by Getty Images. Permission required for reuse.
Cover design: Debra Naylor / Naylor Design Inc.

Contents

Acknowledgments vii
About the Authors ix
Executive Summary xi
Abbreviations xxv

CHAPTER 1: Introduction 1

    Defining out-of-school and at-risk youth 2
    Understanding types of risk factors affecting out-of-school youngsters 2
    The associations between risk factors and outcomes 6
    Characteristics of risks faced by out-of-school adolescents and youth 7
    Overlaps between research on risk, on resilience, and on positive youth development 9
    The integrative view of risk, resilience and positive youth development 11
    Notes 12
    References 13

CHAPTER 2: Educational Disengagement and the Benefits of Reengagement 19

    What is educational engagement and why is it important? 19
    What is reengagement and why is it needed? 24
    Evidence of social and economic benefits of investing in educational reengagement 25
    Notes 26
    References 26

CHAPTER 3: Methodology 29

    Methodological framework 29
    Search strategy 31
    Limitations 32
    Audience 33
    Notes 33
    References 34

CHAPTER 4: Evidence on School Engagement and Reengagement: What Works, How & Why, for Whom, and in What Contexts? 35

What works: reengagement interventions and effect sizes 35
How reengagement interventions work 42
For whom and in what contexts do reengagement interventions work? 54
Why these interventions work: accumulated evidence from multiple disciplines 64
Locating the complex evidence: what, how, why, for whom, and in what contexts? 66
Notes 67
References 69

CHAPTER 5: Understanding the Complex Process of Reengagement 77

Reengagement programs with multiple interventions: the evidence 77
A synthesis of the complex process of reengagement: the interrelation of core and enabling interventions 83
Initial thoughts on generalizable causal mechanisms to guide design 85
Notes 87
References 87

CHAPTER 6: Implications for Program Design and Implementation 89

A theory of change for education reengagement of at-risk and out-of-school adolescents and youth 90
Principles for program development 93
Policy questions 98
Notes 101
References 101

CHAPTER 7: Conclusion 103

Note 104
Reference 104

APPENDIX A: Risk Factors 105

APPENDIX B: Evidence Summary of What Works 107

APPENDIX C: Additional Reading 111

Boxes

ES.1	Potential mechanisms of reengagement	xvi
ES.2	Considering and addressing a complex set of needs	xx
1.1	Gender-related risks vary across regions	4
2.1	The case of Turkey: Reengaging out-of-school at-risk youth	23
4.1	A brief note on the magnitude and implications of effect size estimates	42
4.2	Successful examples of teacher training programs from three studies	47
4.3	Case example: How person-context characteristics moderate intervention effectiveness	55
5.1	The reengagement mechanism: Stages of the mentor-mentee relationship	84
6.1	Lessons learned from the design and implementation of the project: reengaging at-risk and out-of-school youth in education in Turkey	99

Figures

ES.1   Global out-of-school adolescents and youth of secondary school age by region, 2016   xii
ES.2   Out-of-school adolescents and youth of secondary school age by country income group, 2016   xiii
1.1   Integrative view of risk, resilience, and positive youth development   11
2.1   Relationship between social supports, academic self-efficacy, educational engagement, and academic and social-emotional outcomes   21
2.2   Link between social supports, self-efficacy, and educational engagement moderated by risk factors   21
2.3   Hypothesis of the reengagement mechanism   22
2.4   Characteristics of education reengagement   24
2.5   Education reengagement outcomes   25
3.1   Methodological framework for design and implementation of complex developmental challenges   30
4.1   Flexible education reengagement pathways   59
4.2   Framework of quality in flexible learning programs in Australia   60
4.3   Methodological framework: Reengaging at-risk and out-of-school adolescents and youth   67
5.1   Interlinkages between education reengagement mechanisms, interventions, and supporters   85
5.2   Reengagement program design elements   86
6.1   Inputs, products, and services for reengagement   91
6.2   A theory of change for reengaging at-risk and out-of-school adolescents and youth   93
6.3   A proposed theory of change—including what works, how, and why   94

Acknowledgments

This study was prepared by Subhashini Rajasekaran (Economist (YP)) and Joel Reyes (Senior Institutional Development Specialist) to inform the design of a World Bank project, "Reengagement of At-Risk Youth in Education in Turkey." The impetus for this work was provided by the Life Long Learning Department of the Ministry of National Education, Turkey.

Many individuals provided valuable inputs and suggestions for this work. Particular thanks go to the peer reviewers for their valuable comments: Alexandria Valerio (Lead Education Specialist), Juan Manuel Moreno (Lead Education Specialist), Dina N. Abu-Ghaida (Lead Economist), and Marjorie H. Chinen (Consultant).

The team owes gratitude for the guidance and support of the World Bank Senior Management including Keiko Miwa, Director of the Education Global Practice; Harry Anthony Patrinos, Education Practice Manager for the Europe and Central Asia Region; and Mario Cristian Aedo Inostroza, Education Practice Manager for the South Asia Region.

The study benefited immensely from discussions and guidance from colleagues at the World Bank, with special thanks to comments and encouragement received from Veronica Silva Villalobos, Quentin T. Wodon, Peter Darvas, Shahram Paksima, Marelize Gorgens, and Kathy A. Lindert.

Thanks to Marc DeFrancis for patiently editing this work and to Marta Helena Reis de Assis and Sujani Ali for their administrative support. We also thank the World Bank Publishing Program for publishing support.

About the Authors

Subhashini Rajasekaran is an Economist (YP) at the World Bank working in the area of education and skills development. Prior to this, she worked at McKinsey & Co. on education reform with public-private partnerships in India, and over the last nine years, with several governmental and nongovernmental organizations. Her research interest is in strengthening learner engagement and outcomes in preuniversity education, with particular focus on quality of learning environments, teacher management, and effective utilization of data for decision-making at all levels. She completed her bachelor's degree in engineering, and holds a master's degree in education from Tata Institute of Social Sciences (Mumbai) and a postgraduate diploma from the Indian School of Business (Hyderabad).

Joel Reyes is a Senior Institutional Development Specialist (education sector), with 25 years of experience in the World Bank Education Global Practice (in Africa, Europe and Central Asia, Middle East and North Africa, Latin America and the Caribbean, and South Asia). From 2013–15, he cochaired the steering committee of the International Network for Education in Emergencies (INEE). His professional and research interests focus on complex social and education problems, especially in fragile, conflict- and/or violence-affected contexts. His academic background has cut across different levels of social and educational development: he is a doctoral candidate in international education from the University of Sussex (United Kingdom) and has been awarded master's degrees in international development from Columbia University (New York) and organizational development from Johns Hopkins University (Baltimore). He led the design of the World Bank's work on Education Resilience Approaches (ERA), within the System Assessment for Better Education Results (SABER). He is currently Education Team Leader in Turkey, supporting the country in its transition from the emergency response for almost four million Syrian refugees, to institutionalized education services and ongoing development efforts. As part of his doctoral research, he is developing the "Transformative Resilience Framework," aimed at guiding more relevant research of change from adversity to wellbeing, including the use of qualitative approaches.

Executive Summary

RATIONALE

The rationale of this study rests on a protracted social and global problem: the large number of out-of-school adolescents and youth, especially those living in adverse life circumstances. Young people who are excluded from education often face multiple and overlapping disadvantages. Globally, 263 million children, adolescents, and youth in the age group of 6–17 years are out of school, according to United Nations Education, Scientific and Cultural Organization (UNESCO's) Institute of Statistics (UIS dataset, February 2018). Of these, about 76 percent are adolescents and youth of lower- and upper-secondary school age, and more than 150 million youth are from regions facing fragile and conflict situations. Considering that currently 2 billion people are affected by fragility, conflict, and violence, and that by 2030, 46 percent of the global poor are likely to be exposed to fragile and conflict situations, complex life risks such as forced displacement and related educational risks will continue to be prevalent. These also impact displaced youth living in host communities, where they tend to be exposed to socio-economic challenges.

Out-of-school, at-risk adolescents and youth face an array of challenges such as extreme poverty, work and family demands as heads-of-household, early marriage, caregiving for younger siblings or psychologically and physically injured parents, and exposure to risky behaviors. Moreover, those who resettle across international borders often carry out these tasks while managing a new language, education system, and culture, typically under difficult economic and legal circumstances. Aside from this, many youngsters across the world leave school due to factors related specifically to school culture such as lack of teacher attentiveness, segregation and unequal treatment, and a disconnect between the learning content and their interests.

Globally, out-of-school rates have not shown a progressive decline in recent years. The global trend for the upper-secondary age group is flattening at 36 percent, while for lower-secondary it has been at 16 percent since 2012 (UIS dataset 2018). These high rates for older cohorts can be explained by a variety of reasons: many youths never entered school, upper secondary education is often not compulsory, and upper secondary school-age youth may choose employment over continuing their education (UNESCO 2016).

FIGURE ES.1

Global out-of-school adolescents and youth of secondary school age by region, 2016

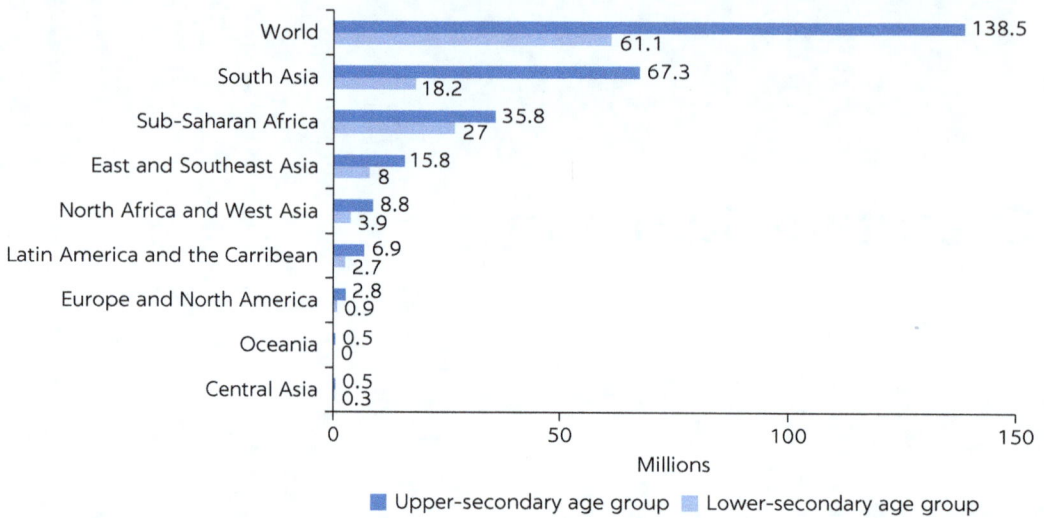

Source: UNESCO UIS Stats; UNESCO 2018.
Note: 61 million, or 23 percent of the total, are adolescents of lower-secondary school age; and 139 million, or 53 percent of the total, are youth of upper-secondary school age.

The global lower-secondary out-of-school rate (16 percent) is nearly twice as high as the primary out-of-school rate (figure ES.1). Three regions are home to nearly nine out of ten out-of-school adolescents of lower-secondary age (12–14 years): Sub-Saharan Africa (27 million), South Asia (18 million), and East and South-East Asia (8 million). Sub-Saharan Africa is also the region with the highest rate of out-of-school adolescents (37 percent), followed by South Asia (17 percent), and North Africa and West Asia (14 percent).

At the upper-secondary level, 139 million school-age youth (15–17 years) were not in school in 2016 (figure ES.1), 14 million more than the combined number of out-of-school children and adolescents of primary and lower-secondary school age. The largest proportion of out-of-school youth, 67 million, live in South Asia, a further 36 million live in Sub-Saharan Africa, and 16 million live in East and South-East Asia. More than half of all youth are out of school in sub-Saharan Africa (58 percent), as are nearly half of all youth in South Asia (48 percent) (UNESCO-UIS 2018).

Given the technological strides being made worldwide and the changing nature of work, failing to educate and train the next generation of workers and leaders in essential skills will contribute to intergenerational persistence of poverty and inequality, lock in gender disparities, obstruct social mobility, and undercut the effective utilization of this demographic capital. This would have substantial, long-term adverse consequences for the shared economic and social well-being of all. A promising pathway to guide these youngsters toward social and economic advancement is through education reengagement interventions that can provide necessary support structures to deliver positive outcomes and help them make a smooth transition into a stable and productive life.

This study specifically focuses on the heterogenous population group of adolescents and youth—ages 12–17 years—who have left school early and face multiple disadvantages, accounting for variation in their individual and

FIGURE ES.2

Out-of-school adolescents and youth of secondary school age by country income group, 2016

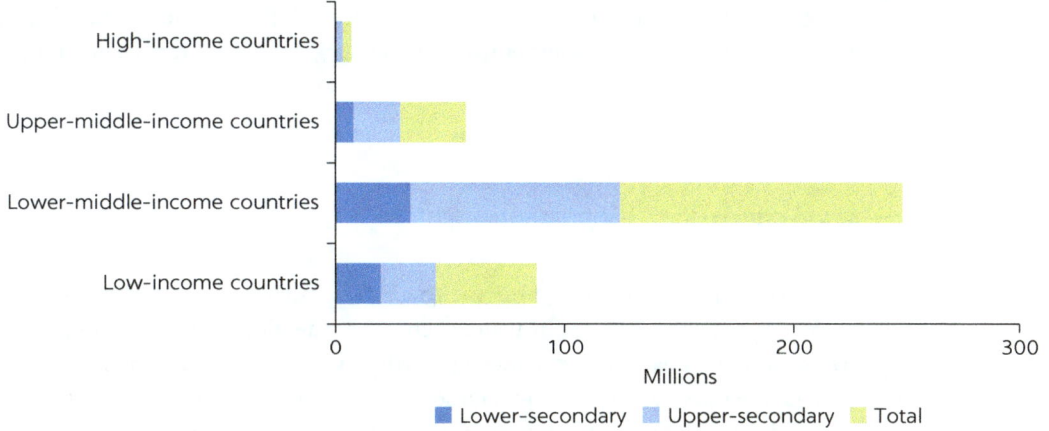

Source: UNESCO UIS Stats; UNESCO 2018.
Note: The largest number of out-of-school adolescents and youth of secondary school age are in lower- and lower-middle-income countries, mainly in South Asia and Sub-Saharan Africa.

contextual characteristics. With limited options for engaging with the formal education system and a history of often difficult past experiences, many are unable to bounce back and reconnect. To break through this impasse, a combination of protective and promotive factors is needed to support these individuals in re-engaging in an education program. Relevant education services can support their resilience through interventions for positive adaptation and development in the context of severe adversity and disadvantage. Comprehensive interventions for young people at risk appear to work better with respect to both positive and negative outcomes when goals include the promotion of competence and positive achievements in addition to the prevention or treatment of symptoms and negative behaviors (Cicchetti et al. 2000; Cowen 2000; Luthar and Cicchetti 2000; Masten 2001; Masten and Coatsworth 1998).

To make these interventions work requires a thoughtfully designed mix of resources. These educational and life resources should not only be available and accessible, they should also nudge the youth to exercise personal agency to navigate their way to identify relevant services they require and to utilize these to meet their developmental needs. These resources can offer protective services to ensure minimum livelihoods and safety; psychological services to promote feelings of self-esteem and a sense of attachment; and institutional services to access health care, schooling and opportunities to grow and display their talents to others (Ungar 2008). Considering the size and nature of the challenge, it is equally important to carefully consider both the scalability and complexity of the interventions for creating impact.

OBJECTIVE

This study aims to identify what works, how and why to re-engage and retain out-of-school and at-risk adolescents and youth in education and explore for whom and in what contexts the identified interventions can be effective. As a working definition for this study, reengagement is a process for out-of-school and at-risk 12-to-17-year-old adolescents and youth—both early school leavers and youth not in education, employment or training (NEETs)—to re-enroll, participate in, and complete their education. Reengagement programs can target a range of outcomes addressing cognitive, psychosocial, protective, and developmental domains.

KEY FINDINGS

Our review of research findings on re-engaging at-risk youth into education shows the complexity of risks faced by youth at both the individual and contextual levels. These multidimensional risks contribute to the education disengagement of youth and adolescents. Reengagement solutions are also multidimensional, including protective and promotive interventions. Following these general findings, the study identified interventions that have shown statistically significant impacts and further examined how, for whom, and in what contexts they work.

Understanding risk, resilience and positive youth development

The stressors young people face are complex and include risk factors related to the individual and to the context. Individual risk factors can be organized into five categories: demographic, geographic, cognitive, emotional, and social/behavioral. Contextual factors comprise of risks related to family and household, school, community, and macro-level structural factors. Risk-related research studies consistently show that persistent experiences of adversity have long-term detrimental effects on the cognitive, emotional, behavioral, and physical functioning of children, adolescents, and youth with long-lasting negative effects in adult life.

Stressors are cumulative and young people face risks as a series of steps along a continuum. The process of exposure to risk moves from minimal risk to remote, imminent, and high risk and then, finally, to participation in the very actions and behaviors that define the risk categories such as dropping out, engaging in risky sexual behavior, and criminality. Young people of school-going age who have left school early without completing their education are highly likely to be facing several adversities and to actively demonstrate imminent to high-risk behaviors (Masten and Powell 2003; McWhirter et al. 2017).

The risk factors faced by out-of-school young people have three characteristic features: they are complex, cumulative, and interact in a social ecology (individuals in context). Using a social ecology frame, risks can be understood to be in an open system, since they emanate from multiple proximal social contexts, such as the individual, family, school, and community, as well as distal factors such as public policies, economic climate, and societal norms. Risks have cumulative impact: research consistently shows that greater the number of risk factors a young person experiences, the worse the academic outcomes, including poorer grades and increased absences. The type of risk appears to be secondary to the number of negative factors experienced. The temporally and culturally dynamic relationship between youth and their environment leads to a complexity of multiple risks, multiple outcomes, and growth processes. The level of risk on a risk gradient is a function of the assets (as an individual) and resources (from the environment) available to the young person in his/her context.

The literatures of risk, resilience and positive youth development offer complementary perspectives on the protective and development process of at-risk youth. All young people are affected by a unique set of risks and protective and promotive factors (individual and contextual), and so need "supports" for achieving positive outcomes. The promotive factors (individual assets and environmental resources) have an inverse relationship with the risks, but they have a direct effect on development outcomes. Increasing the promotive factors has the same effect as reducing the risks, namely, better outcomes. On the other hand, protective factors moderate the supports by counteracting the risks. Thus, there are two pathways—protective and promotive—that mediate the relation between the supports and the development outcomes. Recognizing this complexity, it should also be noted that protective and promotive factors are not always mutually exclusive.

These research findings help infer an integrative view of youth development identifying a minimum of two pathways for healthy outcomes. These two pathways are (1) the protecting pathway, through which *risks* are mediated by protection interventions, leading to positive outcomes; (2) the promoting pathway, through which *assets and resources* strengthen support factors, directly leading to healthier outcomes (see figure 1.1 in chapter 1). Both these pathways are part of a dynamic and interactive system within a social ecology, hence interventions need to attend to all levels of this ecology: individual, family, school, community, and macro-structural. A resilience approach does not aim to build individual assets alone (Reyes 2013). Studies also show that not all risk, protection, and promotion factors are universally relevant, that is, a factor that may be a risk in one context may act as a protective element in another, and vice versa. For example, education can be used as a conduit to generate further social exclusions *or* to promote social cohesion (Bush and Saltarelli 2000).

The complexity of education engagement, disengagement, and reengagement

Educational engagement refers to a multidimensional, person-context process, including three components: behavioral engagement, affective engagement, and cognitive engagement. These components develop as a function of daily interactions between a developing young person and his or her experiences in various academic and social settings. Extensive literature and empirical evidence show that the presence of positive social supports in different settings helps increase academic self-efficacy, which in turn is associated with better academic and social-emotional outcomes (Center for Promise 2014). Emerging research suggests that teacher support plays an important and active role among high-risk youth, along with support from other adults (parents, family, mentors, et al.).

> **BOX ES.1**
>
> ### Potential mechanisms of reengagement
>
> Recognizing and embracing the complexity of interactions and influences in the process of education engagement, we present a hypothesis of the mechanism of reengagement (figure 2.3)—that the risks, protection, and promotion factors mediate the pathways for the social supports, self-efficacy, engagement, and positive developmental outcomes.

Four types of social support have been identified: Emotional, informational, appraisal, and instrumental. Emotional support provides comfort, caring, and trust. Informational support provides useful advice and insights addressing the specific needs of the young person. Appraisal support provides constructive feedback on strengths and developmental areas for informing self-evaluation. Instrumental support provides tangible resources or services. Different types of social supports can be provided by different individuals, including parents, teachers, peers, and other caring adults. Besides the number of supports, the quality, content, and appropriate matching of the support matter.

Early school leaving involves numerous causes and consequences and is a process of disengagement and, eventually, dropping out. This is a long-term process wherein young people may leave due to both academic and nonacademic reasons. Academic reasons could be related to the lack of a curriculum that is interesting or relevant to their future, poor academic "fit" with pace, mode, or language of instruction, or failure to succeed in school, including grade retention, difficult school transitions, and weak academic skills. Nonacademic reasons could be vulnerable life events such as forced displacement, extreme poverty, health issues, pregnancy, parenting, head-of-household responsibilities; a negative school climate, including segregation and a disruptive or unsafe school environment; or disciplinary removal from school due to risky behaviors such as drug use.

Programs to re-engage youth must provide interventions that are both 'protective' (of risks) and 'promotive' (of assets and resources). An outcome to re-engage and retain at-risk youth in the education process needs interventions that address behavioral, affective, cognitive, protection, and developmental needs. To counteract risks, vulnerable youth need protection through the availability, access, and quality of financial, health, and social welfare services. Evidence shows that financial incentives not only help satisfy basic needs but can also have positive psychological effects. Integrated support services help address the complex and diverse needs of at-risk learners such as healthcare, housing, legal services, and childcare services. Promotive interventions must address their emotional, cognitive, and behavioral needs, including strengthening self-efficacy, persistence, goal setting, life planning, developing education skills and attaining relevant qualifications. A combination of protective and promotive interventions, albeit complex, best fit the realities of vulnerable adolescents exposed to multiple risks (box ES.1).

Reengagement involves reaching out to, connecting with and addressing specific needs of at-risk out-of-school young people so that they enroll, participate, and complete their education and strengthen their social, emotional, and cognitive abilities. A successful educational reengagement process would focus on (1) increasing the number and intensity of protective and promotive supports that can mitigate the adverse effect of risk exposure; and (2) provide access to varied and flexible educational pathways to access alternative avenues and gain recognized qualifications and skills. In doing so, such a reengagement process would place youth on a positive life trajectory that opens doors to new opportunities.

Reengagement in education is a cumulative, nonlinear, and complex process that requires time and a variety of supports. A gradual process, it requires a range of interventions with multiple pathways and opportunities for engagement. The range of literature shows complexity in both outcomes and interventions. Also, it is not just an individual process but occurs in a broader context that requires the support of the school and community, as well as of education and other social policies. In designing policies and programs, it is not enough to know only what works to re-engage out-of-school youth, one must also determine how these identified interventions are to be implemented. Developing a nuanced understanding of why certain interventions work provides additional insights that validate the science behind the interventions, sheds light on their generalizability (or, conversely, their context-dependency), and their application to and level of success in other related fields.

Reengagement is not about providing low-cost and low-prestige remediation options, which in themselves can become another cause for exclusion. To be successful, reengagement requires that systemically, more and better educational entry points exist and support at-risk young people to participate and succeed. This would lead to long-term aggregated societal benefits in the form of increased graduation rates, decreased unemployment rates, and expanded availability of and access to multiple options for education and the workplace.

What works to re-engage at-risk and out-of-school adolescents and youth in education?

Mentoring and psychosocial support emerge as core interventions that contribute to positive reengagement outcomes. This is consistently shown by quantifiable and positive size effects in several studies.

- *Mentoring* is defined as a relationship between an adult and an unrelated protégé in which the adult provides ongoing guidance and instruction to develop the competence and character of the protégé (Rhodes 2002). Three meta-analytic quantitative studies (DuBois et al. 2002, 2011; Eby et al. 2008) covering 168 evaluations on youth mentoring programs over the period 1970–2010 show overall average weighted effect sizes of 0.18–0.21 at 95 percent Youth benefited significantly in each of the outcome domains: emotional, behavioral, social, and academic. Research points to the importance of developing "close" mentor-mentee relationships. Mentoring is found to be more effective for youth with pre-existing difficulties or significant risk exposure, with the largest effect sizes between mentoring and mentee's behavioral and attitudinal changes: helping others, school attitudes, and career attitudes. The mentor's background in a helping role or profession was found to be a significant moderator of effect size.

- *Psychosocial Support* describes any type of support that aims to protect or promote psychosocial well-being and encompasses the domains of cognitive, affective, and behavioral competencies (INEE 2016). When directed towards learning, it is called socio-emotional learning (SEL). Three meta-analytic quantitative studies (Durlak et al. 2011; Durlak, Weissberg, and Pachan 2010; Taylor et al. 2017; Wigelsworth et al. 2016) covering 240+ evaluations on social-emotional learning programs up to 2014 (38 interventions outside the US) showed overall average weighted effect sizes in the range of 0.17–0.53 at 95 percent confidence interval (CI). The largest effect sizes found across studies were for social-emotional competence; these effects show strong direct links with academic achievement regardless of students' race, socioeconomic background, or school location. The most effective programs utilized evidence-based skill development activities, which were sequential, active, focused, and explicit (or SAFE) (Durlak and Dupre 2008; Larson and Verma 1999).

How do these interventions work?

Understanding more nuanced processes of successful intervention can help us understand the mechanism underlying their success. For mentoring, there are core stages in the process that leads to better outcomes. *Mentoring* involves four stages: befriending, direction-setting, coaching, and sponsoring. In different stages, the mentors play different roles—informal supporters, academic advisors, administrators, and caregivers. The process works best when it is embedded in an education program and is persistent, adaptive, and intentional about best-fit mentor-mentee matches. Successful interventions include broad psychosocial support and more targeted social-emotional tools for learning. Psychosocial *support* helps re-engaged learners improve interactions with their environment (peers, family, and community). Social-emotional learning (SEL) programs integrate skills training into the curriculum. An example of such an approach is "SAFE." Programs with a focus on *mindsets and climate* (Yeager 2017) entail three practices of success: setting high expectations, celebrating success, having a welcoming environment with respectful, authentic relationships with room for shared decision making.

To address the complex needs of at-risk out-of-school young people, research suggests a set of "enabling" interventions for reengagement. For vulnerable youth, enrolling in school may not be a priority even when options are available. Successful reengagement programs identify and encourage enrolment through awareness and outreach to build trust, connect with social services, and generate the demand for educational opportunities. Once identified, at-risk learners require some level of individualized support and access to other services. This is best done through a case management approach, starting with an assessment of risks and educational levels and referrals for access to other integrated support and financial services and incentives. Mentoring, psychosocial interventions, and financial interventions lead to greater benefits when accompanied by other relevant support services that fulfill basic needs (Kuperminc et al. 2005).

For whom and in what contexts do reengagement interventions work?

Context variation can inhibit or facilitate reengagement interventions requiring nuanced assessment and contextualization. Person-context characteristics and interactions moderate program impact. Hence, we cannot assume homogeneity across global populations in terms of the response to specific interventions by young people facing seemingly similar risks. Programs and interventions successfully evaluated (in terms of impact) elsewhere should still be re-contextualized in a new setting. An international mixed-methods study (Ungar 2006) in 14 communities across 11 countries in five continents offers a framework to guide such re-contextualization. Policy makers, program designers, and practitioners should conduct a more nuanced understanding of extant interventions across the following dimensions: access to material resources, relationships, identity, power and control, cultural adherence, social justice, and cohesion. Other regional studies reviewed offer insights into how these contextual dimensions impact the supply- and demand-side constraints faced by the youth in different contexts. Common across all vulnerable youth is the finding that at least one stable and supportive relationship, positive connections in various settings, and a contextually relevant mix of interventions are essential for these youth to cope.

Therefore, evidence suggests that access to and the availability of flexible and adaptable opportunities for reengagement contribute to the effectiveness of interventions. Permeable and flexible educational pathways and varied platforms of engagement contribute toward effective service delivery of a reengagement program aligned to a particular ecosystem. For example, some at-risk learners cannot attend full-time, center-based programs and face education re-entry barriers. In these contexts, reengagement interventions (such as mentoring and psychosocial support) need to be adapted for open or distance education programs, as well as offer personalized guidance and learning opportunities.

However, for children and youth, non-classroom-based programs may introduce systematic inequities related to teaching and learning quality, adult support, and continuity. Thus, it is important that these provide the same/similar opportunities for success that conventional education options provide. For example, besides offering learners varying levels of flexibility in time, place, path, and pace, it is crucial to have face-to-face interactions with peers and teachers to strengthen self-efficacy and performance expectations. Blended learning environments create such opportunities. There is growing evidence that the outcomes of online and classroom-based instructions are comparable. Online/distance learning platforms support individualized instruction, besides being cost-effective and easily scalable.

Synthesizing the complexity of the reengagement process

Multi-component programs with a mix of interventions are likely necessary to address the multiple and varied needs of young people exposed to multiple and accumulative risks. This study has identified core interventions of mentoring and psychosocial support as well as enabling interventions of outreach, case management, integrated support services, and financial incentives along with blended learning platforms and flexible educational pathways for successful education reengagement outcomes. A recent meta-analytic study (Mawn et al. 2017) of youth reengagement programs has found significant positive effects associated with the use of multicomponent interventions (including such components as classroom-based and jobs-based learning and skills) for cognitive, affective, and behavioral support, along deprivation indicators and high-intensity contact (see box ES.2).

> **BOX ES.2**
>
> **Considering and addressing a complex set of needs**
>
> The creative and individualized environments of educational programs can serve to reconnect and reengage out-of-school youth, providing them with an opportunity to achieve in a different setting using different and innovative learning methods. While there are many kinds of alternative schools and programs, they are often characterized by their flexible schedules, smaller student-teacher ratios, relevant and career-oriented themes, and modified curricula. (Gutherson, Davies, and Daszkiewicz 2011; Ruzzi and Kraemer 2006).

The core interventions of mentoring and psychosocial support form the bedrock on which the enabling interventions (awareness and outreach, case management, and referrals to other protective and promotive services) can operate. Each enabling intervention is associated with underlying 'mechanisms' that contribute to re-engaging at-risk youth successfully: befriending, direction setting, coaching and sponsoring. These mechanisms underline the nature of successful mentor-mentee relationships and psychosocial programs intended to deliver educational outcomes. Uncovering these underlying 'generalizable' mechanisms that seem to support at-risk youth can help trace the core stages of the causal process and identify interventions that can be adapted to different contexts, as needed (see figure 5.1 in chapter 5). This provides a more parsimonious guidance to policy makers and program designers because it allows us to ask specifically what interventions work 'here' and how they can be set up to establish the mechanisms for achieving desired outcomes.

Implications for program design

The evidence on the complex problems and solutions related to out-of-school and at-risk adolescents and youth makes it clear that relevant and adaptive programmatic approaches are needed. This starts with strategic collection and use of data that assess risks and assets for school reengagement across the social ecology where at-risk youth interact. Multi-component programs, although complex, can be designed across core and enabling interventions that provide protective and promotive support and include emotional, behavioral, cognitive, and developmental services.

Multi-component programs require partnerships and context adaptations. A wide network of actors is typically involved including outreach specialists, experienced teachers, mental health professionals, case managers, trained coaches and counselors, experts in cognitive and psychosocial assessments. These adults must be well-qualified, empathic, caring individuals and be institutionally linked to, and supported by, a community of partners who take collective responsibility for disengaged youth, and coordinate action to provide them a pathway to education. Referral services are crucial to guide at-risk youth to a variety of needed protective and promotive services that cannot all be provided by one institution, including schools.

Adaptive monitoring and evaluation approaches are needed to better understand the complex causal process within programs to re-engage out-of-school and at-risk youth. Program design must be evaluated not only at the end for results but must also be monitored and adapted based on context and feedback from learners, mentors, schools, and community. Ongoing and periodic small-scale targeted evaluations to assess progress of program improvements efforts or test incremental impact (Bloom 2010; Duflo 2017) of program enhancements based on the implementation experience are useful to inform the design of program elements. For complex multi-component programs, there is a well-recognized need for diverse research methodologies to understand what components (or combination of components) make a reengagement program effective.

Mixed-methods research strategies are needed to explain the causal process within complex social problems and interventions. A paucity of conclusive empirical evidence relevant to complex social problems makes it difficult to generate relevant theories of change, guide design, and direct resources for new programs and interventions.[1] This may mean that some traditional approaches to evaluation that under explain the mechanisms of change ("black boxes") need to be complemented with mixed-methods approaches (Pawson 2006; Luthar 2003). Finally, additional research is required to build on our current understanding of how reengagement programs work, as well as how they can best be developed, executed, and improved. These may be relevant to the nature of protracted social problems, such as those explored in this study (Reyes 2019, forthcoming).

Conclusion

This study identifies *what* interventions work for reengagement of at-risk and out-of-school adolescents and youth based on effect sizes and systematic evidence. Two core interventions are found: *mentoring* and *psychosocial support*. *How* these can be made effective for addressing the specific needs of at-risk and out-of-school youth further points to *enabling* interventions: awareness building and outreach work, individualized case management along with integrated support services such as housing, healthcare, money management, assessments and referrals, and financial incentives. Vast literature in substantive fields of science (neuro-science, cognitive theory, behavioral economics, resilience, etc.) provide the underlying logic of *why* the above core and enabling interventions contribute to the outcome of interest: school reengagement.

Further, given the different contexts in which at-risk youth live, an education ecosystem that offers flexible and permeable educational pathways is warranted. For example, for youth that cannot attend a full-time education program, blended learning platforms (combining online and face-to-face) encourages them to re-engage and achieve academic and psychosocial outcomes.

Using our methodological framework, we synthesize the complex findings and organize the evidence across 'what works, how, and why.' A broad theory of change is proposed with the intent that this may guide the local design processes, including context-based theories of change for education reengagement programs. We hope this study provides a more parsimonious order of recommendations for policy and programing related to the complex social problem of re-engaging at-risk and out-of-school adolescents and youth exposed to multiple life risks in an education program by analyzing what works, how, and why, as well as for whom and in which contexts.

WHAT THIS STUDY COVERS

In chapter 1, the study identifies and characterizes the risks youth face, explains their association with developmental outcomes, and develops an integrative model of risk, resilience, and positive youth development.

Chapter 2 conceptually unpacks the causal relationship between education (dis-)engagement and outcomes and, building on the integrative model in the previous chapter, develops a hypothesis on the mechanism of education reengagement. The purpose, outcomes, and benefits of reengagement are discussed.

In chapter 3, a methodological framework is developed to identify the factors that can influence reengagement outcomes. This framework embraces more complex explanations of the reengagement process[2]—for whom, in what context, what interventions, how, and why—and is used to analyze the research findings on reengagement, including program evaluations. For this purpose, the study reviews research from a mix of methods and disciplines.

In chapter 4, in addition to identifying interventions with statistically significant effect sizes, we offer further insights about how each of these interventions can shape program outcomes. The study then delves deeper into some of the science that can explain why these interventions work and clarifies for whom and in what context the identified interventions can have impact.

In chapter 5, embracing the complex nature of the reengagement phenomena leads to an analysis of evidence from multi-component programs to develop best practices. We include an initial attempt to identify some underlying generalizable mechanisms across core and enabling reengagement interventions that can guide program design.

Chapter 6 provides some initial guidance on how to use a more complex review of the available literature on re-engaging at-risk adolescents and youth into education by drawing out the interlinkages between the interventions, the stakeholders, and the context for the construction of 'theories of change' for education reengagement. We end with some practical insights and questions for policy makers, practitioners, and implementing agencies entrusted with program design and implementation.

Chapter 7 offers a brief conclusion on the overall findings of the study.

NOTES

1. Reyes 2019, Unpublished doctoral thesis in progress.
2. Our framework is informed by the doctoral thesis research from one of the co-authors of this study (Reyes 2019, unpublished doctoral thesis in progress) and is complemented by a further review of complexity science, realist evaluation methods and analysis, and calls for more complex analysis in the development fields, including from Ramalingam et al. (2008), Duflo (2017), Pawson et al. (2005) and Pawson (2006).

REFERENCES

Alves, V. 2016. "Background Paper on Psychosocial Support and Social and Emotional Learning for Children and Youth in Emergency Settings." Commissioned by the INEE Education Policy Working Group (EPWG) and INEE Standards and Practice Working Group (SPWG). New York, NY: Inter-Agency Network for Education in Emergencies (INEE).

Bloom, D. 2010. "Programs and Policies to Assist High School Dropouts in the Transition to Adulthood." *The Future of Children* 20(1) 89–108.

Bush and Saltarelli. 2000. *The Two Faces of Education in Ethnic Conflict: Towards a Peacebuilding Education for Children*. Inter-Agency Network for Education in Emergencies (INEE).

Center for Promise. 2014. *Supporting Young People's Success in High School Re-Engagement Programs: The Role of Social Support and Self-Efficacy*. Washington, DC: America's Promise Alliance.

Cicchetti, D., J. Rappaport, I. Sandler, and R. P. Weissberg, eds. 2000. *The Promotion of Wellness in Children and Adolescents*. Washington, DC: Child Welfare League of America.

Cowen, E. L. 2000. Community Psychology and Routes to Psychological Wellness. In Rappaport, A. & Seidman, E. (Ed.), Handbook of Community Psychology (pp. 79-99). Boston, MA: Springer.

DuBois, D. L., B. E. Holloway, J. C. Valentine, and H. Cooper. 2002. "Effectiveness of Mentoring Programs for Youth: A Meta-Analytic Review." *American Journal of Community Psychology* 30: 157–97.

DuBois, D. L., N. Portillo, J. E. Rhodes, N. Silverthorn, and J. C. Valentine. 2011. "How Effective Are Mentoring Programs for youth? A Systematic Assessment of the Evidence." *Psychological Science in the Public Interest* 12 (2): 57–91.

Duflo, E. 2017. "The Economist as Plumber—Richard T. Ely Lecture." *American Economic Review* 107 (5): 1–26.

Durlak, J. A., and E. P. Dupre. 2008. "Implementation Matters: A Review of Research on the Influence of Implementation on Program Outcomes and the Factors Affecting Implementation." *American Journal of Community Psychology* 41: 327–50.

Durlak, J. A., R. P. Weissberg, and M. Pachan. 2010. "A Meta-Analysis of After-School Programs that Seek to Promote Personal and Social Skills in Children and Adolescents." *American Journal of Community Psychology* 45 (3–4): 294–309.

Durlak, J. A., R. P. Weissberg, A. B. Dymnicki, R. D. Taylor, and K. B. Schellinger. 2011. "The Impact of Enhancing Students' Social and Emotional Learning: A Meta-Analysis of School-Based Universal Interventions." *Child Development* 82 (1): 405–32.

Eby, L. T., T. D. Allen, S. C. Evans, T. Ng, and D. DuBois. 2008. "Does Mentoring Matter? A Multidisciplinary Meta-Analysis Comparing Mentored and Non-Mentored Individuals." *Journal of Vocational Behavior* 72 (2): 254–67.

Gutherson, P., H. Davies, and T. Daszkiewicz. 2011. *Achieving Successful Outcomes through Alternative Education Provision: An International Literature Review*. Reading: CfBT Education Trust.

Kuperminc, G. P., J. G. Emshoff, M. M. Reiner, L. A. Secrest, P. H. Niolon, and J. Foster, J. D. 2005. "Integration of Mentoring with Other Programs and Services." In DuBois, D. L. and Karcher, M. J. (Eds.) Handbook of Youth Mentoring, Thousand Oaks, CA: Sage Publications Ltd.

Larson, R. W., and S. Verma. 1999. "How Children and Adolescents Spend Time across the World: Work, Play, and Developmental Opportunities." *Psychological Bulletin* 125 (6): 701–36.

Luthar, S. S., ed. 2003. *Resilience and Vulnerability: Adaptation in the Context of Childhood Adversities*. Cambridge University Press.

Luthar, S. S., and D. Cicchetti. 2000. "The Construct of Resilience: Implications for Interventions and Social Policies." *Development and Psychopathology* 12 (4): 857–85.

Masten, A. S. 2001. "Ordinary Magic: Resilience Processes in Development." *American Psychologist* 56 (3): 227.

Masten, A. S., and J. D. Coatsworth. 1998. "The Development of Competence in Favorable and Unfavorable Environments: Lessons from Research on Successful Children." *American Psychologist* 53 (2): 205.

Masten, A. S., and J. L. Powell. 2003. "A Resilience Framework for Research, Policy, and Practice." In *Resilience and Vulnerability: Adaptation in the Context of Childhood Adversities*, edited by S. S. Luthar, 1–25. New York: Cambridge University Press.

Mawn, L., E. J. Oliver, N. Akhter, C. L. Bambra, C. Torgerson, C. Bridle, and H. J. Stain. 2017. "Are We Failing Young People Not in Employment, Education or Training (NEETs)? A Systematic Review and Meta-Analysis of Re-Engagement Interventions." *Systematic Reviews* 6 (1).

McWhirter, J. J., B. T. McWhirter, E. H. McWhirter, and R. J. McWhirter. 2012. *At Risk Youth*. Cengage Learning.

Pawson, R. 2006. *Evidence-Based Policy: A Realist Perspective*. Sage.

Pawson, R., T. Greenhalgh, G. Harvey, and K. Walshe. 2005. "Realist Review—A New Method of Systematic Review Designed for Complex Policy Interventions." *Journal of Health Services Research & Policy* 10 (1_suppl): 21–34.

Quan, A. (Ed.). (2016). Education for people and planet: Creating sustainable futures for all. Global Education Monitoring Report. UNESCO.

Ramalingam, B., H. Jones, T. Reba, and J. Young. 2008. *Exploring the Science of Complexity: Ideas and Implications for Development and Humanitarian Efforts*, vol. 285. London: Overseas Development Institute.

Reyes, J. 2013. "What Matters Most for Education Resilience: A Framework Paper." Systems Approach for Better Education Results (SABER). Working Paper 7, World Bank, Washington, DC.

Reyes, J. 2019. "The Transformative Resilience Framework: Explaining Complex Problems in Education in Emergencies." Unpublished doctoral thesis in progress. Falmer: University of Sussex.

Rhodes, J. E. 2002. *Stand by Me: The Risks and Rewards of Mentoring Today's Youth*. Cambridge, MA: Harvard University Press.

Ruzzi, B. B., and J. Kraemer. 2006. *Academic Programs in Alternative Education: An Overview*. National Center on Education and the Economy. (NJ1).

Taylor, R. D., E. Oberle, J. A. Durlak, and R. P. Weissberg. 2017. "Promoting Positive Youth Development through School-Based Social and Emotional Learning Interventions: A Meta-Analysis of Follow-Up Effects." *Child Development* 88 (4): 1156–71.

UNESCO. 2018. *One in Five Children, Adolescents and Youth Is Out of School*. UIS Fact Sheet 48. http://uis.unesco.org/sites/default/files/documents/fs48-one-five-children-adolescents-youth-out-school-2018-en.pdf.

Ungar, M. 2006. "Nurturing Hidden Resilience in At-Risk Youth in Different Cultures." *Journal of the Canadian Academy of Child and Adolescent Psychiatry* 15 (2): 53.

Ungar, M. 2008. "Resilience across Cultures." *The British Journal of Social Work* 38 (2): 218–35.

Wigelsworth, M., Lendrum, A., Oldfield, J., Scott, A., ten Bokkel, I., Tate, K., & Emery, C. (2016). "The Impact of Trial Stage, Developer Involvement and International Transferability on Universal Social and Emotional Learning Programme Outcomes: A Meta-analysis." Cambridge Journal of Education 46(3): 347–376.

Yeager, D. S. 2017. "Social and Emotional Learning Programs for Adolescents." *The Future of Children* 27 (1): 73–94.

Abbreviations

CCT	conditional cash transfers
CI	confidence interval
DEEWR	Department of Education, Employment and Work Relations, Australia
ES	effect size
HMIC	higher-middle-income country
ICT	information and communication technology
ILP	individual learning plan
ISS	integrated support services
LIC	low-income country
LMIC	lower-middle-income country
MIC	middle-income country
MoNE	Ministry of National Education
NEET	not in education, employment or training
OECD	Organisation for Economic Co-operation and Development
OOS	out-of-school
OL	online learning
PIRLS	Progress in International Reading Literacy Study
PISA	Programme for International Student Assessment
PSS	psychosocial support
PYD	positive youth development
RCT	randomized control trial
ROI	return on investment
SEL	social-emotional learning
TAFE	Technical and Further Education
TIMSS	Trends in International Mathematics and Science Study
UCT	unconditional cash transfer
UIS	UNESCO Institute of Statistics
UNESCO	United Nations Education, Scientific and Cultural Organization
VET	vocational education and training

1 Introduction

This chapter introduces the definitions of the terms "out-of-school" and "at-risk"; discusses the types and characteristics of risk factors vulnerable young people face and their association with developmental outcomes; and presents an integrative model of risk, resilience, and positive youth development.

In a world that is being reshaped by automation and technology, there is an increasing demand for advanced cognitive skills (such as critical thinking and problem solving) and social behavioral skills (such as creativity and curiosity) that are transferable across jobs to compete effectively in the labor market (World Development Report 2019). Failing to educate and train the next generation of workers and leaders with essential skills would contribute to the intergenerational persistence of inequality, lock in income and gender disparities, obstruct social mobility, and undercut the effective utilization of this demographic capital, with substantial, long-term adverse consequences for the shared economic and social well-being of all.

With over 200 million young people in the age range of 12–17 years out-of-school across the world, there is a wave of strong and growing arguments that countries must pay urgent attention to re-engage out-of-school and at-risk youth and support them to attain the knowledge, skills, attitudes, and relevant credentials required for a successful life trajectory as well as for delivering aggregate socioeconomic benefits to society. Recovering these youths and sustaining them in a path of productivity is undoubtedly a challenge, given the lost time in early developmental years, and will require concerted investment and effort.

Although educational access has become almost universal in most countries, many school-age children do not receive relevant, quality education services and are exposed to difficult life situations and adversities, leading to many leaving school early. For older youth, this can be a double disadvantage: neither being enrolled in school nor being gainfully employed. We need a better understanding of (1) how to engage and retain adolescents and youth in education (and prevent dropouts); (2) how to reduce their exposure to risks and support their resilience in the face of adversity; and (3) how to re-engage those that have already left the education system.

This study aims to contribute to develop a better understanding of education modalities for re-engaging and building resilience in at-risk and out-of-school adolescents and youth[1] in the age group of 12–17 years. It offers a review and analysis of the evidence for re-engaging these vulnerable young people into education, synthesizing what interventions work, how and why they work as well as for whom and in what context these can be relevant. Addressing the multiplicity and wide variety of needs of this target group often requires a systemic approach with complex intervention programs.[2] This study can provide guidance for the design of such programs and inform policy making.

By way of introduction, it is useful to first define the terms *out-of-school* and *at-risk,* followed by a discussion of the types and characteristics of risks, their association with outcomes and finally, the role of resilience and strength-based youth development theories in moderating these risks.

DEFINING OUT-OF-SCHOOL AND AT-RISK YOUTH

For this study, *out-of-school* youth refers to young people who have not completed their formal education through higher secondary due to multiple disadvantages linked to characteristics of the school, family, community, and the individual, as well as macro-level socioeconomic political factors. The out-of-school categorization includes students who have never entered school and those who entered but dropped out. In this study, we specifically focus on the latter category of youth who are 12–17 years of age and dropped out of school either before age 12 or between ages 12 and 17 without completing higher secondary education. They are often referred to as early school leavers[3] and not in education, employment or training (NEETs).[4]

At-risk denotes a set of presumed cause-effect dynamics that place an individual young person in danger of future negative outcomes. The term designates a situation that is not necessarily current but can be anticipated in the absence of intervention. Given the complex ecology of stressors all young people face, being *at risk* is less a discrete and unitary diagnostic category than it is a series of cumulative[5] steps along a continuum[6] from minimal risk, to remote risk, to imminent and high risk, and finally to participation in the very actions and behaviors that define the risk categories such as dropping out, risky sexual behavior, violence, and drug abuse (McWhirter et al. 2012). In this analysis, our focus is on re-engaging young people who have left education early and actively demonstrate imminent/high risk behaviors.

Next, we examine (1) the constellation of risks factors affecting youth; (2) the associations between risks and outcomes; and (3) the characteristics of these risks faced by out-of-school adolescents and youth in different contexts.

UNDERSTANDING TYPES OF RISK FACTORS AFFECTING OUT-OF-SCHOOL YOUNGSTERS

A vast literature shows that across different contextual settings, young people facing multiple adversities disconnect and drop out of education due to a wide range and complexity of factors. Several observable predictors of early school leaving have been identified at the level of the individual and at the level of their family, school, community, and society (Ahmadzadeh et al. 2014; Caspi et al. 1998; Center for

Promise 2014, 2015; Cunningham et al. 2008; de Hoyos, Popova, and Rogers 2016; de Hoyos, Rogers, and Szekely 2016; de Witte et al. 2013; Flisi et al. 2015; Garmezy 1985; Inoue et al. 2015; Logan-Greene et al. 2011; Marks and McMillan 2001; Masten and Powel 2003; Mauro and Mitra 2015; Reyes and Elias 2011; Rumberger 2001; Sameroff, Gutman, and Peck 2003; Skinner et al. 2008; UNESCO 2016).

Through an exhaustive exercise of reviewing and synthesizing this evidence on risk factors that can be associated with young people leaving education early (or showing staying power in the face of adversity) in different contexts, we identified two categories of risk: *individual risk factors* and *contextual risk factors*.

Individual risk factors

These risk factors can be organized into five categories: *demographic, geographic, cognitive, emotional,* and *social/behavioral*.

Demographic factors

Some of the main demographic predictors of being out-of-school are age, gender, income group, marital status, and minority group affiliation by race, ethnicity, language, and disability. A UNESCO (2018) study found that upper-secondary school-age youth are four times as likely to be out-of-school as children of primary school age and more than twice as likely to be out-of-school as adolescents of lower-secondary school age. Thus, the likelihood of leaving school increases with age. Studies also found that the likelihood of a young person to reconnect with education decreases with age. Some of main reasons are linked to poverty and the pressure to take up early employment as well as issues related to early marriage, especially among girls. While there appears to be greater gender parity in out-of-school rates for the lower secondary and upper secondary school-age populations, there are significant levels of disparity among regions and countries (box 1.1.). Globally, a gender breakdown of the NEET category (15–24 years) shows variations across country groups: in East Asia and the Pacific, in Europe and Central Asia, and in high-income countries, women are no more likely to be NEET than men. In South Asia, women account for 82 percent of total NEETs, and in the Middle East and North Africa and Sub-Saharan Africa they carry a two-thirds share of NEETs (de Hoyos, Popova, and Rogers 2016). Affiliations to minority groups increase the chances of being out-of-school significantly and can involve a number of reasons such as stigma, lack of awareness, and lack of or limited provision of care.

Geographic risk factors

Research evidence from different regions consistently highlights that rural youth are prone to higher levels of risk with respect to negative outcomes such as early school leaving, early employment, and unemployment, owing mainly to poverty-related economic pressures. Also, it appears that the individual's nationality, country, and region of residence, as well as the country's income level[7] and exposure to conflict can offer insights into the forms and severity of risks faced. While youth living in conflict regions are more at risk than those in non-conflict regions, it is also possible that strong family ties and optimal parental control can offset their negative effects. Yet, a more direct exposure to conflict and violence has significant negative effects.

Risks related to cognitive, emotional, and social/behavioral characteristics

Cognitive risk factors can be indicated by, but need not be limited to, education attainment level, academic performance, IQ scores, attention and

> **BOX 1.1**
>
> ### Gender-related risks vary across regions
>
> Gender-related risk has a lower intensity for females in higher-income countries (Australia, the United States, and other OECD countries) with respect to school completion but not necessarily with respect to labor market outcomes. Conversely, in these contexts males are at a greater risk of leaving school early yet are also more likely to dominate the labor market.
>
> In low- and lower-middle income contexts like Sub-Saharan Africa, education outcomes are dismal for both genders. Females are much more likely than males to face high levels of risk with respect to both education completion and workforce participation (which are found to be linked closely to social norms and practices related to marriage, pregnancy and the role of women in society). But boys may have equally worse outcomes, even though they may remain in school slightly longer on average (Inoue et al. 2015).
>
> In Latin America, a female in the 15–24 age range living in an urban household from the bottom 40 percent of the income distribution is twice as likely as similar males to be out of school and unemployed, with major risk factors attributed to early marriage and teenage pregnancy. Males in the region are more likely to fall in the not in education, employment or training (NEET) category due to early school dropout into the labor market. For both males and females, having any minority group affiliation, by race, ethnicity, language, and disability, is found to be an indicator of higher exposure to risks and poorer academic and mental health outcomes (de Hoyos, Popova, and Rogers 2016; de Hoyos, Rogers, and Székely 2016).
>
> These effects of the risks on outcomes have been explained as a function of (1) insufficient and low-quality resources and learning environments; and (2) sociocultural factors (values, attitudes, and behaviors) of the minority group that influence the individual (Rumberger 2001), leading to internal and external reinforcements of discrimination and prejudice (Szalacha et al. 2003).

executive functioning skills. Risk factors related to emotional characteristics can be indicated by self-efficacy (self-perceptions of competence, worth and confidence, self-esteem); self-regulation skills (impulse control, affect and arousal regulation); outlook on life (hopefulness, belief that life has meaning, faith); perceived value of returns to education; and relatedness (sense of belonging, interest, satisfaction). Risk factors related to social and behavioral characteristics include adaptability, sociability, effort, attention, and persistence (i.e., number of attempts). While the risks related to cognitive, emotional, and behavioral characteristics are widely acknowledged by researchers as contributing factors to outcomes for all youth, there is a greater consistency in attribution to demographic and geographical factors in determining the level of risk.

Contextual risk factors

This set of risk factors relates to family and household, school, community, and macro-level structural factors.

Household and family-related risk factors

These include predictive variables linked to family membership, family structure, socioeconomic status, parental attitudes and behaviors, and family dysfunction. Disaggregating these, factors linked to family membership include number and gender of adults in a household and whether children are below age 12, ages 12–18, or over age 18. Those related to family structure especially focus on the gender, marital status, education level, and occupational field of the head-of-household. Socioeconomic status is a widely acknowledged significant predictor of risk across contexts and can be determined by household income and household earning capacity (proxied by the number of working adults). Parental availability (death, illness, divorce), negative parental attitude towards education, low level of support and involvement with the child as well as family dysfunction and youth victimization such as abuse, violence, corporal punishment, and discord have all been found to be powerful contributors to emotional distress, substance use, school disengagement, and delinquent peer ties and violent behaviors (Banyard, Cross, and Modecki 2006; de Witte et al. 2013; Harachi et al. 2006; Logan-Greene et al. 2011). Thus, low socioeconomic status, large families, single-parent families, step parenting, risky parental behaviors such as drug and alcohol use, and parental absence and illness, as well as quality of parent-child relationship can all have significant influence on the risk levels a young person is exposed to. The nature of parental control (on the continuum of democratic to authoritarian) has also been studied widely and found to influence children's risk exposure[8]. However, these predictors are not fully generalizable and have to be taken together with other predictive factors and in context.

School-related risk factors
These include school climate, education quality, infrastructure, peer affiliations and influence, and school policies and practices. Within the schooling experience of adolescents and youth, a negative *school climate* plays a critical role in pushing students out. This includes practices such as segregation, discrimination, abuse and corporal punishment, violent and unsafe school environment, non-supportive student-faculty interface and interactions, bullying, and negation of students' cultural identity. *Poor education quality* is widely understood across the literature as a predictor of students dropping out. Education quality weaknesses (such as irrelevance of curriculum to the labor market, low expectations, poor instructional and pedagogic quality, barriers due to language of instruction, teacher absenteeism, and poor learning standards) are linked to academic failure, grade retention, disconnection and eventually dropping out. *Infrastructure* related constraints, such as lack of sufficient and clean toilets, unavailability of learning material, and non-conducive physical spaces for learning, physical activities, and sports create additional dropout-related risks. *School policies and practices,* including factors such as class size, school size, program diversity, tracking and learning options, type of school (public/private, selective/non-selective, free/subsidized), are also found to influence the learning experience of young people. Overcrowding, early tracking, inflexible learning paths, selective and capability-based grouping strategies and transition bottlenecks tend to 'push' some young people out of school. Delinquent *peer affiliations* at school are found to further exacerbate the level of risk for young people already facing significant adversities.

Community risk factors
These include social and cultural norms, peer affiliations and influence, quality and availability of schools, and safety. The lack of access to and availability of quality schools, especially in lower- and upper-secondary levels is potentially one of the biggest reasons why during the transition phases, significant levels of dropout are found in low-income and low-middle-income country contexts. Social and cultural norms, practices, and prejudices of communities and neighborhoods contribute to

experiences, beliefs and life choices of young people in important formative years. Thus, community norms that convey reluctance to educate girls and the differently-abled signal the presence of risks related to defying authority and expectations. In neighborhoods where violence and crime are high, there are risks related to safety and security, which can curtail mundane activities like walking alone to and from school and present the need for adult supervision and accompaniment, which may not be available. Finally, when young people are faced with adverse situations such as teenage pregnancy, parental unemployment, death or illness, they need appropriate, accessible and approachable social and health support services. In the absence of a strong network of such services, there is a likely spillover of adverse consequences on education-related outcomes.

Macro-level structural factors
These include economic and political aspects, law enforcement, social and cultural norms, and national and regional education policies and practices. Economic, geopolitical, and sociocultural aspects of a region/country have significant ramifications for the future prospects of young people. Issues around corruption, high inflation and interest rates, poor ease of accessing credit, skewed labor market conditions (pull or push effects), political unrest and instability, conflict, migration, and internal displacement are just some factors. As an instance, the vulnerabilities of young people amongst refugee populations are exacerbated, often due to lack of identity documents. Many refugee students having forcibly fled their homes do not have the needed certificates to re-enter a new education system and progress. Many countries require official identification, visa and legal status requirements, and certification of past schooling to enter the appropriate grade and obtain access to exams and results. Obtaining documents is found to be costly and complicated, leading to the systemic exclusion of refugee youth from education (Ahmadzadeh et al. 2014). Also, an ineffective and poorly enforced judicial system, especially in areas related to education, labor, drug and alcohol use, and marriage, has significant and adverse effects on young people's early experiences. The structure, policies, and practices of the national and regional education system have a more direct influence on the educational options available, directly impacting choices and decisions to complete, leave early, or return later.

THE ASSOCIATIONS BETWEEN RISK FACTORS AND OUTCOMES

Risk-related research studies consistently show that persistent experiences of adversity[9] have long-term detrimental effects on child and adolescent cognitive, emotional, behavioral, and physical functioning and long-lasting negative effects in adult life (Duke et al. 2010; Stambaugh et al. 2013). There is evidence of disruption of healthy and positive development of social-emotional skills and psychosocial outcomes (Afifi et al. 2008; Felitti et al. 1998; Mersky, Topitzes, and Reynolds 2013; Turner et al. 2015) as well as lower levels of academic engagement and higher rates of grade retention and dropping out of high school (Porche, Costello, and Rosen-Reynoso 2016; Porche et al. 2011). Thus, outcomes such as early school leaving are complex, multidimensional phenomena with numerous causes and consequences. Research evidence consistently suggests that none of the above risk factors, taken singly, is uniformly predictive of leaving education across all contexts, and it cautions against making highly generalizable assumptions about risk determinants. While no single risk variable is either a necessary or sufficient determinant of good or bad outcomes, an accumulation of several risk factors (e.g., more than five) carries a greater predictive power for severe levels of adversity that knock young people off positive academic and healthy social trajectories (Center for Promise 2015; Sameroff, Gutman, and Peck 2003). Research consistently suggests that the more risk factors a young person experiences, the worse the academic outcomes, including poorer grades and increased absences (Gutman, Sameroff, and Eccles 2002; Rutter 1979; Sameroff et al. 1987, 1993; Zaff et al. 2014).

The above evidence on the association between risk-related factors and developmental outcomes also highlights the role and relevance of both environmental and individual factors. Studies conducted in the United States show that high-efficacy (more competent) youth in high-risk environmental conditions score worse than low-efficacy (less competent) youth in low-risk conditions, both when measured by IQ and when measured by mental health. Research also shows that environmental risk factors may have a greater influence on outcomes than individual risk factors (Sameroff et al. 1998; Sameroff, Gutman, and Peck 2003).

CHARACTERISTICS OF RISKS FACED BY OUT-OF-SCHOOL ADOLESCENTS AND YOUTH

Research suggests that young people typically experience a multiplicity of risks in complex environments comprising multiple social contexts (family, school, peer group, community) that interact to foster developmental outcomes (biological, emotional, cognitive, and behavioral) of relevance to culturally diverse communities (Sameroff, Gutman, and Peck 2003; Ungar 2011). These risk factors faced by out-of-school young people have three characteristic features. They are *contextual, cumulative,* and *complex.*

Risks are contextual

Using a social ecology frame, risks can be understood to emanate both from more proximal contexts, such as the assets of the individual and the resources and supports offered by family, school and community, and from more distal factors, such as public policies, the economic climate, and societal norms (Center for Promise 2015). The characteristics of youth and the environment in which they live and interact can facilitate or inhibit their developmental outcomes (Ungar 2006). To truly grasp the holistic meaning of a person's risk levels and competence levels, one must examine the pattern of relationships across multiple proximal social contexts (Yoshikawa and Seidman 2000). When growing up under adversity, the locus of change does not reside in either the child or in the environment, but in the processes by which environments provide resources for use by the child (Ungar 2011). The youngster's own individual resources are only as good as the capacity of his or her social and physical ecologies that facilitate their expression and application to developmental tasks (Beckett et al. 2006; Klebanov and Brooks-Gunn 2006; Seccombe 2002; Seidman and Pedersen 2003; Tiet et al. 1998; Ungar 2011, p. 6; Ungar and Liebenberg 2005; Wyman 2003).

As an illustration, poverty is found to be a strong predictor of high environmental risk, as it has cascading effects in limiting access to and the quality of material and financial resources for the young person. Poverty also significantly moderates the psychosocial climates afforded by family, peer group, school, and the community these youths inhabit. But poverty does not always lead all youths to be subjected to a uniform set of psychosocial risk processes, as there are multiple examples of young people who progress despite significant adversity. In some country contexts, such as in Sub-Saharan Africa, girls may be at a significantly greater risk than boys of education exclusion due to practices such as early marriage and social norms related to the role of women or considerations of safety and access to toilets. In other contexts, such as in OECD and Latin American countries, boys may be at a much greater risk of early school leaving than girls due to higher vulnerability to crime and violence, pressure to work, or negative response to bullying at school. Therefore, unique constellations of the salient psychosocial processes that transpire within youths' context—their families, peers, schools, community and other macro-level factors—place them differentially at risk for various negative outcomes (or protect them against these risks, enhancing the possibility of positive developmental outcomes) (Seidman and Pederson 2003; Ungar 2011; Ungar and Liebenberg 2005).

Risks are cumulative

Risk factors typically co-occur with other risk factors, usually encompassing a sequence of stressful experiences rather than a single event, and often pile up in the lives of children over time (Garmezy and Masten 1994; Masten and Powell 2003; Rutter 1979; Sameroff and Chandler 1975; Sameroff and Seifer 1983). While single variables taken alone, such as income level or marital status, on the family side, and gender, race, efficacy, resourcefulness, mental health, or achievement, on the personal side, may have statistically significant effects on youths' behavior, their effects are small in comparison with the accumulation of multiple negative influences that characterize high-risk groups. The kind of risk appears to be secondary to the number of negative factors. Even when the strengths of individual youths are added to predictive models, they do not overcome the effects of high environmental risk (Sameroff, Gutman, and Peck 2003).

Thus, it is neither the individual factors nor singular environmental factors alone that make a difference, but rather the constellation of risks in each youth's life. Multiple risks or vulnerability factors increase the likelihood that an individual or a population will manifest negative developmental outcomes (Seidman and Pederson 2003). The best predictor of problem behaviors seems to be a cumulative risk score that reflects the risk status in the full range of the ecological subsystem. Research increasingly focuses on *cumulative risk*, studied either by aggregating information about stressful life experiences or by aggregating risk indicators (Masten and Powell 2003; Sameroff, Gutman, and Peck 2003).

On average, higher the number of risk factors, more are the problems observed (Masten et al. 1993; Masten and Sesma 1999). High risk often also indicates lower socioeconomic status, poor parenting practices, as well as many stressful life experiences. However, even among homeless families, in which all children are experiencing low SES and the major stressor of homelessness, there is evidence of risk gradients. Homeless children with few or no risk factors may demonstrate positive developmental behaviors compared to their high-risk peers in school and at home. This indicates that the *level of risk* on a risk gradient is a function of the assets (as an individual) and resources (from the environment) available to the young person in his/her context (Masten and Powell 2003).

Risks are complex

There is an increasing consensus among resilience studies that identifying simple relationships between the risks, protective and promotive processes, and predictable outcomes is not a realizable goal. The comprehensiveness and the unity of the child development process requires understanding the complexity of multiple risks, multiple outcomes, and growth processes to avoid a distorted view of the importance of any single risk. Moreover, it is essential to view these risks and the coping mechanisms young people use as contextually, temporally, and culturally embedded processes. Longitudinal studies of child development have shown that the classification of individuals as uniquely resilient or vulnerable are not reliable over time (Phelps et al. 2007; Schoon 2006; Werner and Smith 2001). As a young person grows and moves between different contexts (such as new schools, communities, and relationships), where the contexts themselves are dynamic and variable, there are unexpected consequences to risk exposure, such as those found in post-traumatic growth studies like Solomon and Laufer (2005). Therefore, both the youth and the environment can change their characteristics, as well as their explanatory utility, over time.

Individuals who can overcome certain risks in one context or at a certain point in time may not be able to demonstrate the same capacity for resilience when faced with risks in another context or at another point in time (Masten and Powell 2003, p. 4; Ungar 2011, p. 7; Werner and Smith 2001). Researchers recognize the complex nature of risks (and the resilience processes to overcome these risks) involved in determining the links between context and child. Finally, studies find that the same risk factors affect multiple outcomes, such as depression, conduct disorder, and substance abuse, and that each outcome has multiple risk factors (Coie, Miller-Johnson, and Bagwell 2000; Sameroff, Gutman, and Peck 2003). Such a phenomenon is congruent with the complexity principle of equifinality (Ungar 2011), which states that in open systems, a given outcome can be reached from a number of different developmental paths.

OVERLAPS BETWEEN RESEARCH ON RISK, ON RESILIENCE, AND ON POSITIVE YOUTH DEVELOPMENT

From the bodies of research reviewed and discussed above on risks, adverse childhood experiences, toxic stress, structural barriers to development such as social norms, poverty, violence, and youth resilience to adversity, we can infer a substantial and distinguishable overlap in the perspectives offered by resilience and positive youth development (PYD) (vis-à-vis engagement) research (Li, Lerner, and Lerner 2010; Luthar 2003; Shonkoff et al. 2015; Ungar 2008; Ungar and Liebenberg 2005). Specifically, the linkages between these literatures help us to identify the roles played by risk and by protective and promotive factors and to recognize their interconnectedness within the young person's social ecology that affect healthy development.

Resilience

The literature defines resilience as patterns of positive adaptation in the context of significant risk and adversity (Masten and Powell 2003). Rigorous evidence also confirms that resilience is a culturally and contextually embedded artefact influenced by a youth's environment, and that the repeated interactions between the individual and the social ecologies will determine the degree of positive outcome experienced (Luthar 2003; Luthar, Cicchetti, and Becker 2000; Ungar 2008). Thus, resilience research has extensively focused on the relationship between the individual and contextual risks and on the processes and mechanisms of stress resistance, thus emphasizing protection from negative outcomes. It has examined risk and protective factors as (1) predictors of outcomes such as early school leaving, unemployment, and delinquency, and (2) moderators of the ecological supports. Empirical research provides evidence on the role of parental, peer, school, community, and societal supports as predictors of resilience among at-risk youth (Anghel 2015; Correa-Velez et al. 2017; Dias and Cadime 2017; Oldfield et al. 2018; Tiet, Huizinga, and Byrnes 2009) and recognizes the complexity in this phenomenon (Luthar 2003; Shannon et al. 2007; Ungar 2011).

However, it is being increasingly recognized that resilience processes are protective against risk and promotive of assets and resources within the social ecological framework of family, peer, school, and community environments and broader macro-level structural factors thus affecting the developmental outcomes of young people (Ungar 2011). The conceptualization of interventions is increasingly based on resilience—as *cumulative competence promotion* and *stress protection* (Wyman et al. 2000). The effects of risk factors are counteracted by protective factors, which act as mediators between the risk and the negative outcomes by positively moderating the effect on the supports. The promotive factors include assets and resources. Assets refer to the individual factors, including capacities and strengths while resources refer to the positive supports provided by the youth's environment. Thus, *resilience is both an individual's capacity to navigate the way to positive developmental resources such as psychological, social, cultural and physical resources that sustain well-being, and a condition of the individual's family, community and culture to negotiate for these resources to be provided in culturally meaningful ways* (Ungar 2008). Interventions that counteract risks and offer the necessary assets and resources relevant to the youth's context create protective and promotive pathways to strengthen the supports for optimal development.

Positive youth development

The positive youth development (PYD) research overwhelmingly favors adopting a strength-based conception of adolescence and youth, as opposed to a deficit-focused one. The PYD approach attempts to "move beyond" a problem-oriented focus (on risk and protective factors) and stresses the value of providing supports for youth engagement, and opportunities for bidirectional, constructive youth-context interactions (Larson 2000; Lerner et al. 2007); Snyder and Flay 2012). Thus, it focuses on strengthening developmental assets (also called promotive factors) to directly and positively affect developmental outcomes. These assets refer to internal and external strengths within an individual's social ecology that are predictive of positive outcomes, including health, mental health, and education (Kia-Keating et al. 2011).

While there are varied operational constructs of PYD[10], they share a common focus on building young people's positive personal competencies, social skills, and attitudes (i.e., asset development) through increased positive relationships, social supports, and opportunities that strengthen assets and help youth flourish within their environments (i.e., environmental enhancement) (Taylor et al. 2017). A systematic review of 25 PYD program evaluations (US based) indicated that PYD interventions operating in family, school, and community settings are effective in promoting positive development in a broad range of outcome domains such as self-control, interpersonal skills, problem solving, relationship skills, commitment to schooling and academic achievement (Catalano et al. 2002a, 2002b, 2004). However, it was also found that some interventions decreased substance use, and other problem and risky behaviors. PYD interventions, therefore, can both foster positive outcomes and protect against negative ones.

THE INTEGRATIVE VIEW OF RISK, RESILIENCE AND POSITIVE YOUTH DEVELOPMENT

Both the social ecology perspective of resilience and PYD research identify risk factors to be cumulative, complex and contextual. Further, both fields recognize that development involves the reciprocal interactions between the young person and specific life events, family, school and community factors, macro-level societal conditions and cultural beliefs (Bronfenbrenner 1979; Bronfenbrenner and Morris 2006). These act as developmental factors offering different levels of risks, protection and promotion to the youth to deliver positive outcomes. Interestingly, other researchers (Kia-Keating et al. 2011) corroborate inferences drawn from complementary perspectives offered by these fields, suggesting an integrative view (figure 1.1) that identifies a minimum of two pathways for healthy developmental outcomes. These are (1) the protecting pathway, through which risks are mediated by protective interventions leading to positive outcomes, and (2) the promoting pathway, through which assets and resources strengthen support factors directly leading to healthier outcomes.

Both these pathways are part of a dynamic, interactive system of social ecology. Hence, interventions need to attend to all levels of this ecology (individual, family, school, community, and macro-structural) and not aim to build individual assets alone. Studies also show that not all risk, protection, and promotion factors are

FIGURE 1.1

Integrative view of risk, resilience, and positive youth development

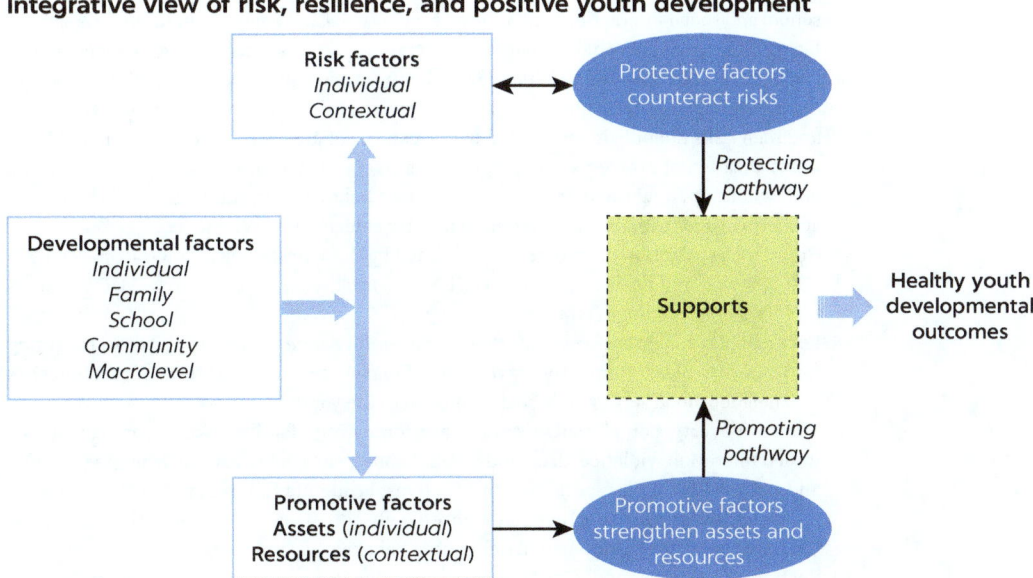

Source: World Bank analysis.

universally relevant, that is, a factor that may be a risk in one context may act as a protective element in another. For example, restrictive and authoritative parental control may be more suited for youngsters growing up in dangerous and highly violent environments, whereas the same may have negative effects on those growing up in less violent neighborhoods. For successful youth outcomes, optimal programs need to take an integrative system-level view, recognizing the multiple levels of interactions and influences as well as the interconnectedness within these systems (Kia-Keating et al. 2011, p. 223; Sameroff, Gutman, and Peck 2003, p. 387). This integrative view will contribute to furthering our understanding of education engagement and to determining contextually relevant reengagement interventions for at-risk youth in education.

NOTES

1. In this study, the words *youth, youngsters, youth and adolescents,* and *young people* are used interchangeably.
2. There are seven key characteristics of a complex social intervention: It is based on a theory/theories; involves the actions of people; is a chain of steps/processes; has processes that are typically non-linear; is embedded in social systems; is prone to modification and adaptation during implementation; and is an open and leaky system that needs to readjust as stakeholders learn and understand it better (Pawson et al. 2004).
3. A European Commission JRC Technical Report (2015) refers to Early School Leavers (ESL) as Early Leavers from Education and Training (ELET), that is, young people 18–24 years age who may have partially completed levels from pre-primary, primary, lower secondary, or upper secondary education of less than 2 years (i.e., Levels 0, 1, 2 or 3c in the United Nations' International Standard Classification of Education [ISCED 1997]). However, in this study, ESL is treated as a category of young people who have not completed their education up to upper secondary and have left early. Since in many parts of the world, youth as young as 12 years or even lower leave education, ESL is considered an appropriate term for this group.
4. NEET refers to young people 15–24 years who are not in education, employment or training. Strong positive correlation is found between NEET 15–24 and NEET 18–24 age ranges (Flisi et al. 2015). Here, we refer to the NEET subgroup in the age range 15–17 years, which is strongly correlated with the characteristics of the overall NEET category.
5. For a detailed analysis of cumulative risk, see Masten and Powell (2003).
6. While minimal risk refers to young people with favorable demographics, positive family, school and social interactions and limited psychosocial and environmental stressors, those facing remote risks may have negative demographic markers (such as lower socioeconomic status, poor access to quality education and opportunity, minority membership, subject to regressive social norms) and be exposed to fewer positive social interactions. Imminent and high risks not only involve the above stressors but are exacerbated by the individual's internalization of problems affecting their sense of self-worth, self-efficacy, and attitudes and beliefs, opening the gateway to even riskier behaviors. In the final stage, the person actively engages in activities that define the risk category (McWhirter et al. 2012).
7. Country classification of income levels defined by the World Bank as low-income country (LIC), lower-middle-income country (LMIC), middle-income country (MIC), higher-middle-income country (HMIC).
8. For example, in an unsafe neighborhood or a conflict zone, more authoritarian parenting for 12-15-year-olds is more protective than stifling whereas the same form of parenting in a safe neighborhood setting may be detrimental to the youth.
9. Such as poverty, homelessness, early labor force entry, family discord, immigration or forced migration, violence, drug and alcohol abuse, early marriage, early pregnancy, war and political turmoil, mental health problems, academic failure, grade retention, age-inappropriate credentials (overage), chronic absenteeism, and perpetration as well as victimization through violent and delinquent behavior.
10. Such as the five Cs model: competence, confidence, connection, character and caring (Lerner 2009; Lerner et al. 2005; Lerner, Lerner, and Benson 2011) or the external and internal developmental assets model (Benson et al. 1998).

REFERENCES

Afifi, T. O., M. W. Enns, B. J. Cox, G. J. Asmundson, M. B. Stein, and J. Sareen. 2008. "Population Attributable Fractions of Psychiatric Disorders and Suicide Ideation and Attempts Associated with Adverse Childhood Experiences." *American Journal of Public Health* 98: 946–52.

Ahmadzadeh, H., M. Çorabatır, J. A. Husseini, L. Hashem, and S. Wahby. 2014. *Ensuring Quality Education for Young Refugees from Syria*. Refugee Studies Centre, University of Oxford.

Anghel, R. E. 2015. "Predictors of Academic Performance among At-Risk Romanian Youth." *Romanian Journal for Multidimensional Education/Revista Romaneasca pentru Educatie Multidimensionala* 7 (1).

Banyard, V. L., C. Cross, and K. L. Modecki. 2006. "Interpersonal Violence in Adolescence: Ecological Correlates of Self-Reported Perpetration." *Journal of Interpersonal Violence* 21 (10): 1314–32.

Beckett, C., Maughan, B., Rutter, M., Castle, J., Colvert, E., Groothues, C., Kreppner, J., Stevens, S., O'Connor, T.G. and Sonuga-Barke, E.J. 2006. "Do the Effects of Early Severe Deprivation on Cognition Persist into Early Adolescence? Findings from the English and Romanian Adoptees Study." *Child Development* 77 (3): 696–711.

Benson, P. L., N. Leffert, P. C. Scales, and D. A. Blyth. 2012. "Beyond the "Village" Rhetoric: Creating Healthy Communities for Children and Adolescents." *Applied Developmental Science* 16 (1): 3–23.

Bronfenbrenner, U. 1979. *The Ecology of Human Development: Experiments by Nature and Design*. Cambridge, MA: Harvard University Press.

Bronfenbrenner, U., and P. A. Morris. 2006. "The Bioecological Model of Human Development." In *Handbook of Child Psychology: Theoretical Models of Human Development*, edited by R. M. Lerner and W. Damon, 793–828. Hoboken, NJ: John Wiley & Sons Inc.

Caspi, A., B. R. E. Wright, T. E. Moffitt, and P. A. Silva. 1998. Early Failure in the Labor Market: Childhood and Adolescent Predictors of Unemployment in the Transition to Adulthood." *American Sociological Review* 63 (3): 424–51.

Catalano, R. F., M. L. Berglund, J. A. M. Ryan, H. S. Lonczak, and J. D. Hawkins. 2002a. "Positive Youth Development in the United States: Research Findings on Evaluations of Positive Youth Development Programs." *Prevention and Treatment* 5 (15).

Catalano, R. F., J. D. Hawkins, M. L. Berglund, J. A. Pollard, and M. W. Arthur. 2002b. "Prevention Science and Positive Youth Development: Competitive or Cooperative Frameworks?" *Journal of Adolescent Health* 31 (6): 230–39.

Catalano, R. F., Berglund, M. L., Ryan, J. A. M., Lonczak, H. S., & Hawkins, J. D. 2004. Positive Youth Development in the United States: Research Findings on Evaluations of Positive Youth Development Programs. *The Annals of the American Academy of Political and Social Science* 591 (1): 98–124.

Center for Promise. 2014. *Supporting Young People's Success in High School Re-Engagement Programs: The Role of Social Support and Self-Efficacy*. Washington, DC: America's Promise Alliance.

Center for Promise. 2015. *Don't Quit on Me: What Young People Who Left School Say About the Power of Relationships*. Washington, DC: America's Promise Alliance.

Coie, J. D., S. Miller-Johnson, and C. Bagwell. 2000. "Prevention Science." In Sameroff, A. J., Lewis, M., Miller, S. M. (Eds.) *Handbook of Developmental Psychopathology*, 93–112. Boston, MA: Springer.

Correa-Velez, I., S. M. Gifford, C. McMichael, and R. Sampson. 2017. "Predictors of Secondary School Completion among Refugee Youth 8 to 9 Years after Resettlement in Melbourne, Australia." *Journal of International Migration and Integration* 18 (3): 791–805.

Cunningham, W., L. McGinnis, R. G. Verdú, C. Tesliuc, and D. Verner. 2008. *Youth at Risk in Latin America and the Caribbean: Understanding the Causes, Realizing the Potential*. Washington, DC: World Bank.

de Hoyos, R., A. Popova, and H. Rogers. 2016. *Out of School and Out of Work: A Diagnostic of Ninis in Latin America*. Washington, DC: World Bank.

de Hoyos, R., H. Rogers, and M. Székely. 2016. *Out of School and Out of Work: Risk and Opportunities for Latin America's Ninis*. Washington, DC: World Bank.

de Witte, K., S. Cabus, G. Thyssen, W. Groot, and H. M. van den Brink. 2013. "A Critical Review of the Literature on School Dropout." *Educational Research Review* 10: 13–28.

Dias, P. C., and I. Cadime. 2017. "Protective Factors and Resilience in Adolescents: The Mediating Role of Self-Regulation." *Psicología Educativa* 23 (1): 37–43.

Duke, N. N., S. L. Pettingell, B. J. McMorris, and I. W. Borowsky. 2010. "Adolescent Violence Perpetration: Associations with Multiple Types of Adverse Childhood Experiences." *Pediatrics* 125 (4).

Felitti, V. J., R. F. Anda, D. Nordenberg, D. F. Williamson, A. M. Spitz, V. Edwards, and J. S. Marks. 1998. "Relationship of Childhood Abuse and Household Dysfunction to Many of the Leading Causes of Death in Adults: The Adverse Childhood Experiences (ACE) Study." *American Journal of Preventive Medicine* 14 (4): 245–58.

Flisi, S., V. Goglio, E. C. Meroni, and E. Vera-Toscano. 2015. *School-to-Work Transition of Young Individuals: What Can the ELET and NEET Indicators Tell Us*. Luxembourg: Publications Office of the European Union, EUR-Scientific and Technical Research Reports.

Garmezy, N. 1985. "Stress-Resistant Children: The Search for Protective Factors." *Recent Research in Developmental Psychopathology* 4: 213–33.

Garmezy, N., and A. Masten. 1994. "Chronic Adversities." *Child and Adolescent Psychiatry* 3: 191–208.

Gutman, L. M., A. S. Sameroff, and J. S. Eccles. 2002. "The Academic Achievement of African-American Students during Early Adolescence: An Examination of Multiple Risk, Promotive, and Protective Factors." *American Journal of Community Psychology* 39: 367–99.

Harachi, T. W., C. B. Fleming, H. R. White, M. E. Ensminger, R. D. Abbott, R. F. Catalano, and K. P. Haggerty. 2006. "Aggressive Behavior among Girls and Boys during Middle Childhood: Predictors and Sequelae of Trajectory Group Membership." *Aggressive Behavior: Official Journal of the International Society for Research on Aggression* 32 (4): 279–93.

Inoue, K., E. Di Gropello, Y. S. Taylor, and J. Gresham. 2015. *Out-of-School Youth in Sub-Saharan Africa: A Policy Perspective*. Washington, DC: World Bank.

Kia-Keating, M., E. Dowdy, M. L. Morgan, and G. G. Noam. 2011. "Protecting and Promoting: An Integrative Conceptual Model for Healthy Development of Adolescents." *Journal of Adolescent Health* 48 (3): 223.

Klebanov, P., and J. Brooks-Gunn. 2006. "Cumulative, Human Capital, and Psychological Risk in the Context of Early Intervention: Links with IQ at Ages 3, 5, and 8." In *Resilience in Children*, edited by B. M. Lester, A. S. Masten, and B. McEwen, 63–82. Boston, MA: Blackwell.

Larson, R. W. 2000. "Toward a Psychology of Positive Youth Development." *American Psychologist* 55 (1): 170–83.

Lerner, R. M. 2009. "The Positive Youth Development Perspective: Theoretical and Empirical Bases of Strengths-Based Approach to Adolescent Development." *Oxford Handbook of Positive Psychology* 149.

Lerner, R. M., J. B. Almerigi, C. Theokas, and J. V. Lerner. 2005. "Positive Youth Development a View of the Issues." *The Journal of Early Adolescence* 25 (1): 10–16.

Lerner, R. M., J. V. Lerner, and J. B. Benson. 2011. "Positive Youth Development: Research and Applications for Promoting Thriving in Adolescence." *Advances in Child Development and Behavior* 41: 1–17.

Lerner, R. M., E. Phelps, A. Alberts, Y. Forman, and E. Christiansen. 2007. "The Many Faces of Urban Girls: Features of Positive Development in Early Adolescence." In *Urban Girls Revisited: Building Strengths*, edited by B. Leadbeater, and N. Way, 19–52. New York: New York University Press.

Li, Y., J. V. Lerner, and R. M. Lerner. 2010. "Personal and Ecological Assets and Academic Competence in Early Adolescence: The Mediating Role of School Engagement." *Journal of Youth and Adolescence* 39 (7): 801–15.

Logan-Greene, P., P. S. Nurius, J. R. Herting, C. L. Hooven, E. Walsh, and E. Adams Thompson. 2011. "Multi-Domain Risk and Protective Factor Predictors of Violent Behavior among At-Risk Youth." *Journal of Youth Studies* 14 (4): 413–29.

Luthar, S. S., ed. 2003. *Resilience and Vulnerability: Adaptation in the context of childhood adversities*. Cambridge University Press.

Luthar, S. S., and D. Cicchetti. 2000. "The Construct of Resilience: Implications for Interventions and Social Policies." *Development and Psychopathology* 12 (4): 857–85.

Luthar, S. S., D. Cicchetti, and B. Becker. 2000. The Construct of Resilience: A Critical Evaluation and Guidelines for Future Work." *Child Development* 71 (3): 543–62.

Marks, G., and J. McMillan. 2001. *Early School Leavers: Who Are They, Why Do They Leave, and What Are the Consequences?* http://research.acer.edu.au/research_conference_2001/2.

Masten, A. S., and N. Garmezy. 1985. "Risk, Vulnerability, and Protective Factors in Developmental Psychopathology." In Lahey B.B., Kazdin A.E. (Eds.), *Advances in Clinical Child Psychology*, Volume 8, pp 1-52. Boston, MA: Springer.

Masten, A. S., D. Miliotis, S. Graham-Bermann, M. Ramirez, and J. Neemann. 1993. "Children in Homeless Families: Risks to Mental Health and Development." *Journal of Consulting and Clinical Psychology* 61: 335–343.

Masten, A. S., and J. L. Powell. 2003. "A Resilience Framework for Research, Policy, and Practice." In *Resilience and Vulnerability: Adaptation in the Context of Childhood Adversities*, edited by S. S. Luthar, 1–28. New York, NY: Cambridge University Press.

Masten, A. S., and A. Sesma. 1999. "Risk and Resilience among Children Homeless in Minneapolis." *CURA Reporter* 29 (1): 1–6.

Mauro, J. A., and S. Mitra. 2015. *Understanding Out-of-Work and Out-of-School Youth in Europe and Central Asia* (English). Washington, DC: World Bank Group. http://documents.worldbank.org/curated/en/103971468187482224/Understanding-out-of-work-and-out-of-school-youth-in-Europe-and-Central-Asia

McWhirter, J. J., B. T. McWhirter, E. H. McWhirter, and R. J. McWhirter. 2012. *At Risk Youth*. Cengage Learning.

Mersky, J. P., J. Topitzes, and A. J. Reynolds. 2013. "Impacts of Adverse Childhood Experiences on Health, Mental Health, and Substance Use in Early Adulthood: A Cohort Study of an Urban, Minority Sample in the US." *Child Abuse and Neglect* 37: 917–25.

Oldfield, J., A. Stevenson, E. Ortiz, and B. Haley. 2018. "Promoting or Suppressing Resilience to Mental Health Outcomes in at Risk Young People: The Role of Parental and Peer Attachment and School Connectedness." *Journal of Adolescence* 64: 13–22.

Pawson, R., T. Greenhalgh, G. Harvey, and K. Walshe. 2004. *Realist Synthesis: An Introduction*. Manchester: ESRC Research Methods Programme, University of Manchester.

Phelps, E., A. B. Balsano, K. Fay, J. S. Peltz, S. M. Zimmerman, R. M. Lerner, and J. V. Lerner. 2007. "Nuances in Early Adolescent Developmental Trajectories of Positive and of Problematic / Risk Behaviors: Findings from the 4-H Study of Positive Youth Development." *North American Clinics of Child and Adolescent Psychiatry* 16: 473–96.

Porche, M. V., D. M. Costello, and M. Rosen-Reynoso. 2016. Adverse Family Experiences, Child Mental Health, and Educational Outcomes for a National Sample of Students." *School Mental Health* 8: 44–60.

Porche, M. V., L. R. Fortuna, J. Lin, and M. Alegria. 2011. "Childhood Trauma and Psychiatric Disorders as Correlates of School Dropout in a National Sample of Young Adults." *Child Development* 82: 982–98.

Reyes, J. A., and M.J. Elias. 2011. "Fostering Social–Emotional Resilience among Latino Youth." *Psychology in the Schools* 48 (7): 723–37.

Rumberger, R. W. 2001. *Why Students Drop Out of School and What Can Be Done*. UCLA, The Civil Rights Project / Proyecto Derechos Civiles.

Rutter, M. 1979. "Protective Factors in Children's Response to Stress and Disadvantage." In *Primary Prevention of Psychopathology*, edited by J. S. Bruner and A. Garden, vol. 3, 49–74. Hanover, NH: University Press of New England.

Sameroff, A. J., W. T. Bartko, A. Baldwin, C. Baldwin, and R. Seifer. 1998. "Family and Social Influences on the Development of Child Competence." In *Families, Risk, and Competence*, edited by M. Lewis and C. Feiring, 161–85. Mahwah, NJ, US: Lawrence Erlbaum Associates Publishers.

Sameroff, A. J., and M. J. Chandler. 1975. "Reproductive Risk and the Continuum of Caretaking Casualty." In *Review of Child Development Research*, edited by F. D. Horowitz, M. Hetherington, S. Scarr-Salapatek and G. Siegel, vol. 4, 187–243. Chicago, IL: University of Chicago Press.

Sameroff, A., Gutman, L. M., & Peck, S. C. 2003. Adaptation among youth facing multiple risks: Prospective research findings. In S. S. Luthar (Ed.), Resilience and vulnerability: Adaptation in the context of childhood adversities, 364–391. New York, NY, US: Cambridge University Press.

Sameroff, A. J., and R. Seifer. 1983. "Familial Risk and Child Competence." *Child Development* 54: 1254–68.

Sameroff, A. J., R. Seifer, A. Baldwin, and C. Baldwin. 1993. "Stability of Intelligence from Preschool to Adolescence: The Influence of Social and Family Risk Factors." *Child Development* 64: 80–97.

Sameroff, A. J., R. Seifer, M. Zax, and R. Barocas. 1987. "Early Indicators of Developmental Risk: Rochester Longitudinal Study." *Schizophrenia Bulletin* 13: 383–92.

Schoon, I. 2006. *Risk and Resilience: Adaptations in Changing Times*. Cambridge, England: Cambridge University Press.

Seccombe, K. 2002. "'Beating the Odds' versus 'Changing the Odds': Poverty, Resilience, and Family Policy." *Journal of Marriage and Family* 64: 384–394.

Seidman, E., and S. Pedersen. 2003. "Holistic Contextual Perspectives on Risk, Protection, and Competence among Low-Income Urban Adolescents." In *Resilience and Vulnerability: Adaptation in the Context of Childhood Adversities*, edited by S. S. Luthar, 318–42). New York: Cambridge University Press.

Shannon, K. E., T. P. Beauchaine, S. L. Brenner, E. Neuhaus, and L. Gatzke-Kopp. 2007. "Familial and Temperamental Predictors of Resilience in Children at Risk for Conduct Disorder and Depression." *Development and Psychopathology* 19 (3): 701–27.

Shonkoff, J., P. S. Levitt, J. Bunge, J. Cameron, G. Duncan, P. Fisher, and N. Fox. 2015. *Supportive Relationships and Active Skill-Building Strengthen the Foundations of Resilience*. (PDF). National Scientific Council on the Developing Child.

Skinner, E., C. Furrer, G. Marchand, and T. Kindermann. 2008. "Engagement and Disaffection in the Classroom: Part of a Larger Motivational Dynamic?" *Journal of Educational Psychology* 100 (4): 765.

Snyder, F. J., and B. R. Flay. 2012. "Positive Youth Development." In *Handbook of Prosocial Education*, edited by P. M. Brown, M. W. Corrigan, and A. Higgins-D'Allessandro, vol. 2, 415–443. New York, NY: Rowman & Littlefield.

Solomon, Z., and A. Laufer. 2005. "Israeli Youth Cope with Terror: Working with Children and Youth—Vulnerability and Resilience." In *Handbook for Pathways to Resilience across Cultures and Contexts*, edited by M. Ungar, 229–46. Thousand Oaks, CA: Sage.

Stambaugh, L. F., H. Ringeisen, C. C. Casanueva, S. Tueller, K. E. Smith, and M. Dolan. 2013. *Adverse Childhood Experiences in NSCAW*. Washington, DC: OPRE Report.

Szalacha, L. A., S. Erkut, C. García Coll, J. P. Fields, O. Alarcón, and I. Ceder. 2003. "Perceived Discrimination and Resilience." In *Resilience and Vulnerability: Adaptation in the Context of Childhood Adversities*, edited by S. S. Luthar, 414–35. New York: Cambridge University Press.

Taylor, R. D., E. Oberle, J. A. Durlak, and R. P. Weissberg. 2017. "Promoting Positive Youth Development through School-Based Social and Emotional Learning Interventions: A Meta-Analysis of Follow-Up Effects." *Child Development* 88 (4): 1156–71.

Tiet, Q. Q., H. R. Bird, M. Davies, C. Hoven, P. Cohen, P. S. Jensen, and S. Goodman. 1998. Adverse Life Events and Resilience." *Journal of the American Academy of Child & Adolescent Psychiatry* 37 (11): 1191–200.

Tiet, Q. Q., D. Huizinga, and H. F. Byrnes. 2010. "Predictors of Resilience among Inner City Youths." *Journal of Child and Family Studies* 19 (3): 360–78.

Turner, H. A., A. Shattuck, D. Finkelhor, and S. Hamby. 2015. "Effects of Poly-Victimization on Adolescent Social Support, Self-Concept, and Psychological Distress." *Journal of Interpersonal Violence* 1 (26).

UNESCO. 2016. *Education for People and Planet: Creating Sustainable Futures for All*. Global Education Monitoring Report.

UNESCO. 2018. *One in Five Children, Adolescents and Youth Is Out of School*. UIS Fact Sheet No. 48.

Ungar, M. 2006. "Nurturing Hidden Resilience in At-Risk Youth in Different Cultures." *Journal of the Canadian Academy of Child and Adolescent Psychiatry* 15 (2): 53.

Ungar, M. 2008. "Putting Resilience Theory into Action: Five Principles for Intervention." In *Resilience in Action*, edited by Liebenberg and Ungar, 17–38.

Ungar, M. 2011. "The Social Ecology of Resilience: Addressing Contextual and Cultural Ambiguity of a Nascent Construct." *American Journal of Orthopsychiatry* 81 (1): 1.

Ungar, M., and L. Liebenberg. 2005. "Resilience across Cultures: The Mixed Methods Approach of the International Resilience Project." In *Handbook for Working with Children and Youth Pathways to Resilience across Cultures and Contexts*, edited by M. Ungar, 211–26. Thousand Oaks, CA: Sage.

Werner, E. E., and R. S. Smith. 2001. *Journeys from Childhood to Midlife: Risk, Resilience, and Recovery*. Ithaca, NY: Cornell University Press.

World Development Report. 2019. *The Changing Nature of Work*. World Bank.

Wyman, P. A. 2003. "Emerging Perspectives on Context Specificity of Children's Adaptation and Resilience: Evidence from a Decade of Research with Urban Children in Adversity." In *Resilience and Vulnerability: Adaptation in the Context of Childhood Adversities*, edited by S. S. Luthar, 293–317. Cambridge, England: Cambridge University Press.

Wyman, P. A., I. Sandler, S. Wolchik, and K. Nelson. 2000. "Resilience as Cumulative Competence Promotion and Stress Protection: Theory and Intervention." In *The Promotion of Wellness in Children and Adolescents*, edited by D. Cicchetti, J. Rappaport, I. Sandler, and R. P. Weissberg, 133–84. Washington, DC: Child Welfare League of America.

Yoshikawa, H., and E. Seidman. 2000. Competence among Urban Adolescents in Poverty: Multiple Forms, Contexts, and Developmental Processes." *Advances in Adolescent Development* 10: 9–42.

Zaff, J. F., K. K. Ginsberg, M. J. Boyd, and Z. Kakli. 2014. "Reconnecting Disconnected Youth: Examining the Development of Productive Engagement." *Journal of Research on Adolescence* 24: 526–40.

2 Educational Disengagement and the Benefits of Reengagement

This chapter defines and discusses educational engagement, the problem of disengagement, and the characteristics, outcomes, and benefits of reengagement. It sets the stage for the review of the literature on education reengagement of out-of-school and at-risk youth, including NEETs.

WHAT IS EDUCATIONAL ENGAGEMENT AND WHY IS IT IMPORTANT?

Educational engagement (or academic engagement) refers to a relational, person-context construct. It is thought to develop as a function of daily interactions between a developing young person and his or her experiences in various academic and social activities and with different individuals (Li 2011). A student's level of engagement is demonstrated by the interest, psychological investment, and active effort he or she directs toward learning and educational attainment. It is a multidimensional construct, including three components: behavioral engagement, affective engagement, and cognitive engagement (Fredricks, Blumenfeld, and Paris 2004). Each of these components is affected by a student's internal resources and contextual factors.

Behavioral engagement refers to active participation and an absence of disruption by the student in his/her learning activities with the intent to gain skills and competencies. Emotional engagement refers to a sense of belonging to and a building of trust toward an educational entity—the school, its adult members, schoolmates, and related activities. Cognitive engagement refers to the student's intent, commitment, and investment in learning by setting academic goals and navigating and negotiating the path leading to these goals by identifying resources as well as persisting and overcoming potential barriers (Center for Promise 2014b, 2015).

It is important to distinguish between educational engagement and school engagement. While these are related, school engagement, as demonstrated by attendance and completion of assignments, does not necessarily indicate educational engagement. That is, it does not signify that a student is engaged at all three levels—behavioral, emotional, and cognitive—for learning and educational attainment. The absence of readily observable behavioral indicators of disengagement is not the same as active engagement (Li 2011). Further, research also suggests that internal forms of engagement (emotional and cognitive) may be precursors to external forms (behavioral) (Li and Lerner 2013; Pietarinen, Soini and Pyhältö 2014; Skinner et al. 2008).

In sum, extensive literature and empirical evidence have shown that educational engagement is strongly and positively associated with higher academic achievement and higher likelihood of healthy social and emotional outcomes for young people (Fredericks, Blumenfeld and Paris 2004; Hébert and Reis 1999; Rumberger 2011). The next section discusses the role of contextual and individual factors that influence these outcomes.

The mediating role of social supports

Substantive research literature shows that contextual factors influence a student's internal assets such as persistence, self-control, and self-efficacy (for review, see Center for Promise 2014). Research further shows that the presence of positive "social supports" from adults and peers in the family and from school and community help increase *academic self-efficacy*, which refers to perceived competence in oneself to execute actions and attain academic goals. Students with more and better social supports are more likely to develop positive academic attitudes and beliefs and greater confidence in their academic competencies. Such supports also make them more aware of the importance of education and may promote aspirations for academic pursuits. Conversely, empirical studies have found that disengagement from school has significant and adverse implications for concurrent psychological and behavioral wellbeing and for long-term development (Hancock and Zubrick 2015; Johnson, Crosnoe, and Elder 2001).

Four types of social support have been identified: *emotional support* provides comfort, caring and trust; *informational support* provides useful advice and insights addressing the specific needs of the young person; *appraisal support* provides constructive feedback on strengths and developmental areas for informing self-evaluation; and *instrumental support* provides tangible resources or services, such as accompanying a student for a college visit, making introductions for pursuing academic or nonacademic interests, or providing financial support. Different types of social supports can be provided by different individuals including parents, teachers, peers and other caring adults in the school and community.

Besides the number of supports, the quality, content and appropriate "matching" of the support matter (for review, see Center for Promise 2014b, 2015; Li 2011; Li and Lerner 2013; Li, Lerner and Lerner 2010). Thus, there is a direct relationship between academic self-efficacy and supports. Increased self-efficacy, in turn, predicts academic engagement and is found to be associated with better academic and social emotional outcomes (Ryan and Deci 2000; Wang and Eccles 2013) (see figure 2.1). These associations are also in cognizance with motivational frameworks of engagement (Skinner et al. 2008; Wang and Eccles 2013).

While empirical evidence on the association between social supports, self-efficacy, and educational engagement has been studied widely in traditional education settings, there is relatively limited evidence available for re-engaged

FIGURE 2.1
Relationship between social supports, academic self-efficacy, educational engagement, and academic and social-emotional outcomes

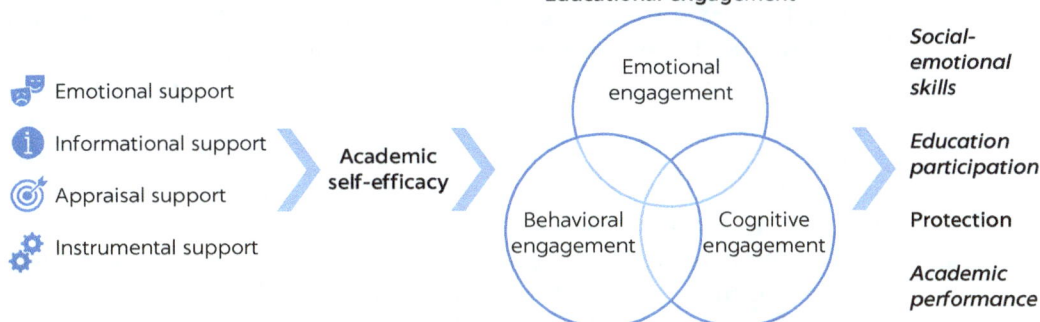

Source: World Bank analysis.
Note: Presence of positive social supports helps increase academic self-efficacy, and increased academic self-efficacy is associated with better academic and social emotional outcomes.

youth facing severe levels of adversity. One recent study by Pan, Zaff and Donlan (2017) has investigated the associations among teacher and parent supports, student academic self-efficacy and education engagement for a sample of 938 reconnected youth[1] in the United States who returned to academics after dropping out, using the multidimensional construct of education engagement. It also examined how youths' adverse life experiences moderated their pathways and outcomes. The main finding was that students' academic self-efficacy mediated parent and teacher support as well as youth academic engagement. Parent and teacher support significantly predicted academic self-efficacy, which in turn significantly predicted emotional and cognitive engagement[2] (see figure 2.2). Relative to parent support, teacher support had a stronger effect on academic self-efficacy and emotional and cognitive engagement. Another key finding was that parental support positively predicted academic self-efficacy and engagement for students with lower risk levels, but associations were not significant for those with high levels of risks (>5) (Pan, Zaff, and Donlan 2017). Thus, teacher support appears to play an important and active role among high-risk youth, though the role of parental support must be contextually examined and cannot be undermined.

FIGURE 2.2
Link between social supports, self-efficacy, and educational engagement moderated by risk factors

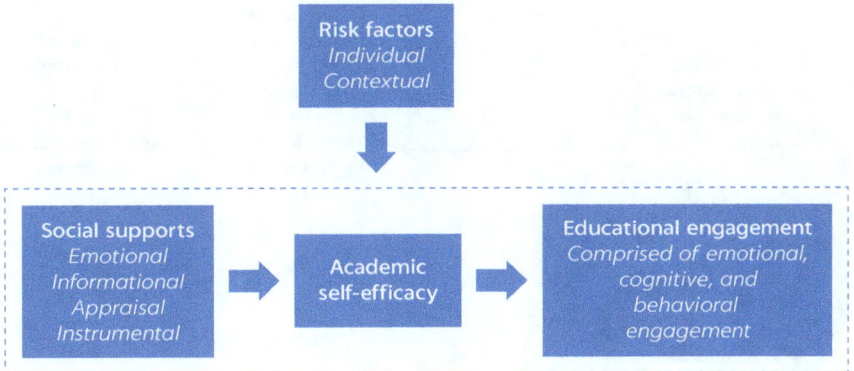

Source: World Bank compilation based on Pan, Zaff, and Donlan 2017, Center for Promise 2014.

Hypothesizing the mechanism of reengagement

From the above (including the analysis in chapter 1), we can *recognize the complexity of interactions and influences in the process of education engagement*. In summary, the following four points emerge. (1) An integrated view of risk, resilience and positive youth development can help determine contextually relevant reengagement interventions for at-risk youths in education (see figure 1.1 in chapter 1). (2) Educational engagement predicts academic achievement and healthy social emotional outcomes. (3) Social supports predict academic self-efficacy, which in turn moderates educational engagement. (4) Risks have an inverse moderating effect on supports and hence on self-efficacy, education engagement, and outcomes. Taken together, we can *hypothesize that the mechanisms of risks, protection and promotion mediate the pathways for support, self-efficacy, engagement and positive developmental outcomes* (as represented in figure 2.3).

Increasing promotive factors has the same effect as reducing risks, because they are on the same dimension for most youth most of the time; and increasing protective factors has a counteractive effect on risks. Thus, the mechanisms of reengagement should be both protective against risks and promotive of assets and resources. Undeniably, there is a need to build an evidence-backed understanding of what the predictors and mediators of educational reengagement are and their relevance in different contexts.

The problem of education dis-engagement

Learners who experience insufficient academic and social supports, low expectations of adults, seemingly limited life choices, adverse life events, work and family demands, and high exposure to risky behaviors like alcohol and drug use tend to disconnect and disengage from education (Center for Promise 2014b, 2015; Masten and Powell 2003), that is when the number and intensity of the risk factors overwhelms the number and intensity of the available protective and promotive supports.

FIGURE 2.3

Hypothesis of the reengagement mechanism

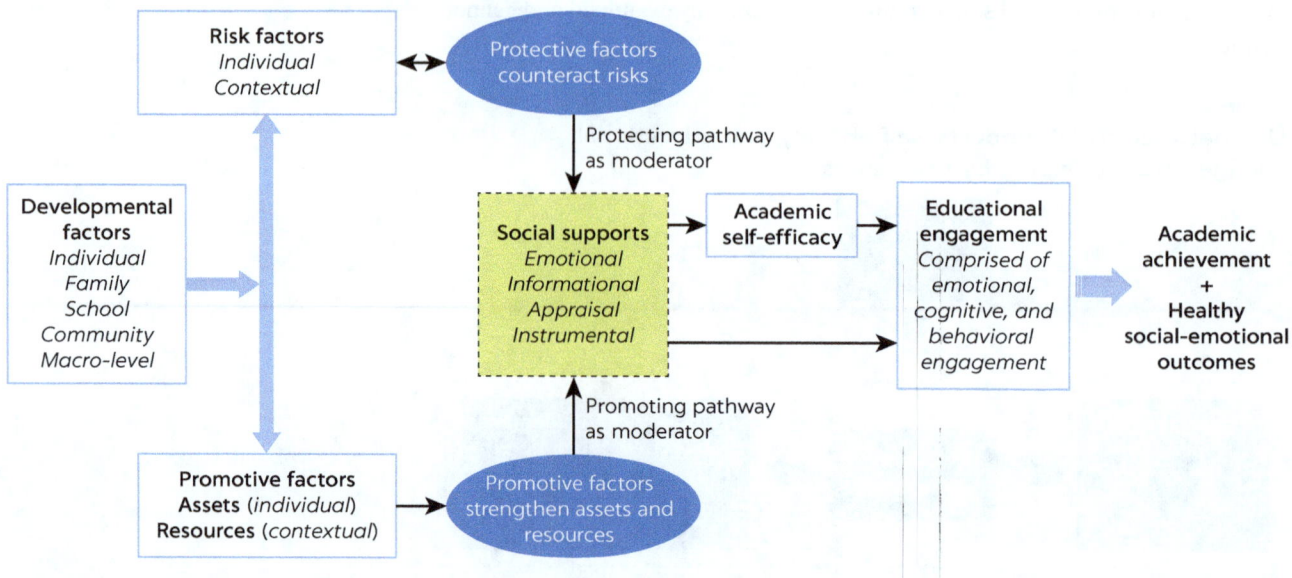

Source: World Bank analysis.
Note: Presence of positive social supports helps increase academic self-efficacy, and increased academic self-efficacy is associated with better academic and social-emotional outcomes.

Disengagement is a consequence of the dynamic and complex relationship between individual characteristics and contextual characteristics such that the adversities are inextricably bound up and disentangling their effects would be a tremendous challenge (Rumberger 2004) and likely to be too noisy (De Witte et al. 2013; Smeyers and Depaepe 2006). Out-of-school youth in vulnerable life situations (such as extreme poverty, working and head-of-households, displacement, etc.) face compounded life risks and are relatively more exposed to this complex problem:

> disengaging from school… [is] a result of the dynamic relationship among individual characteristics (e.g., race, gender, income) and risk factors (e.g., failing courses, low attendance, behavior problems, or being overage for a particular grade) and contextual characteristics (e.g., school climate; the interest teachers take in students; relationships with adults in the community; the poverty level of the community surrounding the school) (Center for Promise 2014b, p. 11).

There are academic and nonacademic reasons due to which young people disengage from education. For learners facing difficult life situations such as health issues, parenting, family demands and pressure to earn, engaging in traditional schools is more challenging. For displaced populations, services for accreditation, curriculum and language of instruction are additional obstacles to surpass in an education program which must be made adaptable to the realities of students from communities such as internally displaced, migrant laborers, and refugees (Ahmadzadeh et al. 2014).

Aside from the disruptive role of displacement and conflict on young people's lives, strictly school-related factors such as a negative school climate can play a significant role in pushing students out of the education system. When youngsters face a school environment that is disruptive, unsafe, has a deep-rooted culture of segregation or lacks an inclusive culture in lower and upper secondary schools, they are highly likely to exit early. Young people also leave school early due to academic reasons such as curriculum and pedagogic methods that seem

BOX 2.1

The case of Turkey: Reengaging out-of-school at-risk youth

This study was originally conducted for the design of a project in Turkey, "Re-Engaging At-Risk and Out-of-School Youth." The project aims to provide intensive, education reengagement support for early school leavers through the Open Education Program of the Ministry of National Education (MoNE). In Turkey, despite ample school-based and open education offers, many vulnerable youths discontinue their education and could benefit from complementary services to reengage them in a relevant education program.

In 2016, Turkey had more than 350,000 out-of-school youth, or 7.1 percent youth in the 14–18 age group. Reducing the rates of early school leavers (including "reparticipation" or reengagement of those that have dropped out) is a national goal as stated in the Turkey's 10th Development Plan 2014–18, the Education Sector Plan and the National Lifelong Long Learning Strategy 2014–18. Regionally, in Europe, reducing the stock of early school leavers is one of its key development indicators (Education and Training in Europe, ET 2020).

The 2012 UNICEF study on Out-of-school children in Turkey identified various barriers and bottlenecks that lead to exclusion from education. It cites sociocultural and psychosocial factors, community-based social capital, and health and economic barriers. It further highlights that these barriers are exacerbated by gender and disability related values (UNICEF 2012). In eastern Turkey, for example, the main problem faced by refugee children is the lack of Turkish language ability, absence of tailored education, and at times tense relations with host communities (Şeker and Sirkeci 2015).

irrelevant and non-interesting, poor fit with the pace, mode and language of instruction, failure to succeed in school due to weak academic skills, poor school transitions and grade retention.

Evidence shows that disconnection from school is a long-term process, not a sudden event (Center for Promise 2014a). Through time, when students' disempowering attitudes and negative behaviors get reinforced by negative environmental factors both inside and outside school, it lowers their emotional and cognitive engagement. This may be exhibited by poorer behavior engagement such as absenteeism, disruption, passive aggression, low academic performance. Thus, "dropping out" of school is just the final stage in a dynamic and cumulative process of disengagement (Finn 1989; Newmann 1992; Rumberger 1987; Rumberger and Lim 2008, pp. 2–4; Wehlage et al. 1989). Actively re-engaging out-of-school learners is crucial to both help them re-enter education and retain them.

WHAT IS REENGAGEMENT AND WHY IS IT NEEDED?

In this analysis, the term "reengagement" refers to the process of creating and advancing the "mechanisms" for reaching out to, connecting with and addressing the needs of at-risk individuals in the target age group of 12–17 years so that they re-enroll, participate and complete their education, and strengthen their social, emotional and cognitive abilities.[3] These mechanisms need to provide these young people (1) protective and promotive supports that can mitigate the adverse effect of the risk exposure and; (2) varied and flexible educational pathways to access alternative avenues, gain recognized qualifications and skills placing them on a positive life trajectory that opens doors to new opportunities.

Characteristics of reengagement

Reengagement (sometimes also called "dropout recovery") is a complex, non-linear and gradual process, much like disempowerment and dis-engagement, and hence requires time and multiple and varying supports and pathways through the involvement of a range of stakeholders at all levels—leaders of schools/education programs, community partners, policymakers and private enterprises—for delivering successful outcomes (figure 2.4). Wyman et al. (2000) argue for a conceptualization of interventions based on resilience as *cumulative competence promotion and stress protection*. While some aspects of the reengagement process may be standardized, several customizations are required every step of the way to meet the specific needs of the at-risk, out-of-school adolescent or youth. For severely disadvantaged individuals, this can be an even longer and arduous process. Even as a starting point, some programs propose a minimum of 8–10 months for youth to acclimate to an educational setting (Zaff et al. 2014).

FIGURE 2.4

Characteristics of education reengagement

Cumulative	Gradual	Non-linear	Multiple stakeholders	Multiple and varying pathways	Complex

Source: World Bank analysis.

Reengagement: Outcomes and impact

A successful educational reengagement process would focus on increasing the number and intensity of protective and promotive factors affecting out-of-school and at-risk young people and provide them flexible pathways to re-enter and continue. Successful gains made in these areas can lead to a range of near-term outcomes—the acquisition of the necessary skills, mindsets and behaviors that will set them on a path of recovery. In the intermediate- to long-term, individual outcomes would include relevant credential acquisition such as acquiring a formal diploma, degree or certification or an equivalent educational qualification, an industry-specific training, an internship and an apprenticeship, as well as strengthening the social and emotional skills. Thus, reengagement outcomes (figure 2.5) would include (1) development of social and emotional skills of the young person, (2) fulfillment of basic needs, (3) participation in education (enrolment, persistent engagement and completion) and, (4) academic performance in term of grades and attainment levels. The overall expected impact is that these youngsters would be able to secure employment, earn a stable source of income with improved education, health and welfare outcomes.

What reengagement is not

Reengagement is not about providing low-cost and low-prestige remediation options which in themselves can become another cause for exclusion. To be successful, reengagement requires that systemically, more and better educational entry points and pathways exist and support at-risk young people to participate and succeed. This would lead to long-term aggregated societal benefits in the form of increased graduation rates, decreased unemployment rates and expanded availability of and access to multiple options to education and workplace (Kim and Taylor 2008, p. 207; Mills, Renshaw, and Zipin 2013; Sumbera 2017, pp. 49,119).

EVIDENCE OF SOCIAL AND ECONOMIC BENEFITS OF INVESTING IN EDUCATIONAL REENGAGEMENT

Review of the literature on young people not in employment, education or training (NEET) shows that changing the developmental trajectory of disconnected youth has a significant benefit for the youth and society at large. The social benefits include: (1) welfare outcomes and reduction in reliance on public assistance; (2) health-related outcomes including general health, healthy behaviors and psychological health indicators; (3) significant improvement in educational attainment levels; and (4) reduced costly behaviors such as crime and higher civic participation. The economic benefits reported include: (1) added tax

FIGURE 2.5

Education reengagement outcomes

Needs	Outcomes
Promotive	
• Emotional	*Socioemotional skills*: Positive change in social and emotional indicators
• Behavioral	*Education participation*: Awareness, reenrolment, persistent engagement, and completion
• Cognitive	*Academic performance*: Academic outcomes and attainment level
Protective	*Protection*: Availability, access, and quality of financial, health and social welfare services

Source: World Bank analysis.

revenues; (2) decreased expenditure for public services; (3) increased employment and hence, overall long-term productivity gains.

Mawn and collaborators (2017) showed a statistically significant increase in youth employment and hence a stable source of personal income for individuals, as well as positive effects on earnings and expected earnings through nine experimental and nine quasi-experimental trials of multiple reengagement interventions for youth. Cohen and Piquero (2009) found that providing a productive and healthy life trajectory to an 18-year-old youth at-risk of criminal and violent activities can save society anywhere between $2.6 million and $5.3 million (based on US data). Levin et al. (2007) estimated that the average social benefits or cost reductions per student attributable to graduating versus non-graduating from high school in the US is $209,200. It also showed that every $1 invested in prevention would yield between $1.5 and $3 in social benefits.

Catterall (2011) showed comparable gains in his study *"Societal Benefits and Costs of Dropout Recovery."* This research focused on re-enrolling and re-engaging 15–17-year old youth in 9 public charter schools in the US. A one-dollar expense in the charter school recovery program generated three dollars' worth of social benefits. In another case, the Australian Department of Education, Employment and Work Relations (DEEWR) conducted a social ROI analysis of five organizations that were part of a School-Business-Community Partnership Brokers program for re-engaging out-of-school disadvantaged youth. The analysis demonstrated that the program created a "positive return on the DEEWR cash investment where every $1 invested led up to $3.7 worth of social value" (te Riele 2014).

It is also important to note here that the social and economic costs of not investing in at-risk young people has been researched and documented for some regions such as Latin America and the Caribbean (Cunningham et al. 2008) and Australia (te Riele 2014). However, more rigorous analysis is required, especially in low-income country (LIC) and low-middle-income country (LMIC) contexts, to be able to quantify the benefits and the relative cost savings of investments made on at-risk and out-of-school young people, to be able to make a solid argument of the expected gains from such efforts.

NOTES

1. In the sample, the mean age was 16.5 years; the sample was 52.33 percent female; SD was 1.78.
2. Emerging evidence shows that emotional and cognitive engagement may be precursors to external forms of behavioral engagement.
3. From the definition of reengagement (also called dropout recovery) defined in Rennie Center for Education Research & Policy 2012.

REFERENCES

Ahmadzadeh, H., M. Çorabatır, J. A. Husseini, L. Hashem, and S. Wahby. 2014. *Ensuring Quality Education for Young Refugees from Syria*. Refugee Studies Centre, University of Oxford.

Beleli, Özsel, S. J. 2012. *Turkey Country Study, Global Initiative on Out-of-School Children*. Ankara: UNICEF.

Catterall, S. J. 2011. *The Societal Benefits and Costs of School Dropout Recovery*. Hindawi Publishing Corporation. Los Angeles: Education Research International.

Center for Promise. 2014a. *Don't Call them Dropouts: Understanding the Experiences of Young People who Leave High School before Graduation.* Washington, DC: America's Promise Alliance.

Center for Promise. 2014b. *Supporting Young People's Success in High School Re-Engagement Programs: The Role of Social Support and Self-Efficacy.* Washington, DC: America's Promise Alliance.

Center for Promise. 2015. *Don't Quit on Me: What Young People who Left School Say about the Power of Relationships.* Washington, DC: America's Promise Alliance.

Cohen, M. and A. R. Piquero. 2009. "New Evidence on the Monetary Value of Saving a High-Risk Youth." *Journal of Quantitative Criminology* 25(1): 25–49.

Cunningham, W., L. McGinnis, R. G. Verdú, C. Tesliuc, and D. Verner. 2008. *Youth at Risk in Latin America and the Caribbean: Understanding the Causes, Realizing the Potential.* Washington, DC: World Bank.

de Witte, K., S. Cabus, G. Thyssen, W. Groot, and H. M. van den Brink. 2013. "A Critical Review of the Literature on School Dropout." *Educational Research Review* 10: 13–28.

European Commission. 2010. European Policy Framework for European Cooperation in Education and Training (ET2020). https://ec.europa.eu/education/policies/european-policy-cooperation/et2020-framework_en

Finn, J. D. 1989. "Withdrawing from School." *Review of Educational Research* 59: 117–42.

Fredricks, J. A., P. C. Blumenfeld, and A. H. Paris. 2004. "School Engagement: Potential of the Concept, State of the Evidence." *Review of Educational Research* 74 (1): 59–109. doi:10.3102/00346543074001059

Hancock, K. J., and S. Zubrick. 2015. *Children and Young People at Risk of Disengagement from School.* Commissioner for Children and Young People, Western Australia.

Hébert, T. P. and S. M. Reis. 1999. "Culturally Diverse High-Achieving Students in an Urban High School." *Urban Education* 34 (4): 428–57.

Johnson, M. K., R. Crosnoe, and G. H. Elder, Jr. 2001. "Students' Attachment and Academic Engagement: The Role of Race and Ethnicity." *Sociology of Education* 74 (4): 318–40.

Kim, J. and K. Taylor. 2008. "Rethinking Alternative Education to Break the Cycle of Educational Inequality and Inequity." *The Journal of Educational Research* 101 (4): 207–19.

Levin, H., C. Belfield, P. Muennig, and C. Rouse. 2007. *The Costs and Benefits of an Excellent Education for all of America's Children.* New York: Teachers College, Columbia University.

Li, Y. 2011. "School Engagement: What It Is and Why It Is Important for Positive Youth Development." *Advances in Child Development and Behavior* 41: 131–60.

Li, Y., and R. M. Lerner. 2013. "Interrelations of Behavioral, Emotional, and Cognitive School Engagement in High School Students." *Journal of Youth and Adolescence* 42 (1): 20–32.

Li, Y., J. V. Lerner, and R. M. Lerner. 2010. "Personal and Ecological Assets and Academic Competence in Early Adolescence: The Mediating Role of School Engagement." *Journal of Youth and Adolescence* 39 (7): 801–15.

Masten, A. S., and J. L. Powell. 2003. "A Resilience Framework for Research, Policy, and Practice." In *Resilience and Vulnerability: Adaptation in the Context of Childhood Adversities,* edited by S. S. Luthar, 1–28. New York, NY: Cambridge University Press.

Mawn, L., E. J. Oliver, N. Akhter, C. L. Bambra, C. Torgerson, C. Bridle, and H. J. Stain. 2017. "Are We Failing Young People Not in Employment, Education or Training (NEETs)? A Systematic Review and Meta-Analysis of Re-Engagement Interventions." *Systematic Reviews* 6 (1).

Mills, M., P. Renshaw, and L. Zipin. 2013. "Alternative Education Provision: A Dumping Ground for 'Wasted Lives' or a Challenge to the Mainstream?" *Social Alternatives* 32 (2): 13–18.

Newmann, F. M. ed. 1992. *Student Engagement and Achievement in American Secondary Schools.* New York: Teachers College Press.

Pan, J., J. F. Zaff, and A. E. Donlan. 2017. "Social Support and Academic Engagement among Reconnected Youth: Adverse Life Experiences as a Moderator." *Journal of Research on Adolescence* 27 (4): 890–906.

Pietarinen, J., T. Soini, and K. Pyhältö. 2014. "Students' Emotional and Cognitive Engagement as the Determinants of Well-Being and Achievement in School." *International Journal of Educational Research* 67: 40–51.

Rennie Center for Education Research and Policy. 2012. *Forgotten Youth: Re-Engaging Students through Dropout Recovery*. Cambridge, MA: Rennie Center for Education Research and Policy.

Ryan, R. M., and E. L. Deci. 2000. "Self-Determination Theory and the Facilitation of Intrinsic Motivation, Social Development, and Well-Being." *American Psychologist* 55 (1): 68.

Rumberger, R. W. 1987. "High School Dropouts: A Review of Issues and Evidence." *Review of Educational Research* 57: 101–21.

Rumberger, R. W. 2004. "Why Students Drop Out of School?" In *Dropouts in America: Confronting the Graduation Rate Crisis*, edited by G. Orfied, 131–55. Cambridge. MA: Harvard Education Press.

Rumberger, R. W. 2011. *Dropping Out: Why Students Drop Out of High School and What Can Be Done about It*. Cambridge, MA: Harvard University Press.

Rumberger, R. W., and S. A. Lim. 2008. *Why Students Drop Out of School: A Review of 25 Years of Research*. California Dropout Research Project, UC Santa Barbara.

Şeker, B.D., and I. Sirkeci. 2015. "Challenges for Refugee Children at School in Eastern Turkey." *Economics and Sociology* 8 (4): 122–33.

Skinner, E., C. Furrer, G. Marchand, and T. Kindermann. 2008. "Engagement and Disaffection in the Classroom: Part of a Larger Motivational Dynamic?" *Journal of Educational Psychology* 100 (4): 765.

Smeyers, P. and M. Depaepe. 2006. "On the Rhetoric of 'What Works': Contextualizing Educational Research and the Picture of Performativity." In *Educational Research: Why 'What Works' Doesn't Work*, edited by P. Smeyers and M. Depaepe, 1–16. Dordrecht: Springer.

Sumbera, B. G. 2017. *Model Continuation High Schools: Social-Cognitive Promotive Factors that Contribute to Re-Engaging At-Risk Students Emotionally, Behaviorally, and Cognitively towards Graduation*. Doctoral dissertation, Pepperdine University.

Te Riele, K. 2014. *Putting the Jigsaw Together: Flexible Learning Programs in Australia*. Final report. Melbourne: The Victoria Institute for Education, Diversity and Lifelong Learning.

Wang, M., and J. Eccles. 2013. "School Context, Achievement Motivation, and Academic Engagement: A Longitudinal Study of School Engagement Using a Multidimensional Perspective." *Learning and Instruction* 28: 12–23.

Wehlage, G. G., R. A. Rutter, G. A. Smith, N. Lesko, and R. R. Fernandez. 1989. *Reducing the Risk: Schools as Communities of Support*. New York: Falmer Press.

Wyman, P. A., I. Sandler, S. Wolchik, and K. Nelson. 2000. "Resilience as Cumulative Competence Promotion and Stress Protection: Theory and Intervention." In *The Promotion of Wellness in Children and Adolescents*, edited by D. Cicchetti, J. Rappaport, I. Sandler, and R. P. Weissberg, 133–84. Washington, DC: Child Welfare League of America.

Zaff, J. F., K. K. Ginsberg, M. J. Boyd, and Z. Kakli. 2014. "Reconnecting Disconnected Youth: Examining the Development of Productive Engagement." *Journal of Research in Adolescence* 24: 526–40.

3 Methodology

This chapter develops a methodological framework to identify the factors, interventions and processes that can influence educational outcomes for vulnerable young people by embracing complex explanations of the phenomena of interest: educational reengagement of at-risk out-of-school adolescents and youth.

This study synthesizes some of the available evidence on educational engagement and reengagement for at-risk and out-of-school adolescents and youth living in difficult life situations. It includes a collection of evidence on interventions associated with the education reengagement of this target group. The articles reviewed include quantitative and qualitative methods—while some measure the effect sizes of interventions on the outcome of interest, others describe the details of program design and implementation leading to desired outcomes. The study covers three types of analysis[1]:

(1) To identify *'what'* interventions work using outcome-based analysis using effect sizes (through Randomized Control Trials, Quasi-Experimental Studies, and Impact Evaluations);
(2) To identify *'how'* to provide relevant services by uncovering the enabling interventions, along with breakdown and sequencing of key activities for engagement of at-risk youth;
(3) To explain *'why'* single apostrophe interventions work and *'in which contexts'* using broader research across relevant fields of study (psychology, neuroscience, economics) and theoretical foundations (realist, critical realist, and behavioral and social science research).

Finally, when contradicting evidence was found, we tried to reconcile opposite findings by understanding the complexity of the problem and the effect of context and multiple interventions to address similar problems.[2]

METHODOLOGICAL FRAMEWORK

This review embraces complex explanations of the phenomena of interest: educational reengagement of at-risk adolescents and youth. It does so by consulting inter-disciplinary and mixed-methods research and identifying associative links between interventions, mechanisms of change, and outcomes. An emerging theory of change is identified. Theories of change are the basis for program design and evaluations, to be tested for their validity and adapted to different contexts. For each program intervention, we first assess its impact (through effect sizes), then identify literature that explains further how the intervention is implemented and review a few fields of study that explain why impact is expected to happen. Evidence on what works, how, and why helps us better infer the causal linkages between interventions and outcome (i.e., to help begin to open the "black box"). We acknowledge that as a first attempt to embrace analysis of more complex evidence, there would still be some methodological and content gaps. However, we believe it is a step in the right direction given the increasing calls for a more relevant analysis of complex social programs in development fields (Reyes 2019; unpublished doctoral thesis in progress).

Our methodological framework is presented in figure 3.1. It guides the following components of this study on education reengagement of at-risk youth:

1. **Embrace complex explanations of phenomena:** Acknowledging and *embracing the interconnectedness* of the elements of a phenomenon (asking *what works, how, for whom and in what context*).
2. **Use a multi-disciplinary, mixed-methods approach:** This allows a more comprehensive understanding especially in multi-component programs.
3. **Build causal, correlational and associative links:** Understanding the *mechanisms* through which change can happen along with the impact of *context*[3] and the *processes that support behavior change*.
4. **Identify the theory of change:** This can be developed by noting the *causal links across interventions and mechanisms of change*.

FIGURE 3.1

Methodological framework for design and implementation of complex developmental challenges

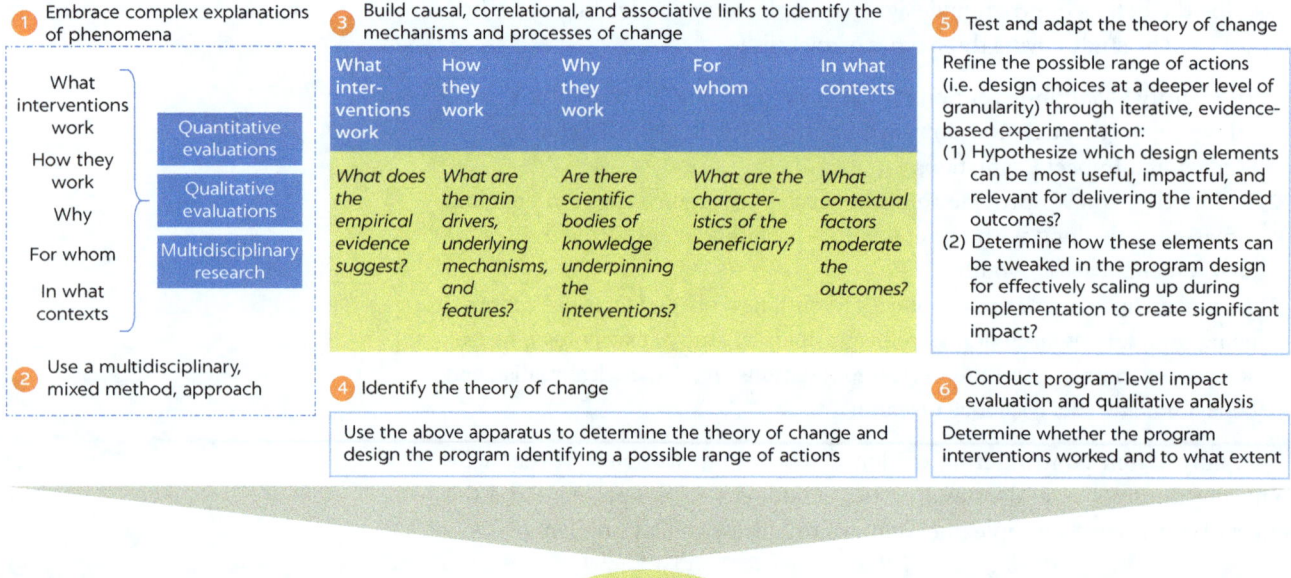

Source: World Bank analysis.
Note: This study covers step 1 through 4.

5. **Test and adapt the theory of change in the real-world context[4]:** This will be informed and iterated based on locally experienced needs and constraints.
6. **Conduct program-level impact evaluations and qualitative analysis:** This will generate the evidence to develop a better understanding of whether the program worked and to what extent.

SEARCH STRATEGY

A purposeful, mixed-method,[5] multi-disciplinary review process was used to cast a wide net for identifying related and relevant outcomes of reengagement programs for at-risk adolescents and youth in the age group of 12–17 years. This evidence base included meta-analysis and systematic reviews, randomized control trials, quasi-experimental studies, realist evaluations, case studies, program evaluations, process evaluations and theoretical studies.

Sources of information

To identify relevant literature in peer-reviewed academic journals, the team conducted systematic searches of electronic databases (including EBESCO, JSTOR, ProQuest, Eric, Wiley, Sage and Google Scholar) using a set of relevant key words and search terms. This was supplemented with web searches and forward and backward citation tracking to identify reports by practitioners, research institutions, program websites and reports by international organizations. The search was conducted during the period October 2017 to June 2018. The empirical evidence that focuses on what works is based on publications during the period 2000–18. The evidence on 'how interventions work and why' is based on a broader publication period until 2018.

Some of the key search words used were "engagement," "youth at-risk," "vulnerable adolescents," "realist evaluation," "impact evaluation," "open education," "meta-analysis," "outreach," "mentoring," "social emotional learning," "community-based," "scholarships," "conditional cash transfers," "psychosocial skills," "distance education," "blended learning," "dropping out predictors," "reengagement predictors," "youth outcomes moderators." The studies, books and reports reviewed are presented in the references at the end of each chapter with additional readings in Annex C.

Selection criteria

This study included three categories of relevant literature:

- Category 1 focused on answering What Works and included meta-analyses and program evaluations that are randomized controlled experiments with an experimental design and quasi-experimental designs.
- Category 2 focused on answering How Programs Work and included meta-analysis using realist and critical realist evaluation methods, surveys of program participants, program descriptions, case studies, white papers, theoretical studies, reports on policy and design practices.
- Category 3 focused on Why Programs Work and included multiple disciplines that informed intervention designs.

It is important to note that these categories do not relate to the quality or strength of the studies but contribute to the methodology for informing the analysis.

Quantitative studies were selected based on following criteria:

- Included an explicit definition of its expected outcomes
- Included outcomes expressed in a measurable way
- Included collected evidence on credible information on participants' outcomes
- Excluded evaluations focused on age groups solely 11 years and below or 25 years and above
- Excluded evaluations focused on prevention-based interventions alone

Qualitative studies were selected based on below criteria:

- Included evidence focused on the target group and the problem definition
- Included evidence that demonstrated credibility based on website linkages, presence of beneficiary narratives, number of citations and references
- Included globally relevant evidence.
- Excluded evidence that focused on prevention-based interventions alone.

LIMITATIONS

Various evaluation methods including randomized control trials (RCTs), quasi-experimental studies, case studies and mixed methods analysis, with varying levels of rigor have been used to assess the impact of a reengagement program on its targeted audience. Systematic study of reengagement as a complex phenomenon is recent and hence, requires further study. Thus, some the main limitations of this study are identified as below:

Limited empirical evidence
Empirical evidence on reengagement programs is thin. There are limited number of systematic evaluations to understand what components (or combination of components) make a reengagement program effective. More rigorous research is needed to identify what practitioners in schools, youth centers, post-secondary institutions, and community-based organizations are doing to effectively reengage this population to support them through graduation and guide their transition to work and/or further education.

Noise in complex, multi-component systems
Noisy variables in complex, multi-component systems make causality attributions difficult. While this study has tried to unravel the underlying elements that makes programs successful, we acknowledge that there are limitations with evaluations of multi-component programs in specifically determining the statistically-measurable component-level contributions to program and youth success.

Issues of rigor in program evaluations
While the section on 'What works?' has focused on using RCTs, quasi-experimental studies and systematic evaluations, the rigor of these evaluations maybe limited by issues of low statistical power, participant attrition, short-term measures of effectiveness rather than longitudinal effects and effects of confounders such as motivation of voluntary participants. Other types of published

research used to inform this work are limited by potential sources of biases due to self-reporting and use of various interpretative techniques.

Scarcity of research on program impacts in low- and middle-income countries
The evidence search involved purposefully looking for empirical evidence from different contexts. However, a larger number of such studies are based on programs located in the US although there is some coverage of programs in other geographic contexts such as Europe, Africa and South America as well. This points to the strong need to intensify rigorous evaluation efforts and program responses, especially if one wants to see how contextual factors mediate program participation, outcomes and impacts.

Limited evidence for specific risk categories of the adolescent and youth groups
While the evidence targeted to needs of the young person is available for the US context, there is a need for a broader understanding of youth risk categories and gather evidence on what works and how for those facing different types of risks.

Lack of consensus in definitions and indicators
While a multidimensional understanding of engagement has emerged, there are various definitions, operationalizations and measurement indicators used across the literature. Such lack of clarity has led to inconsistent use of terminology, cloudy evidence of relations, and poor measurement. This lack of clarity also reflects on the different theories used to frame the study of student engagement.

AUDIENCE

The audience for this study includes policy makers, researchers, practitioners and World Bank staff—to deepen our understanding of the reengagement process, inform policy dialogue and provide direction to program design and implementation.

Also, this initial attempt to methodologically embrace a more complex analysis of evidence for programing may be useful to researchers interested in complex social problems that merit a mixed-methods approach for causal explanations.

NOTES

1. While the evidence from outcome-based impact evaluations provided inputs into which programs are yielding results, we use more explanatory research from the behavioral and social sciences, as well as available synthesis from a 'realist' approach, to coax out more nuanced evidence on the processes that lead the identified interventions to contribute to the outcome of interest. The examples of programs showed a range of different strategies used and possible context influences.
2. The initial impetus for a methodology to analyze more complex evidence came from prior work of one of the co-authors of this study (Reyes 2019, unpublished doctoral thesis in progress).
3. Even small differences in context, convenience and salience have large effects on crucial choices (see World Bank 2015).

4. Using methods such as the PDIA (Problem Driven Iterative Adaptation) from: Andrews, Pritchett, and Woolcock (2017); Duflo 2017.
5. A mixed-method approach helps address the need for greater specificity in how protective factors are linked with the risks they mitigate (Guerra 1998; Luthar, Cicchetti, and Becker 2000).

REFERENCES

Andrews, M., L. Pritchett, and M. Woolcock. 2017. *Building State Capability: Evidence, Analysis, Action*. Oxford University Press.

Duflo, E. 2017. "The Economist as Plumber—Richard T. Ely Lecture." *American Economic Review* 107 (5): 1–26.

Guerra, N. G. 1998. "Serious and Violent Juvenile Offenders: Gaps in Knowledge and Research Priorities." In *Serious and Violent Juvenile Offenders*, edited by R. Loeber and D. Farrington, 389–404. Thousand Oaks, CA: Sage.

Luthar, S. S., D. Cicchetti, and B. Becker, B. 2000. "The Construct of Resilience: A Critical Evaluation and Guidelines for Future Work." *Child Development* 71 (3): 543–62.

Reyes, J. 2019. *The Transformative Resilience Framework: Explaining Complex Problems in Education in Emergencies*. Unpublished doctoral thesis in progress. Falmer: University of Sussex.

World Bank. 2015. *World Development Report 2015: Mind, Society, and Behavior*. Washington, DC.

4 Evidence on School Engagement and Reengagement: What Works, How & Why, for Whom, and in What Contexts?

This chapter summarizes the empirical evidence on what interventions work for educational reengagement, reviews examples to synthesize how they work, and examines their scientific basis, referencing multiple disciplines. It then examines for whom and in what context these interventions have an impact and elaborates on the role of the platforms and pathways of reengagement.

The review of interventions to prevent early school leaving and to engage/re-engage at-risk learners in an education program yielded a range of strategies. In this chapter we identify and distinguish the interventions as *core* and *enabling*, evidenced by their positive effects on relevant outcomes and by identifying how their composite elements, events, or activities relate to each other in the process of change. Mentoring and psychosocial support (PSS), are classified as *core interventions* and the *enabling interventions* determined are outreach, case management, integrated support services and referrals, and financial incentives. Then we examine some of the substantive evidence from different fields of science to infer why these interventions and processes work. Lastly, we examine for whom and in what contexts these interventions have an impact and explain the role played by blended learning platforms and flexible educational pathways.

WHAT WORKS: REENGAGEMENT INTERVENTIONS AND EFFECT SIZES[1,2]

Based on the summary of various quantitative systematic reviews, we identified two core interventions that have a quantifiable effect on outcomes related to school reengagement: (1) mentoring and (2) psychosocial support (PSS) with a focus on social-emotional learning (SEL). The level of contribution of each intervention is assessed through its effect size (ES) (also see box. 4.1). From available effect size analysis, mentoring and PSS provide the most contributions to the cognitive, emotional and social skills of at-risk learners (see Annex B for a table summarizing the evidence on what works).

Mentoring

Quantitative evidence shows that mentoring interventions have a positive impact on outcomes for at-risk youth. Mentoring has been defined as a "relationship between an older, more experienced adult and an unrelated, younger protégé—a relationship in which the adult provides ongoing guidance, instruction, and encouragement aimed at developing the competence and character of the protégé" (Rhodes 2002, p. 3). The study results from randomized controlled trials of mentoring programs such as Across Ages, Big Brothers Big Sisters of America, and Friends of the Children provide evidence of statistically significant improvements in academic performance and belief in self-efficacy and point to the importance of developing close relationships between mentors and mentees for success (Bayer, Grossman and DuBois 2013; Center for Promise 2015; Converse and Kraft 2009; Eddy et al. 2017; Herrera et al. 2011; Komosa-Hawkins 2012; Meyer and Bouchey 2010; Taylor et al. 1999).

A meta-analysis, *"Does mentoring matter?"* by Eby and colleagues (2008), reviewed three major areas of mentoring research (youth, academic, workplace) to determine the overall effect size associated with the following mentoring outcomes for mentees: behavioral, attitudinal, health-related, interpersonal, motivational, and career. It identified 112 quantitative studies where the sole or primary intervention was mentoring, comparing mentored and non-mentored individuals on these individual-level outcomes. Youth mentoring was defined as a naturally occurring (informal) or formally arranged (such as Big Brother Big Sister program) relationship between a nonparental adult and a child, adolescent, or young adult (Blinn-Pike 2007).

The analysis provides evidence that mentoring is significantly and positively correlated with all aforementioned outcome variables, albeit at different levels. Although all effect sizes (ES) were small in magnitude, they showed a positive trend. The largest effect was found between mentoring and the mentee's behavioral and attitudinal changes: helping others, school attitudes, and career attitudes. Reviews of youth (DuBois et al. 2002) and academic (Sambunjak et al. 2006) mentoring found an association between mentoring and both career and employment outcomes. Other reviews link youth mentoring (DuBois et al. 2002; DuBois and Silverthorn 2005), academic mentoring (Dorsey and Baker 2004; Sambunjak et al. 2006), and workplace mentoring (Underhill 2006) to outcomes such as positive self-image, emotional adjustment, and psychological well-being, positive social relationships, higher performance, and less problem behavior, although several also have small ES.

Two meta-analyses of youth mentoring programs in the United States posited that social, emotional, cognitive, and identity processes, when interconnected, created caring and meaningful relationships between youth and nonparental adults (or older peers) that promoted positive developmental trajectories (DuBois et al. 2002, 2011). Here, the mentoring intervention focused on promoting resiliency among youth from at-risk backgrounds (Rhodes 1994). The above analyses covered 55 evaluations for the period 1970–98 and 73 evaluations for the period 1999–2010, respectively.

Both studies found positive effects of mentoring programs intended to promote positive youth (18 years or less) outcomes.[3] The 2002 study results indicated an overall average weighted effect size of 0.14 at the 95 percent confidence interval (CI) (ranging from 0.10 to 0.18), and an overall average weighted effect size of 0.18 at the 95 percent CI (ranging from 0.11 to 0.25) for fixed and random effects, respectively. The 2011 study indicated an effect size of 0.21 for end-of-program assessments averaged across all its 73 studies, with a 95 percent CI. The 2011 study thus reconfirmed the previous findings, indicating significant improvement for mentored youth (0.25 ± 0.14) and significant decline for comparison youth (−0.17 ± 0.11). Additionally, it indicated a positive impact of mentoring programs on school attendance, grades, and academic achievement test scores but not on substance use. DuBois and colleagues also provide a word of caution that mentoring programs targeting at-risk youth facing cumulative effects of both personal and contextual risk may be less effective than programs targeting those facing fewer risks. Kuperminc and colleagues highlight that youth mentoring leads to greater benefits when accompanied by other support services (2005). Thus, the program design becomes a crucial factor and resources are likely to get stretched.

Furthermore, researchers have also identified moderators that influence the effect size, including characteristics of participating youth (gender, race, and ethnicity, developmental level, single-parent household, socioeconomic background, at-risk status), mentor–mentee relationships (actual frequency of contact, average length), and program features (mentoring alone or in a multicomponent program, using psychosocial or instrumental outcomes or both, in a large urban geographic location or not, and by gender of mentor, mentor background, implementation monitoring, etc.). This analysis noted the following (DuBois et al. 2002, 2011).

Mentee and mentor characteristics

- **At-risk status of mentee.** Youth from backgrounds of environmental risk and disadvantage appear most likely to benefit from participation in mentoring programs. In the 2002 study, at-risk status was found to be a significant moderator of effect size. This means that youth exposed to risk benefited more from mentoring interventions. The largest effect size of 0.26 was found for youth experiencing both individual and environmental risk factors, while an effect size of 0.17 was found for those facing environmental risk alone. Larger effect sizes (= 0.19) were reported for youth from primarily low socioeconomic backgrounds than for other samples (= 0.11).
- **Mentee characteristics.** Similar and favorable effects of mentoring programs were found across youth with varied demographic and background characteristics, such as age, gender, race, ethnicity, and family structure, and also across different types of outcomes and data sources, suggesting that mentoring is a universally applicable intervention for young people.
- **Mentor characteristics.** For mentor characteristics, gender, race, and ethnicity were not found to be significant moderators of effect size; however, a background in a helping role or profession (for instance, as a teacher) was a significant moderator of effect size. Evaluations of programs that used these types of mentors reported larger ES (= 0.26) than those that did not (= 0.09). Also, no significant relationship was found with mentor compensation.

Program characteristics

- **Evidence Based Programs.** For youth exhibiting individual-level risk factors, positive effects of mentoring were evident for programs engaged in a majority of theory-based and empirically-based "best practices" (0.20 and 0.24 for fixed and random effects, respectively, with 95 percent CI). These best practices in program features included: ongoing training with structured

activities for mentors, expectation setting with youth on frequency of contact, mechanisms for support and parental involvement, and monitoring of overall program implementation. In multivariate analyses, these practices were consistently represented among the strongest predictors of greater reported positive effects for mentoring programs.
- **Mentor-mentee relationship:** DuBois and colleagues (2002) showed that program effects are enhanced significantly when strong relationships are formed between mentors and youth, using nine independent samples with a total of 35 ES on average. Among youth participating in mentoring programs, those for whom relationships of greater intensity or quality were evident scored between one-quarter and one-third of a standard deviation higher in a favorable direction on outcome measures (average effect size = 0.30 under random effects and = 0.29 with fixed effects, 95 percent CI, range 0.15–0.45).
- **Characteristics with less significant or nonsignificant ES:** The ES did not demonstrate a significant relationship with geographic program location or the setting in which mentoring activities took place. ES was found to be unrelated to whether mentoring was an isolated intervention or in a multicomponent program and to whether it involved psychosocial or instrumental outcomes.

Another meta-analytic evaluation of 46 studies, by Tolan et al. (2014), reviewed mentoring interventions in the United States (1970–2011) for effects on delinquency and three associated outcomes (aggression, drug use, and academic functioning) for at-risk youth. These youths were identified by conduct problems, aggressive behavior, and high-crime environmental characteristics. Mean effects sizes were significant and positive for each outcome category (0.11 for academic achievement, 0.16 for drug use, 0.21 for delinquency, 0.29 for aggression). The study found heterogeneity in ES for all four outcomes, with stronger effects when the mentor's motivation was his/her 'professional development and advancement', (as opposed to 'personal motivation or civic duty'). Significant improvements in effects were found when advocacy and emotional support were emphasized in the mentoring process.

Finally, reviews of emerging research by Kuperminc (2016) and Kuperminc and Thomason (2013) point to the potential relevance of *group mentoring*. Evidence is beginning to accumulate that supports at least the short-term effectiveness of formal group mentoring programs. There is some preliminary evidence that:

- Group mentoring programs can produce an array of positive outcomes for youth (behavioral, emotional, academic, etc.) and seem to be effective across a wide range of youth participants (of varying ages, ethnicities, and so on).
- Additional relational processes, such as group cohesion and belonging and a strong group identity, may also contribute to the outcomes youth experience from group mentoring. The group identity could be based on specific interests such as a sport, gaming, or specific challenges such as teenage pregnancy or others.
- Group mentoring programs offer a context for activities that develop mentee skills, change mentee attitudes, and offer positive peer interactions; and these processes can lead to behavioral outcomes for participants.

Psychosocial support and learning

Positive impact, using quantitative research studies, was found from PSS and SEL interventions. *Psychosocial support* "describe[s] any type of local or outside support that aims to protect or promote psychosocial well-being and/or prevent or treat mental disorders for people in crisis situations" (INEE 2016, p. 8). It is an umbrella term that encompasses three domains of cognitive, affective, and behavioral competencies, and includes trauma recovery, family and community guidance, and learning support. Psychosocial interventions, when directed towards learning, are referred to as social-emotional learning or SEL. SEL aims to foster the development of five interrelated competencies, namely: self-awareness, self-management, social awareness, relationship skills, and responsible decision-making. These five competencies cut across the cognitive, social, and emotional domains (INEE 2016).

A growing body of research evidence (Carneiro and Heckman 2003; Cunha et al. 2006; Heckman 2000) summarized by Inoue et al. (2015) suggests that so-called soft skills—behavior and personality traits, goals, motivations, and preferences—strongly influence schooling decisions and a wide variety of risky decisions among youth (Heckman, Stixrud, and Urzua 2006; Rumberger and Lamb 2003). Thus, even when youth know the longer-term financial benefits of attending school, the decision to exit early can be considered a consequence of high "psychic costs" faced due to attending, such as poor skills for academic success and low sense of academic self-efficacy and self-esteem (Heckman and Kautz 2012). Thus, universal SEL programs that offer substantial benefits to counteract these psychic costs are likely to be effective.

A meta-analysis found positive follow-up effects of 82 school-based SEL interventions, including classroom-based activities, classroom or school climate enhancement efforts, various school wide initiatives, and parent involvement (Taylor et al. 2017). The interventions involved 97,406 students from kindergarten through high school (37.8 percent in kindergarten to 5th grade, 45.1 percent in 6th to 8th grade, and 13.4 percent in 9th to 12th grade). The studies targeted at least one of the five SEL interrelated competency domains described earlier. The analysis found statistically significant positive effects of SEL interventions at follow-up for each of the seven outcome categories (social and emotional skills; attitudes toward self, others, and school; positive social behaviors; academic performance; conduct problems; emotional distress; and substance use). Mean ES ranged from 0.13 to 0.33 (95 percent CI, $p < 0.05$) with SEL program participants benefiting significantly more than controls across all social and emotional assets and positive and negative indicators of well-being.

The review also found positive impact across ethnic and socio-economic backgrounds, but with no significant differences across them. Fourteen interventions covered by the review included at least 75 percent children from poor and working-class families, which formed a lower-income comparison group. Across ethnic backgrounds, for 6 months or more post-intervention, no significant differences were observed in the impact of SEL between interventions involving predominately white students (n = 21, ES = 0.23, 95 percent CI [0.14, 0.32]), predominately students of color (n = 13, ES = 0.18, 95 percent CI [0.06, 0.30]), or interventions containing a diverse student population (n = 19, ES = 0.17, 95 percent CI [0.08, 0.27]). No significant difference was found in follow-up ES between interventions involving predominately low- and working-class students (n = 13, ES = 0.21, 95 percent CI [0.08, 0.33]) compared with those of another SES status (i.e., either predominately middle- and upper-class or diverse SES samples (n = 36, ES = 0.23, 95 percent CI [0.15, 0.30]). Further, comparison of follow-up effects for interventions conducted in the United States (n = 43, ES = 0.20, 95 percent

CI [0.14, 0.26]) and abroad (n = 38, ES = 0.16, 95 percent CI [0.09, 0.22]) revealed comparable positive effects in both contexts. Thus, this meta-analytic study, although focused on school-based interventions, mainly suggests that SEL may be effective for middle and high school students, with no significant differences across ethnic, socioeconomic, and geographical backgrounds.

Another meta-analytic study of 73 after-school programs in the United States promoting social and personal skills for adolescents and youth found that there is an overall positive and statistically significant impact on participating youth. Improvements were seen in three major areas: feelings and attitudes (i.e., their self-perceptions and bonding), behavioral adjustment (i.e., increases in positive social behaviors and decreases in problem behaviors and drug use), and school performance (i.e., grades and level of academic achievement). The average effect size of +0.22 (95 percent CI, [0.16,0.29]) indicates that these programs have an overall positive and statistically significant impact on the program participants. The most effective programs utilized evidence-based skills-development training activities that were sequential, active, focused, and explicit (Durlak and Weissberg 2007).

Another meta-analytic review, also by Durlak and colleagues (2011), reviewed 213 school-based, universal social and emotional learning (SEL) programs involving 270,034 students, kindergarten through high school. The study found direct links between competencies in social and emotional learning, with an overall 11-percentile gain in academic achievement and an effect size of 0.31 (95 percent CI, [0.26,0.36]) for targeted socio-emotional skills. Compared to controls, SEL participants demonstrated significantly improved social and emotional skills, attitudes, behavior, and academic performance. It was found that school teaching staff can successfully conduct SEL programs. This study also found that the incorporation of evidence-based SEL programing, using the four recommended practices (sequential, active, focused, and explicit) for developing skills moderated program outcomes as did the presence of implementation problems. These studies by Durlak and Weissberg (2007) and Durlak et al. (2011) point us to some of the features of effective programming that lead to positive academic and nonacademic outcomes, both in after-school and school-based interventions.

Further, in terms of program features, a meta-analysis (Wigelsworth et al. 2016) of 89 studies conducted between 1995 and 2013 reported the effects of school-based, universal SEL programs on seven outcome variables related to the five SEL competency domains of self-awareness, self-management, social awareness, relationship skills, and responsible decision making. The program features analyzed included the international transferability of the design, level of participation of the program developer in the evaluation, and evaluation results for efficacy versus efficiency. International transferability was used as a proxy to measure the impact of program implementation in its country of origin or outside. The level of the developer's involvement in evaluation was defined as 'led', 'involved', or 'independent' according to whether the evaluation was led by the same developer, was receiving some developer support, or was executed completely independently. Efficacy studies demonstrate the internal validity of a program (for example whether it has highly trained and carefully supervised implementation staff), while effectiveness is used to test whether and how an intervention works in real-world contexts and naturalistic settings (such as using just the staff and resources that would normally be available). The findings may be summarized as below:

- **Statistically significant size effects across studies.** Size effects were significant, although the magnitude varied by outcome type, with the largest effects for social-emotional competence (0.53) and the smallest for attitudes toward self (0.17).
- **Local design vs. external design.** Studies implemented within the same country in which they were developed showed greater effects than those transported abroad for four of seven outcome variables, and in all four the effects were statistically significant. Notably, two outcome variables—conduct problems (such as anti-social behavior, bullying, and aggression) and academic attainment—showed significantly higher ES for studies coded as "away," indicating a higher transferability of design elements associated with these outcome variables.
- **Developer involvement in evaluation.** Developer involvement was associated with a potential inflation of outcome ES, compared with effects that might be expected in a real-world situation.
- **Efficacy and effectiveness.** Lastly, 61 studies were coded for efficacy (the intervention producing the expected result) and 25 were coded for effectiveness (having a beneficial effect in a real-world setting). Six of seven outcome variables showed greater size effects for efficacy than for effectiveness, while the outcome variable "social-emotional competence" showed a greater effect size for effectiveness (0.47) than for efficacy (0.31). This calls for a better understanding of field forces in context that can facilitate or inhibit the intervention (see the next section, "How reengagement interventions work").

Regarding youth affected by conflict and forced displacement, a recent experimental study (Panter-Brick et al. 2018) tested the impact of an 8-week PSS program and found medium to small ES for all psychosocial outcomes. The program included structured activities informed by a profound stress attunement framework for advancing adolescents, delivered in group-format to youth ages 12–18 in communities heavily affected by the Syrian crisis, including both Syrian refugees and Jordanian youth. The intervention improved insecurity, distress, and mental health difficulties but not prosocial behavior and post-traumatic stress reactions. Beneficial impacts were strongest for adolescents who had experienced four or more lifetime traumas. With respect to levels of insecurity, youth engaged in the psychosocial intervention had sustained benefits relative to youth who did not.

Lastly, family and community support form an integral part of the affective and behavioral support for at-risk youth. For example, a study measured the impact of adolescent friendships and/or family support in adolescents exposed to early-life stresses before age 11, such as bullying. It found that close family and social support was negatively associated with subsequent depressive symptoms (van Harmelen et al. 2016). Another study that analyzed the impact of family characteristics on the school success of 211 at-risk adolescents found that both family cohesion and parental monitoring predicted school engagement, but neither family characteristic predicted the grade-point average (Annunziata et al. 2006).

While systematic evaluation of SEL programs in school and after-school settings may not be considered directly useful for at-risk and out-of-school adolescents and youth, the literature on programs using positive youth development and resilience approaches as well as those addressing significantly disadvantaged young people highlight the need for psychosocial supports that act

> **BOX 4.1**
>
> ### A brief note on the magnitude and implications of effect size estimates
>
> While the overall average estimated effect size (ES) for mentoring and psychosocial support (PSS) interventions may seem quite modest, well-recognized researchers (DuBois et al. 2002; Taylor et al. 2017; Tolan et al. 2014) argue that Cohen's benchmarks of effects as small (.20), medium (.50), or large (.80) are not applicable for universal promotion or prevention studies nor are they relevant for interpreting follow-up data. A mean ES of 0.33 of SEL interventions on academic performance (obtained from eight studies) compares to post effects obtained by strictly educational interventions (Hill et al. 2008). For other outcomes, there are no current empirical standards for comparing the ES of positive youth development interventions. As current data is new to the fields of social-emotional learning and positive youth development, the reported mean effects may serve as initial benchmarks for comparing the success of future efforts.
>
> Furthermore, since numerous programmatic and other environmental variables are likely to be critical for fully realizing potential benefits of youth mentoring and PSS programs, there is a need for greater consideration of specific context-based factors influencing effectiveness. Also, outcomes for youth at risk due to personal vulnerabilities vary substantially in relation to program characteristics (for instance, evidence shows that poorly implemented programs may have an adverse effect on such youth). Hence, there is a need for greater caution in adherence to guidelines for the design and implementation of effective programs as well as more in-depth assessment of relationship and contextual factors in the evaluation of programs. This calls for systematic and specific programmatic reporting on processes and implementation features, which can help make mentoring and PSS-based interventions more effective.

as protective and promotive forces (see chapters 1 and 2 of this study). Thus, there is an urgent and important effort required to conduct empirical evaluations of social-emotional and psychosocial programs for out-of-school disadvantaged youth in different contexts to gather evidence on their effectiveness.

HOW REENGAGEMENT INTERVENTIONS WORK

In addition to the evidence of the impact of mentoring and PSS for at-risk youth, the literature provides evidence on how to implement these interventions. *This is important because key activities, processes, and contextual factors can have a causal impact—either inhibiting or facilitating the achievement of expected outcomes.* Given the cumulative risks and complex needs of out-of-school youth, outreach, integrative case management and referral services along with financial support can enable these youth to re-engage. Blended learning platforms and multiple educational pathways can help address the common need for flexibility. This section presents evidence of some how-to processes and mechanisms related to these interventions to support at-risk learners.

Lessons learned on how to implement mentoring

As noted before, mentoring interventions have had a statistically significant positive impact on a variety of outcomes for at-risk youth, including educational outcomes. Given the extensive evidence, it is important to capture the lessons learned on how these services are provided. To recap, mentoring is a "relationship between an older, more experienced adult and an unrelated, younger protégé—a relationship in which the adult provides ongoing guidance, instruction, and encouragement aimed at developing the competence and character of the protégé" (Rhodes 2002, p. 3). The most important processes are focused precisely on the inter-relationship between mentor and mentee: the type of support, the relational approach, the relevant skills of the mentor, and the predisposition and aspirations of the mentee.

The positive impact of a mentor relationship in an educational setting is founded on the principles of protection and promotion. In a realist synthesis evaluation of nine diverse studies, Pawson (2006) extracts the constituent mechanisms of an interpersonal mentor-mentee relationship. The process of change depends on a combination of trust, support in direction setting, coaching to acquire skills and other resources, and help with contacts and networking. This set of functions is facilitated in four mentoring stages:

- **Befriending:** Creating bonds of trust and sharing new experiences so that the mentee recognizes the legitimacy of other people and other perspectives.
- **Direction-setting:** Promoting a sense of self-reflection by discussing alternatives and possible actions and having the mentee reconsider his or her range of loyalties, values, and ambitions.
- **Coaching:** Advising, cajoling, or even coaxing the mentee into acquiring the skills, assets, credentials, and testimonials required to enter and engage with mainstream education modalities.
- **Sponsoring:** Advocating and networking on behalf of the mentee to help them gain the requisite contacts and information about opportunities.

An array of mentor skills and qualities are required to achieve a successful and sustained reengagement of mentees in education and technical programs. Following from the four stages above, mentor skills range from peace-making at the befriending stage to fence-mending as the mentee tests out alternative goals, and finally trouble-shooting, brainstorming, and brokering channels for education and career guidance. As a sponsor of the mentee, the mentor also needs to step up to engage with and build bridges with different agencies and agents at various stages of the mentoring process. These connections include family and close relatives at the befriending stage, the mentee's community and its authority figures in the direction-setting stage, and training and career guidance professionals at the coaching and sponsoring stages.

Finally, the evaluation finds other success conditions. Mentoring works better if it is embedded in a program offering support for further education, training, and career aspirations. The built-in resilience and aspirations of mentees play a significant role in their progress. Also, different mentors will have different experiences and sets of skills. As youth progress in their education and life plans, they need access to a variety of mentors who operate in the different stages in which they need support. A recent qualitative study of 61 youth by Ungar and Ikeda[4] (2017) corroborates the above synthesis and further expands the understanding of the multiple roles a mentor needs to play in the mentor-youth relationship. In the study, the authors describe the roles in the below terms:

- **Informal supporters** are mentors who de-professionalize their role and flatten hierarchies, emphasizing empathy and enforcing few rules. This aligns to

the skills required at the befriending stage, where mutual respect and trust-building are essential.
- **Administrators** are mentors who enforce rules that are in the youth's best interest, being a source of structure and consequences with firm boundaries but with little tolerance for flexible case planning or emotional engagement. This role can be loosely mapped onto the direction-setting stage, where youth feel supported but also begin taking responsibility.
- **Caregivers** are mentors who hold reasonable expectations and impose structures but are flexible in their negotiations with youth when rules are broken, thus combining the qualities of the first two categories. This positions mentor workers as authoritative parent-like caregivers with permeable but enforceable boundaries and well-articulated expectations. This role offers coaching and networking support while also enforcing structures and holding the youth accountable.

The Ungar and Ikeda study found that all three engagement strategies (informal support, administrator, and caregiver) were optimal according to the circumstances and depending on the level of risk, the age appropriateness of the rules, and the cultural norms for expected behavior. Thus, no single strategy for engaging young people as a mentor is ideal. Mentoring involves a process of negotiation and renegotiation that balances (1) the need to build a trusting relationship in which young people feel protected and are full participants and (2) the provision of enough structure to promote and help them succeed. Overall, the role conceptualizations of mentors and the organizational culture within which the mentors work are important in helping at-risk youth succeed (Lakind, Eddy, and Zell 2014). The mentee's progress is nonlinear, and the mentoring relationship needs to have a persistent adaptive element for rebuilding trust at every step, strengthening resilience against new forms of obstacles, and building confidence to accomplish success in acquiring new skills.

Other meta-analytic studies of mentoring programs by Tolan et al. (2013, p.183), DuBois et al. (2002, 2011) and Rhodes (2002) also included a review of mentoring process models, which identified four processes as central to mentoring:

- **Emotional support and friendliness** to promote self-efficacy, confidence, and sense of mattering;
- **Provision of information or teaching that might aid the recipient** in managing social, educational, legal, family, and peer challenges;
- **Identification of the recipient with the mentor,** which helps with motivation, behavior, and bonding or investment in prosocial behavior and social responsibility; and
- **Advocacy for the recipient** in various systems and settings.

These findings from meta-analytic reviews strengthen and emphasize the above findings by Pawson (2006) and Ungar and Ikeda (2017).

Lessons learned on how to implement psychosocial services

There is overwhelming evidence of the positive impact of psychosocial interventions for the emotional, behavioral, and cognitive reengagement of at-risk youth. For these learners, psychosocial services provide the pathways of protection (i.e., the reduction of negative behaviors, drawn from risk and resilience research) and promotion (i.e., the increase of positive behaviors, drawn from positive youth development research) (Kia-Keating et al. 2011; Rutter 1987). School context (policies, curricular and extracurricular programs and practices) can provide learning opportunities that scaffold the development of students' emotional, behavioral, and cognitive engagement (INEE 2016, pp.61; Khanlou and Wray 2014; Main and Whatman 2016; Sumbera 2017, pp. 174–93; Zins et al. 2004).

Psychosocial interventions must include processes for emotional engagement of students to create trust, confidence, and a motivation to succeed. These processes strengthen the students' affective relationship with educators and the school, creating a positive shift in their mindset toward their education. Schools in turn must provide the policies, programs, and practices to support the engagement of at-risk learners (Eccles et al. 1983; Fredricks, Blumenfeld and Paris 2004; Sumbera 2017; Voelkl 1997; Yazzie-Mintz 2007). Positive emotional experiences that initiate an alteration in self-belief open the pathways that strengthen cognitive and behavioral engagement of learners. Schools and teachers can promote these emotional and behavioral changes in several ways:

- **Environment.** Creating a welcoming, mutually respectful, clean, and safe learning environment.
- **Expectations.** Setting high expectations and communicating clearly, frequently, and openly, based on mutual respect and trust.
- **Decision making.** Shared decision making, such as through flexible scheduling.[5]
- **Participation.** Creating opportunities for active student participation on a continuous basis in high-quality, meaningful work such as community services and co- and extra-curricular activities.
- **Individualized support.** Offering individualized support opportunities and experiences such as through counseling, one-on-one activities.
- **Celebrating progress.** Celebrating small successes and acknowledging student progress.

Emotional engagement in a student's own social and physical environment can lead to cognitive engagement, required for learning and school success (Bandura 1977; Weiner 2007). An educational site can provide the mechanism for this process by offering:

- **A structured but adaptable learning environment.** This includes multiple intake dates, different pathways for earning course credits, and consistent routines.
- **Relevant educational experiences.** This includes individualized academic plans and career programs that match students' interests and potential.
- **Integrating social-emotional components in the learning process.** This includes adapted curriculum, pedagogical practices, and classroom management.

Evidence exists on how to integrate SEL into the curricular content and delivery. One such emerging evidence-based curriculum design is known as SAFE, an acronym that stands for: *sequenced, active, focused, and explicit* (Durlak et al. 2011; Durlak, Weissberg, and Pachan 2010). Core curricular content (such as in reading, math, and science) can contribute to social-emotional engagement, and in turn to cognitive engagement, through: (1) *sequenced* activities led in a coordinated and connected way to skills, (2) *active* forms of learning, (3) *focused* on developing one or more social skills, and (4) *explicit* about targeting specific skills. Other researchers have also identified the importance of one or more of these elements in after-school programs (Larson and Verma 1999; Miller 2003; and National Research Council and Institute of Medicine 2002).

Other SEL applications within school programs include student centered pedagogy, learner participation in classroom management, and sports and artistic activities in the formal curriculum. Other options are to support SEL only through limited and fixed slots of time, such as for cognitive-behavioral group work, self-esteem enhancement programs, conflict resolution training, and peer mediation (Martin 2012). The more completely SEL interventions are integrated into the regular educational program, the more likely they are to succeed. Similarly, who is trained and to what extent they are trained in relevant SEL and PSS practices have implications for effectiveness. Greater the extent (in both range and depth) of training and wider the participation of different stakeholders (both adults and youth), better the implementation (Jones and Bouffard 2012).

In another study, Yeager (2017) finds that effective universal SEL that positively transforms adolescents' lives focuses on *mindsets* and *climate* rather than solely on *skills* (see box 4.2). Harnessing adolescents' developmental motivations, U.S.-based programs such as Becoming A Man and Teen Outreach aim to make them feel respected by adults and peers and offer them the chance to gain status and admiration from people whose opinions they value. Less encouragingly, typical SEL programs—which directly teach skills and invite participants to rehearse those skills over the course of many classroom lessons—were found to have a poor track record with middle adolescents (roughly ages 14–17), even though they work well with younger children. Yeager advocates for programs to take the *climate and mindset* approach when working with adolescents and include three elements: (1) creating a mindset that harnesses the adolescent desire for status and respect; (2) creating a climate that is more respectful toward adolescents; and (3) creating a mindset that blunts the power of threats to peer status and respect. Based on empirical program evaluations, three elements of highly effective SEL programing for adolescents were identified:

- **Make classrooms more rigorous and set high expectations of performance.**
- **Reduce unfairness** since young people act out against rules and disciplining systems that are biased, unjust, and disrespectful.
- **Encourage and support authentic adolescent relationships with adults**, achieved by honoring young people's desire to feel respected.

Finally, the study offers successful examples of teacher training programs to create such intellectually challenging and respectful learning environments (Gregory et al. 2016; Okonofua, Paunesku and Walton 2016) that have shown substantial positive effects (see box 4.2).

As a last overarching note, psycho-social and social-emotional skills are learnt over time and need continuous and consistent support and encouragement. This requires an enabling environment that is intentional about continuously supporting and monitoring student behavior, is inclusive of parental involvement as well as of other relevant stakeholders such as mentors and outreach workers, and is based on localized knowledge related to the day-to-day functioning of students' lives. It can take place through both promotion and prevention efforts. Four broad, mutually inclusive approaches can be adopted: (1) infusing SEL in teaching practices to create a learning environment supportive of SEL, (2) infusing SEL instruction into an

> **BOX 4.2**
>
> ## Successful examples of teacher training programs from three studies
>
> **Becoming a Man—a psychosocial support program**
>
> Becoming a Man (BAM), which aims to reduce youth violence in Chicago and involves a weekly school-based discussion group for 7th to 10th grade male students at high risk of failure, was found to produce dramatic effects. BAM features open-ended, student-led discussions with mentors from the neighborhood, along with a series of activities that build relationships and a sense of community with others in a small group. Based on two randomized control trials (2009–10 and 2013–15), BAM reduced arrests among participants by 28–35 percent and violent crime by 45–50 percent and increased high school graduation rates by 12–19 percent at long-term follow-up. The program also involves an appealing act of defiance: students have to skip class to attend. Paradoxically, skipping class to attend BAM led to higher graduation rates (Heller et al. 2013; Yeager 2017).
>
> The program *does not*
>
> - encourage young men to suppress their desire to fight or retaliate when facing disrespect, or
> - tell young people what they should do or suggest right and wrong.
>
> The program *does*
>
> - acknowledge that sometimes it is important to retaliate to protect one's reputation, and
> - help develop new mindsets for interpreting threats and identify alternate ways to demonstrate their masculinity (focusing on integrity, personal accountability, saving face, and maintaining status).
>
> **My Teaching Partner-Secondary—a teacher training and mentoring program**
>
> This is a comprehensive teacher training and mentoring program by Anne Gregory (Rutgers University) to help 86 high school teachers (covering more than 2,000 students) create an intellectually challenging but respectful classroom climate. Yeager (2017) argues that this is not a typical social-emotional learning (SEL) program—it does not train teachers to teach students self-control skills or how to manage their emotions. Instead, it trains teachers to create a climate that treats students with respect, takes them seriously, and gives them more autonomy in choosing meaningful work. This helps teachers exhibit care and create a sense of belonging. The study showed that students in treatment classes
>
> - engaged in higher-order thinking and reasoning, rather than tedious 'seat work'
> - were less likely to be disciplined for breaking rules, and
> - exhibited significant reduction in the racial gap in discipline infractions, even 2 years after the teacher training ended, which was strongest when teachers created academically demanding classrooms that respected students' intellectual competence.
>
> That is, making school easier does not lead students to respect rules, but challenging students and treating them as though they could develop competence can.
>
> **Online teacher training module—to encourage an empathetic mindset about discipline**
>
> This was a minimal teacher-training intervention that included an online activity for middle school teachers, which they could complete in their own time without guidance from researchers, that was intended to change their beliefs about discipline. Teachers were persuaded that discipline should be empathetic, not 'zero tolerance' and lacking in compassion for students' reasons for acting out. In an evaluation with over 35 teachers and 1,200 middle-school students, the researchers found that students in treatment classrooms reported fewer experiences of disrespect and received half as many suspensions, which fell from 9 percent of students to 4.5 percent. When students felt that the climate was more respectful, they behaved in ways that showed they could manage their frustrations and emotions (Okonofua, Paunesku, and Walton 2016). The authors claim that this intervention can be delivered at near-zero marginal cost to large samples of teachers and students.
>
> *Source:* Yeager 2017.

academic curriculum, (3) creating policies and organizational structures that support students' social and emotional development, and (4) directly teaching SEL skills in free-standing lessons (CASEL Guide 2015). No matter *how* the program communicates with the youth, the most effective universal SEL interventions need to impact mindsets and climate, as focusing on skills alone would not be enough (Yeager 2017).

Identifying and reaching out to vulnerable learners

Although mentoring and SEL have been evaluated for quantifiable ES related to protection and promotion of at-risk youth, evidence suggests there are other enabling interventions that have a decisive impact on whether at-risk learners succeed. The first and foremost intervention is about *access*. An effective outreach activity is a crucial step to engage at-risk youth in support services. Outreach work is "a contact-making and resource-mediating social activity targeted at individuals and groups who otherwise are hard-to-reach and who need easily accessible linkages to support" (Andersson 2013, p. 184).

A mixed-methods meta-analysis of 16 outreach programs found that 63 percent of the youth contacted through outreach participated in the offered service. Notably, the qualitative analysis also found that the greater the risks of exclusion for the target group, the more difficult it is to identify and engage those youth in services, such as stigmatized youth at-risk of HIV/STI infections and street-involved youth. An analysis of the research literature (Andersson 2013; Connolly and Joly 2012) suggests that there are common components in successful outreach work, including:

- **Contact making:** Meeting youth in their environment is the first step to engagement. Making contact involves understanding the history and social support systems of the hard-to-reach youth and adapting trust-building contact approaches that minimize tensions. For example, at-risk youth may have had negative experiences with authority figures, so a highly formalized first-contact approach may discourage their participation.
- **Relation building:** This involves forming a relationship of care, respect, confidentiality and trust with a vulnerable youth. An outreach worker must motivate through his/her presence, dialogue, and support. This requires patience (ability to wait and observe), facilitating opportunities to engage, and taking actions that build a relationship of trust and support.
- **Social support:** This involves providing youth with information, connecting them to a slew of services, handing out supplies and materials, and providing training. Youth-centric services and information can be provided through social media, local radio announcements, and creative arts and music. Outreach workers also become a key social support pillar, making themselves available at different hours of the day.

To accomplish the above outreach foundation, youth surveys and experimental studies have highlighted the critical role of outreach workers as front-line agents (Chui and Chan 2012; Pollack et al. 2011). The outreach workers need the following skills and professional qualities (Mikkonen et al. 2007; Pollack et al. 2011):

- **Know the context.** Have familiarity with locations where encounters will likely take place.
- **See the strengths in at-risk youth.** Use a client-centered and strength-based approach focused on the potential and qualities of at-risk youth.

- **Give and promote respect.** Use engagement skills to promote respect and comfort. Be sociable and respectful, even in the absence of reciprocity from disengaged youth.
- **Be adaptive.** Be comfortable with ambiguity and have the ability to manage contingencies and open-ended situations.
- **Network.** Have the skills to develop extensive networks and connections to other referral services.

For staffing outreach workers, a study by Kryda and Compton (2009) points to how funding must not be organized on a per-contact basis, because this encourages the workers to go for quick fixes rather than for sustained support (pp. 148–49). In addition to creating access through traditional youth outreach workers, there are emerging case studies on using innovative ways to reengage at-risk youth, such as through social media and shopping malls (Chalker and Stelsel 2009; Chan and Holosko 2017; Dekelver, Van den Bosch and Engelen 2011) that require further evaluations.

Protection and promotion through financial incentives

Financial assistance is popularly seen as a tool for incentivizing enrolments and retention in education and as a protective factor against education and health risks. It aids in meeting the minimum basic needs of the most vulnerable, facilitating access to social services. However, there is also evidence of positive contributions to psychosocial outcomes, such as a sense of efficacy as well as belonging to an educational community. Emerging evidence also suggests that incentives such as conditional cash transfers may have a greater impact on young people (age 12 and over) than on children (under age 12). For youth, therefore, the outcomes and mechanisms of change due to financial support go beyond addressing budget constraints (Cunningham et al. 2008b, pp. 53–57).

Financial incentives provide a flexible way to target multiple outcomes of both protection and promotion. In Turkey, for example, the implementation of conditional cash transfers through its Social Risk Mitigation Project has been quite successful for education and health outcomes. In education, this project conditioned financial support on the enrollment and maintenance of 80 percent school attendance. Impact assessments conducted by Ayala Consulting (2006) and Akhter et al. (2007) showed that there was an increase in enrolment rates and school attendance and in the use of health services such as vaccination and hospital births. The program design indicated the value attached to the status of women, as payments were made to them (Yildirim, Ozdemir and Sezgin 2014; Zulkhibri 2015).

In Indonesia, a scholarship program was implemented with dual objectives: (1) to preserve access to education for the poor during the economic crisis of 1998, relieving pressure on educational costs, and (2) to reduce the pressures on families that necessitate child labor. It followed a decentralized geographic and individual targeting approach to increase enrollment and smooth consumption, with notable success (Sparrow 2007). Similar impact evaluations of programs in several countries, including Bangladesh, Columbia, Jamaica, Mexico, Pakistan, and the United States, show increases in enrolments and completion rates and reductions in dropout rates (Cunningham et al. 2008a, pp. 53–57; McCaig et al. 2016; Morris et al. 2017; OFFA 2014; Wolf et al. 2013). Reed and Hurd (2016) showed that for disadvantaged students, scholarships not only incentivized enrolment but also enabled successful participation in an education program.

Additionally, a limited number of emergent studies have uncovered evidence that the provision of financial aid to students in need can have a powerful psychological effect, with a range of associated impacts. For instance, in addition to decreasing financial anxiety related to housing, family support, and medical expenses (West et al. 2006), studies have suggested that scholarships can act as a gesture of recognition that acknowledges and legitimizes the students' inclusion at school or university, increasing the bonds they feel with the institution (Hatt et al. 2005). Studies have also found that scholarships inspire greater motivation and engagement, which in the minds of these young people then become a means of paying back for the financial support they receive (Harrison, Baxter, and Hatt 2007). An impact evaluation of a scholarship program for students from disadvantaged backgrounds at Macquarie University in Sydney, Australia, provides evidence of improved retention rates and also suggests other positive developmental outcomes, such as security, independence, motivation, engagement, confidence, and a sense of belonging (Reed and Hurd 2016).

Evidence also suggests that financial aid can improve self-efficacy (Oler 2011), career decision-making, and even early labor market performance (Yang 2011) and may also embolden students to take additional positive risks they would not otherwise have taken. Reed and Hurd (2016) found that the extra financial resources not only paid for study materials but also created extra time by reducing the amount of paid work students needed to undertake. This extra time enabled recipients to better compete with their peers, engage in other opportunities that the students felt they would not have otherwise had (such as engaging outside formal classes with their peers), take part in extracurricular activities, or make plans for their future careers, such as by researching and applying for other study opportunities.

For financial incentives, and especially for conditional cash transfers, the following design insights are available from the World Bank's Policy Toolkit to support at-risk youth in middle-income countries (2008):

- **Align amounts with level of risk.** Transfers should be higher in situations where children and youth are most at risk, but they should generally be lower in value than a young person's potential earnings while having the flexibility to increase with age, considering the increased opportunity costs to families of sending older children to school and the greater availability of risky opportunities.
- **Transitional periods are crucial.** Transfers are implemented best during transitions (i.e., when young people are moving up from one level of school to another and going from one developmental stage to the next) due to the high probability of making risky decisions in these phases.
- **Provide referrals and access to other services.** Transfers need to be accompanied by increased resources for schools, health centers, and other complementary services, because young peoples' lack of access to these services will undermine the incentive and reduce the quality of these services for the entire youth population.

A considerable and growing body of evidence suggests that the effects of incentives depend on how they are designed, the form in which they are given (especially monetary or non-monetary), how they interact with intrinsic motivations and social motivations, and what happens after they are withdrawn. Incentives do matter but can have various consequences, sometimes in unexpected ways (Gneezy, Meier, and Rey-Biel 2011). As an example, a randomized control trial of a large-scale program in Bogota, Columbia, involving 13,000 youth showed that conditional cash transfers for upper-secondary students were particularly effective when the financial subsidy was deferred until re-enrollment (with a 4 percent increase in secondary and a 9.4 percent in tertiary) or until re-enrollment in a tertiary institution (a large 49 percent increase) (de Hoyos et al. 2016a, 2016b).

It is important therefore to reflect on the specific behavior changes the program seeks to create, the possible incentive mechanisms that can drive these changes, whether they need to be monetary, and how these can be framed and instituted to have the necessary effect. The design of the programs offering financial incentives must be careful to answer the following questions:

- **For whom?** Who is the program targeting (youth, parents, mentors, teachers, schools, etc.) and on which criteria is it based (e.g., past academic experiences, motivation to progress, gender, other social barriers such as health issues)?
- **For what?** Which actions or outcomes are to be rewarded? Is it those that demonstrate positive behavior changes, such as enrolling in a school/course or improvement in, say, one SEL element?
- **To what extent (amount, how long)?** Providing too much or too little financial aid can be detrimental to instituting behavioral changes. Similarly, time periods for the provision matter.
- **Which instrument?**[6] Consider the differences between scholarships and bursaries (such as competitive vs. automatic assignment), and between cash transfers and vouchers (such as conditional vs. unconditional payments).
- **In what form?** Framing the incentive appropriately is found to have significant effects on its uptake. Considerations include the number of choices, default options, ordering of options, and timing and modalities of engagement.

In sum, the current evidence of the impact of financial incentives indicates moderate, short-run positive effects on some subgroups of students, at least while the incentives are in place. There is clearer evidence for increasing attendance and enrolments, but mixed results on effort and achievements. Context also plays a role: financial incentives work for some students but not for others (e.g., as a function of gender, past academic achievement, or drive and motivation) (Gneezy, Meier, and Rey-Biel 2011).

Case management of the multiple needs of at-risk youth

As noted, research consistently suggests that at-risk youth and their families have multiple needs and interrelated problems. These cannot be successfully addressed by a single service or service provider. Indeed, the education system and schools alone cannot respond to a myriad of issues such as child protection, homelessness, and unemployment. A case management approach with service integration can support clients with multiple needs to achieve the desired outcomes. This can include, for instance, individualized assessments and follow-ups (using the case management approach) and referring at-risk students to specialized providers.

Service integration refers to procedures and structures that help several service agencies coordinate their efforts for a full range of services for at-risk youth and families. This involves interagency collaborations and partnerships as common institutional arrangements. Formal collaborations and partnerships can contribute by co-locating staff and extending referrals and coordination of services. The following steps have been identified in this process:

- **Identify the services needed.** Evaluate the types of services available along with the breadth and intensity of services required by the at-risk youth based on local needs and resources.
- **Build partnerships.** Broad-based collaborations are best accomplished through institutional arrangements and formal agreements (MOUs or contracts) with providers that can have a major impact on client needs. The providers may include schools, law enforcement, juvenile and family courts, employers, social services, health and mental health services, among others. Each collaborative may consist of colocated staff and may promote service coordination and ensure that clients referred to different agencies are provided services. More ad-hoc, informal, flexible, or trust-based arrangements may also be preferred.
- **Share information and decision making.** Partner organizations make concerted efforts during their formative stages to exchange information explicitly about the mission, services, flexibility, and limitations of each partner and have parity in decision-making.
- **Select the service site.** Service provision, using institutions such as schools or community centers or through mobile arrangements or home visits, will depend on the nature of the service itself, and it should maintain a careful balance between providing ease of access to learning opportunities and providing a safe, respectful and welcoming space.
- **Provide centralized client intake and a shared facility.** Setting up a centralized client intake, assessment, and referral system reduces service barriers and increases usage. Such a centralized set-up creates opportunities for cross-disciplinary staffing, joint fund-raising, and a sharing of resources and co-locating of staff from a range of agencies in the same facility, on a full- or part-time basis. It also enhances collaboration among practitioners and can eliminate the need for youth to travel to different locations to obtain different services.
- **Staff interaction and development.** This is the encouragement of formal and informal interagency interactions to discuss client issues and changes in needs, progress, and options for service provision. This kind of collaboration can lead to professional development and growth for staff, better understanding of the capabilities and limitations of other agencies, and enhanced knowledge for accessing local resources.
- **Design and use of evaluations effectively.** Extensive early collaboration with program personnel enables the evaluation measures to be more meaningful. Impact information should be tied to youth and family outcomes rather than only to the services delivered.

Overall, local programs may face difficulties in implementing an integrated slew of services, but there is evidence that it is possible through formalized, active and colocated staffing, collaboration with joint objectives, effective targeting and management of caseloads, appropriate training and practice, and adaptive monitoring of outcomes (Morley and Rossman 1997).

Case management offers individualized support for identifying and providing access to a wide array of services that can be customized to meet the specific needs of at-risk clients. The case team aims to determine service needs, provide inter-agency linkages, and monitor service delivery and outcomes (Melaville and Blank 1991; Morley and Rossman 1997). It makes use of service integration through collaboratives and partnerships. At a minimum, it involves a limited needs assessment of at-risk youth and the provision of referrals to appropriate services. In its most extensive form, it would include detailed diagnostics, development of individual service plans, coordination with service providers and referral services, crisis intervention or provision of emergency services, advocacy with schools and other institutions, and counseling and family outreach. Effective case management requires relatively smaller caseloads as the needs of clients increase. The case manager's qualifications need to match the functional requirements of the task (Morley and Rossman 1997). In general, the case manager and case team would: (1) work with youth and their families to determine service needs; (2) provide inter-agency linkages, and (3) monitor service delivery and outcomes (Melaville and Blank 1991). It is critical that diagnostics and assessments of the young person take a positive youth development approach and aim to measure both strengths and areas of improvement (Kerka 2006; Luthar 2003; Ungar 2006).

A realist synthesis evaluation of 53 sources of empirical evidence and various comparative studies has found that case management works because of the quality of the relationship between the client and the case manager or case management team. These qualities include persistence, reliability, intimacy, and respect (Bedell, Cohen, and Sullivan 2000; Coldwell and Bender 2007; Gronda 2009; Morse 1999; Wolff et al. 1997). To deliver comprehensive and practical support, evidence further identifies some key dimensions in the case manager's relationship with at-risk youth that must be actively managed during programing:

- **Genuine caring.** A genuine emotional connection creates a relationship through the intimate nature of some case management activities, such as accompanying to doctor's appointments and advising in financial management. Hence, intimacy is both an unavoidable part of these activities to deliver comprehensive, practical support and a key element of the emotional bond. This generates challenging issues in practice, such as emotional ambiguity, power differences, professional boundaries and expectations, and differing perspectives of clients and workers (Angell and Mahoney 2007; Beresford, Croft, and Adshead 2007; Dickson-Gomez et al. 2007).
- **Relevant skills.** To be effective, the case management relationship relies on highly skilled staff with advanced assessment, communication, and relationship skills, relevant field experience of regular supervision, and access to different resources that can offer specialist support (for example, expertise in psychiatric and substance use issues) (Gronda 2009).
- **Multi-disciplinary effort.** The empirical evidence is not conclusive about whether an individual or a team-based support is better for case management, but higher complexity tends to demand multidisciplinary efforts. Comparative research shows that the direct provision of comprehensive, practical support produces better client outcomes than brokerage or referral to other services.
- **Self-care capacity.** Case management must integrate and balance the multiple and individualized needs of at-risk youth, providing direction to a variety

of service providers, and building the capacity of clients for self-care. Although this approach is time- and resource-intensive in the medium term, it is cost-effective because it increases a person's self-care capacity and consequently reduces other long-run systemic expenditures. Further, the support duration must be individually negotiated based on the assistance required, the satisfaction of minimum needs, and a realistic level of self-care as an outcome goal (Gronda 2009).

In the next section, we discuss the potential role and contextual relevance of the interventions identified so far by reviewing for whom and in what contexts these can work, and present some ways to address the varied learning needs of all youths, including those facing multiple adversities.

FOR WHOM AND IN WHAT CONTEXTS DO REENGAGEMENT INTERVENTIONS WORK?

Determining for whom and in what context interventions work is crucial to achieve the expected education reengagement of at-risk youth. Adaptations are needed even in programs that have been successfully evaluated elsewhere. We assert this because

(1) the characteristics of the youth facing severe adversities and the environments in which they live and interact facilitate or inhibit program interventions and their impact;
(2) at-risk youth inherently experience cumulative risks (in terms of type, level and variety of risks);
(3) a mix of interventions along with at least one stable and supportive relationship and positive connections in various settings are essential for these youth to cope; and
(4) evidence suggests that permeable education systems,[7] multiple educational pathways, and varied platforms of engagement together constitute an ecosystem for the effective service delivery of a reengagement program.

Needs and interventions for at-risk youth may differ not only due to individual characteristics, but also because of dynamic life contexts. This person-context characteristic must be understood to design and adapt the core and enabling interventions discussed earlier (mentoring, psychosocial support, etc.).

Person-context characteristics and interactions moderate program impact

A constellation of individual and environmental risk factors affects positive youth development (Luthar 2003). Some researchers argue that we cannot assume homogeneity across global populations in terms of the response by young people facing seemingly similar risks and in their ability to use a predefined set of assets. While aspects of healthy functioning such as self-efficacy, hope, participation, sense of belonging, and identity are properties inherent in all individuals, unchecked risks in context can inhibit their expression (Cartwright 2007; Cartwright and Hardie 2012; Luthar 2003; Ungar 2008).

To understand how the variability in the settings in which young people face risks affects their ability to bounce back, Ungar (2006) conducted a

> **BOX 4.3**
>
> ### Case example: How person-context characteristics moderate intervention effectiveness
>
> Quotations of two participants in the International Resilience Project led by Michael Ungar highlight how person-context characteristics moderate how interventions play out and their effectiveness.
>
> Sasha, a 17-year-old teenage mother from Winnipeg, Canada, explains that her school and teacher are the most important factors contributing to her success: *"The guidance counsellor right now at my school was my teacher last year, and at the time I had an eight-month-old son, and it was really hard for me to get to school and to do well and stuff. I had a big attitude when I came. And one day I decided I wasn't going to come to school no more and I told my teacher, Pat, and she just said that everything was going to be okay if I made it okay and that she would help me every day to get to school. She would pick me up. She would phone me. She would give me bus tickets. She bought my son a sled and she just told me it was going to be okay. And I came, and I did it and I finished the whole year…if she wasn't there I would have just probably dropped out."*
>
> A second teenaged mother, Akili, from Njoro Tanzania, an impoverished community at the base of Kilimanjaro, provides a very different account of what contributes to a young woman's resilience: *"I am not independent as I still depend on my mother. Previously, I was depending on my father and my mother, but since I got pregnant my father deserted me and he doesn't like to see me… I depend on my mother for everything…. The main protector of my life is myself and it is not proper to disturb my mother. I feel as I made a mistake of getting pregnant before the right time, I have to take care of myself… My mother is helping me to get employed so that I can live a good life… If I have money I think I can solve my problems. I have no money because I am not running any business… My goals are to have a job or a business which will let me rent my own room, where I can live with my child, so that I can depend on my own instead of depending on my mother."*
>
> While the first experience highlights the teacher and school as key success factors, in the second case it is the mother and access to opportunity that are identified as pivotal to success. Traditional schooling may be relevant for Akili, but micro-enterprise grants are potentially a better way to engage her in a productive activity while also creating pathways for learning. The different success factors in the experiences of these two teenage mothers highlight the importance of understanding contextual nuances necessary to ensure that intervention designs work.
>
> *Source:* Ungar 2006, p. 54.

mixed-methods investigation of resilience of over 1,500 youth (694 males = 47.9 percent; 757 females = 52.1 percent, mean age = 16 years, SD = 2.653) in 14 communities in 11 countries[8] across five continents. This investigation, called the International Resilience Project, examined global as well as *culturally and contextually specific* aspects of risk and resilience (both outcomes and processes) in youth, the mediating factors associated with resilience, and localized definitions of positive outcomes (see box 4.3). The study found that even when faced with similar adversities, there is significant variation across cultures in how youth cope. These differences led to the identification of seven "tensions" in any context—from the perspective of at-risk youth—which can inhibit or facilitate recovery, functioning, and positive change in the face of adversities:

(1) **Access to material resources:** Availability of financial, educational, medical and employment assistance and/or opportunities and access to food, clothing, and shelter;

(2) **Relationships:** With peers and adults within one's family and community;

(3) **Identity:** Personal and collective sense of purpose, self-appraisal of strengths and weaknesses, aspirations, beliefs, and values, including spiritual and religious identity;
(4) **Power and control:** Experiences of caring for one's self and others; the ability to affect change in one's social and physical environment to access resources;
(5) **Cultural adherence:** Adherence to local and/or global cultural practices, values, and beliefs;
(6) **Social justice:** Finding a meaningful role in community and social equality; and
(7) **Cohesion:** Balancing one's personal interests with a sense of responsibility to the greater good; feeling part of something larger than oneself, socially and spiritually.

Ungar's international study offers a frame to study cultural and contextual influences and how these can affect proposed programs and interventions for at-risk and out-of-school youth. Does this context provide access to material resources, to relationships, and to a sense of identify and cultural adherence? What are the power and control issues, who makes decisions, who is included and excluded, and how do these tensions lead to social justice or injustices and to social cohesion or lack thereof? Rather than controlling for contextual variables in the analysis, these can be embraced by understanding how interventions for youth influence and are influenced in these seven areas. Including context in any type of interventions analysis (including impact analysis) can contribute to more culturally and contextually grounded designs of future programs or to adaptations of existing interventions designed and evaluated elsewhere (Cartwright and Hardie 2012).

At a broader level, from the perspective of supply- and demand-side constraints faced by out-of-school youth, other studies can also provide an image of contextual differences to take into account within and across countries (Cunningham et al. 2008b; de Hoyos, Rogers, and Szekely 2016; Mauro and Mitra 2015; Inoue et al. 2015). Not surprisingly, research finds strong linkages between a country's socioeconomic and demographic characteristics and the magnitude of its out-of-school youth population. Those living in poverty, from rural households, or belonging to ethnic minorities are more likely to be exposed to greater levels of risk. The incidence of out-of-school youth is also found to be lower in countries that spend a larger share of their gross domestic product on education and have adequate public provision of secondary education. Countries with high population growth rates also tend to experience a higher incidence of out-of-school youth. Strong formal labor markets and the availability of stable jobs encourage more young people (or their parents) to choose school over work. Moreover, social norms and expectations around gender roles are important factors influencing young people's life experiences and decisions on continuing and completing education and participating in the labor market. When a larger share of the labor force holds wage and salaried jobs, youth tend to attend and stay in school, reminding one that labor policies, education policies, and the business climate in a country are deeply connected to one another.

Need for a comprehensive intervention mix, supportive relationships, and connections in multiple settings

For young people experiencing a cumulative and complex set of risks across different levels of a social context, it is unlikely that a "magic bullet" of interventions will be found (Masten and Coatsworth 1998) that will lead to consistently significant program impact. Evidence suggests successful programs require a mix of adaptable interventions. Yet some underlying common mechanisms, such as positive and supportive relations, emerge as generalizable across contexts.

Comprehensive interventions for young people at risk appear to work better with respect to both positive and negative outcomes when goals include the promotion of competence and positive achievements, in addition to protection against negative outcomes (Cicchetti et al. 2000; Masten 2001; Masten and Powell 2003). For those facing high to severe levels of risk, a targeted mix of protective and promotive interventions is necessary—protective against risks and promotive of assets and resources. Also, increasing promotive factors has the same effect as reducing risks, because they are on the same dimension for most youth most of the time. But protective and promotive processes in one context may prove to be risky in another (Sameroff, Gutman, and Peck 2003).

Positive and supportive relationships and *connections in multiple settings* are important for every young person. The capacity to adapt and thrive despite adversity develops through the interaction of supportive relationships, gene expression, and adaptive biological systems (Shonkoff et al. 2015). Positive engagement provided in two or more settings is more likely to enhance positive and reduce negative developmental outcomes, whereas in only a single setting it may be insufficient to produce similar outcomes even when interventions are targeted (such as toward the family, school, or peer group) (Sameroff, Gutman, and Peck 2003; Seidman and Pederson 2003). In settings where adults can communicate a sense of relatedness and foster autonomy, youth are more likely to become engaged (Allen et al. 1994).

Overall, the reliable presence of at least one supportive relationship and multiple opportunities for developing effective coping skills emerge as essential to building the capacity for youth to do well in the face of significant adversity.

Flexible learning pathways create opportunities and reduce learning barriers

Flexibility to access quality learning opportunities is important for all learners. The main principle of offering multiple pathways, multiple entry points, and various modalities of engagement into education is to offer choices, not close doors. Inbar and Sever (1989) have suggested three basic criteria for genuine reengagement frameworks, namely that they should (1) be accessible for all; (2) be effective in improving educational attainment; and (3) provide the same/similar opportunities for success that conventional education opportunities provide. When youth have the opportunity and support to carve their own educational pathways, this is likely to increase their engagement and motivation and help them develop a sense of ownership of their future and an empowering belief in their self-efficacy. Moreover, being actively involved in developing one's own goals and plans creates the opportunity to develop the skills needed to continue to plan and manage one's future life.

Out-of-school young people facing significant levels of adversity need specialized support to develop tailored career and learning plans based on individualized interest and learning styles. These tailored approaches should include, access to assessment and need-based special education and other social and health related supports. Flexible options can range from programs delivered outside normal study hours, through distance or blended learning, to opportunities for work and study, such as apprenticeships (CEDEFOP 2017). Addressing the high variability in the risk profile of vulnerable youth, in terms of type, level and variety of risks, requires adaptability in the quantum and types of support. Multiple and permeable educational pathways and flexible platforms of education engagement can reduce barriers of time, location, and pace of learning.[9]

Examples of multiple and permeable educational re-entry pathways

Systematic provision of multiple and permeable pathways in education systems enables individuals to personalize their learning choices and experiences. Out-of-school youth need educational options that are feasible, interesting, and sufficiently challenging to utilize their assets effectively (Ungar 2008). In a 2008 OFSTED survey of 29 secondary schools in the United Kingdom covering 32,987 students, 3,404 students (78 percent) of 4,347 students who had been identified previously as disaffected (chronic absenteeism, aggressive, and disruptive) were re-engaged successfully using a multicomponent intervention approach including outreach, parental engagement, mentoring, and integrated services. The selected schools had shown a decrease in absenteeism and had a record of sustained good practices in re-engaging young people. One of the findings was that successful efforts involved actively personalizing the curriculum, such as by using part-time college courses, revision courses, and offsite experiences, and by incorporating local languages in the pedagogic practice, establishing different forms of authentic accreditations, and offering incentives and rewards.

A longitudinal three-cohort study of re-engaging early-school-leaving Australian youth into education, by Polidano, Tabasso and Tseng (2015), found that second-chance programs that encourage an early return to study (that is, reducing the amount of time out of education) and that help youth develop post-education career plans may be more effective than programs that concentrate only on improving numeracy and literacy scores. Other studies (Gutherson, Davies, and Daszkiewicz 2011; Myconos 2014) do signify the need to address literacy and numeracy skills besides vocationally relevant and "applied" skills, while making the case for flexible, individually-tailored and multimodal support based on the youth's goals and aspirations.

On the supply side, ensuring the provision of needs-based engagement pathways and additional support that can break down barriers to learning requires serious policy commitment. It also requires sustainable funding support catalyzed by both public and private sector provisioning and vibrant partnership networks between schools, businesses, and communities. These flexible pathways must be aligned to youth's transition needs, because getting this pathway design right will enable the transitions, which are complex and multifaceted. Hence, the following need to be recognized (see figure 4.1):

- **The pathways are not unidirectional for all young people.** Youth facing many risks and building resilience often go through a 'yo-yo' process, whereby movements can reverse or shift in other directions based on extraneous factors related to family, peers, political turmoil, or personal aspirations and self-perceptions.
- **The pathways are not always visible and clearly accessible.** The path of progress through school and then from school to work does not have clear milestones and access routes. Instead, for young people facing severe adversities, there is a dynamic relation between the supply of multiple pathways and entry points and individual and contextual factors that affect their ability to navigate and negotiate their way to their goals.

FIGURE 4.1
Flexible education reengagement pathways

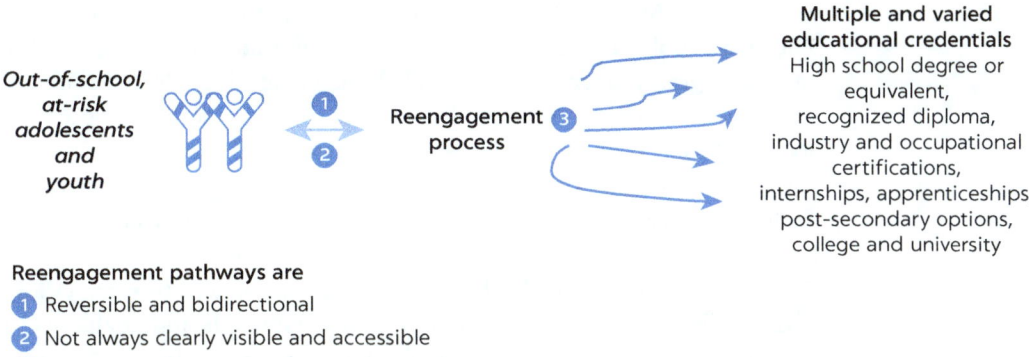

Reengagement pathways are
① Reversible and bidirectional
② Not always clearly visible and accessible
③ Have low predictability and equitability in outcomes

Source: World Bank representation based on Ross and Gray 2005.

- **The pathway outcomes are difficult to predict and not always equitable.** The traditional path of progress through school and then from school to work has a fixed destination. However, for youth willing to re-engage, the outcomes are a function of their resilience, the labor market conditions, and other contextual and individual risk factors (Clayton et al. 2010; Ross and Gray 2005).

In Australia, there is well-regarded diversity in the provision of flexible learning pathways in terms of program structure, the types of credentials and activities offered, and the characteristics of the at-risk young people that these programs cater to. A meta-analytic review by Te Riele (2014) of the access and diversity of flexible learning programs in Australia—concerning their outcomes, interventions, and mechanisms for disadvantaged youth—recognizes the need for non-traditional pathways (often referred to in the literature as alternative, second-chance, flexible, or reengagement education programs) to achieve the policy goals of educational attainment and to improve productivity while meeting the needs of the young people for whom mainstream schools are inaccessible, disengaging, and/or obstructive. Te Riele's review included a systematic database of 913 programs covering 70,000 students per year (age >11 years, July 2014) selected based on the following criteria: use of an adaptive approach, provision of recognized secondary-school level credentials, targeting disadvantaged youth at risk of non-completion and early school leavers, and focused on learning with choice of attendance. The key findings were:

- **The primary target group of these flexible programs is the 15–19 year age cohort who are at risk of non-completion or are early school leavers.** Over 40 percent of the programs target the 15–19-year age group while about 200 programs cater to the 11–14-year group and the 15–19-year group. A very small number (<20) focus on the full spectrum of students from age 11 to 20+ years. Over 600 programs focus on early school leavers and over 200 programs focus on suspended/expelled youth. There are also specialized programs that cater to a wide range of needs such as for the homeless, pregnant women, young parents, refugees and indigenous people.
- **There are three structural arrangements.** Programs are fairly evenly distributed across three arrangements–within schools, within VET institutes (called Technical and Further Education or TAFE) and community colleges, and as stand-alone programs (in 2014). While TAFE, community colleges, and

stand-alone programs usually lead to directly earning recognized school-level credentials, the within-school programs offer indirect (nontraditional) ways to earn the same. Most programs are quite small (fewer than 100 students).

- **There are multiple levels and types of credentials.** There is variability among programs in terms of the number and choice of credentials offered. Programs offer only junior secondary-level certificates (at three levels, with about 400+ sites) or only senior secondary-level certificates (at two levels, with about 200 sites) or both (about 300+ sites). There are also equivalent qualification certificates offered at every level, such as a Certificate in General Education for Adults or a Tertiary Preparation certificate.
- **The curriculum includes both vocational education and training (VET) and learning activities responsive to students' needs and goals.** About 50 percent of the reviewed programs offer formal and accredited VET courses covering a wide array of industries, such as sports, information and communication technology (ICT), construction, community health, and hospitality. The remainder offer nonaccredited VET certificates. Eight out of nine programs offer literacy, numeracy, and life skills and about one-third offer mentoring and job seeking services.

FIGURE 4.2

Framework of quality in flexible learning programs in Australia

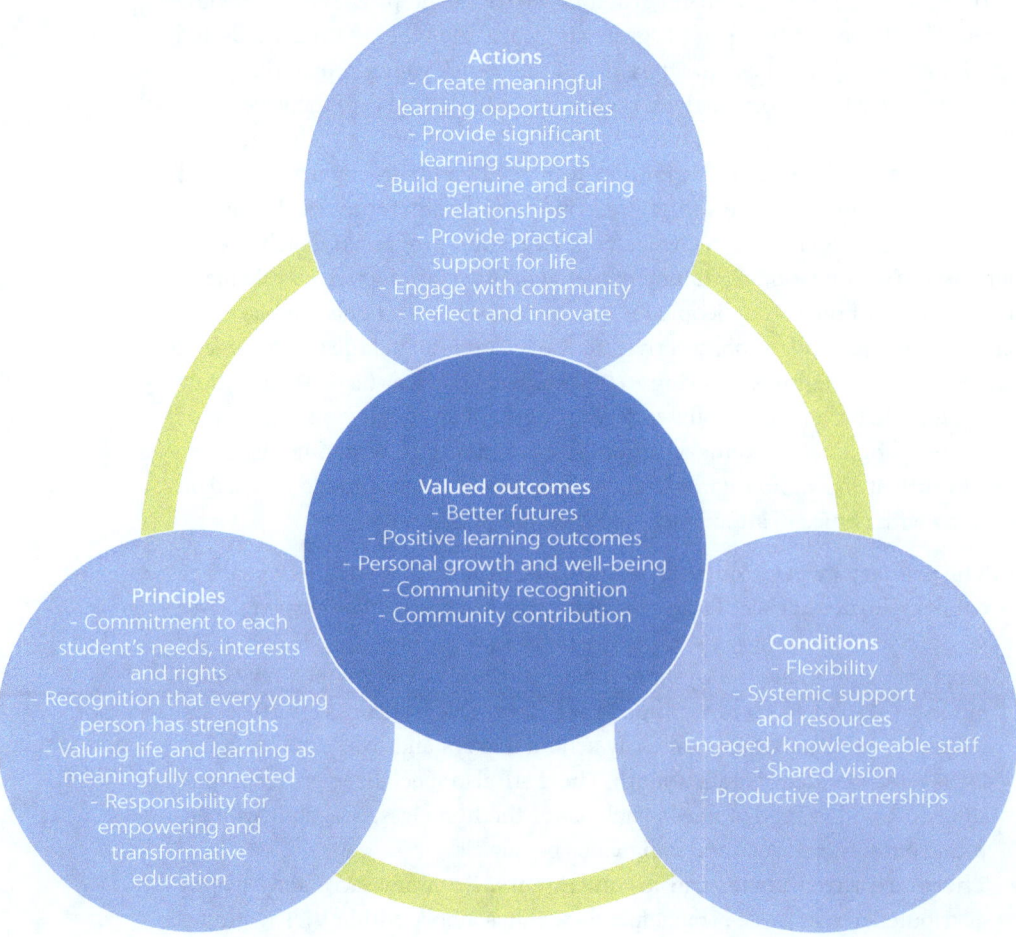

Source: The Victoria Institute (Te Riele 2014). Used with permission; further permission required for reuse.

- **Framework of quality in flexible learning programs.** Te Riele's (2014) review identifies four dimensions of flexible programs (see figure 4.2): valued outcomes, actions, principles, and conditions relevant for youth facing multiple adversities that need to be contextually adapted and operationalized in multiple ways. Interestingly, this framework renders support to the findings of this study on what and how interventions work. Some barriers to engagement, retention, and transition have also been identified and include the status of vocational and technical education, logistical problems, the high costs of supporting alternative programs and associated funding issues, and a lack of data to accurately monitor engagement, completions and transitions for further study or employment (Clayton et al. 2010).

Blended learning platforms offer flexibility and personalization

Research suggests that children and youth learn best in environments where they feel safe and free to explore and learn, and where they have secure relationships with caring and responsive adults. The modalities of delivering content and skills have expanded in recent years from face-to-face and asynchronous distance learning platforms to online and digital platforms. This is especially important for youth who cannot attend a full-time, center-based educational program. The learning environments are influenced by the modalities of engagement and interactions, hence they deserve attention, especially for students facing significantly higher risks and less supportive environments.

Open education is a system of teaching and learning that makes study materials (open education resources) freely available to students. The materials typically include textbooks, quizzes, class exercises, videos, and other learning objects. These are usually openly licensed, that is, they can be retained, reused, revised, remixed, and redistributed freely. *Distance education* is a subset of open education that has the goal of reaching students with constraints to access.[10] Distance education and, more recently, online learning are viewed as 'anytime, anywhere' education, having five distinguishing instructional qualities (Keegan 1996; Rekkedal et al. 2003):

(1) **Location:** Quasi-permanent separation of teacher and learner;
(2) **Systemic student support and resources:** Influence of an educational organization in planning, preparation, and provision of student support;
(3) **ICT tools:** Use of technical media, computers and digital networks for course content;
(4) **Communication channels:** Provision of one-way or two-way communication; and
(5) **Group learning opportunities:** Quasi-permanent absence of colocated learning groups; can be either asynchronous or synchronous.

Researchers have compared the effectiveness of open/distance education to classroom instruction. Bernard and colleagues (2014) have identified 16 major meta-analyses undertaken since the year 2000 to assess the differences between classroom-based instruction and distance education/online learning. The broad consensus across studies is that there is little difference in the effectiveness of the instructional forms of distance education (including online learning) compared with classroom-based instruction. The average ES are 0.00 for distance education (both synchronous and asynchronous) and 0.05–0.15 for online learning, which is similar to that of classroom-based instruction. Arguably, there is wide variability among studies, from those strongly favoring distance education to those favoring classroom-based instruction, making it relatively difficult to draw strong conclusions about effectiveness yet. Further, quantitative interpretation of the nuances of what works has also been difficult. For example, evidence is so far inconclusive on what specifically is effective—is it the distance, the media, the instructional strategies, or some combination of these? How these factors work is also unclear.

There is qualitative evidence on the benefits and value of online learning for both at-risk students and the education programs serving them (Bernard et al. 2014). The value-added is especially accrued by at-risk youth, as evidenced by increased enrolment and time spent on learning activities. From the analysis of case studies on online learning courses for at-risk students by Watson and Gemin (2008), we can identify some of the desirable characteristics of online learning programs and the challenges these address for at-risk youth.

- **Increased flexibility** can help recover lost time and reduce the social stigma they may face in a face-to-face classroom setting.
- **Improved access to the hard-to-reach and underserved regions** can provide resources and instructors that are not locally available.
- **Increased mobility** reduces the opportunity costs of being in school during a specific time and place.
- **Individualized and self-paced instruction and learning** are particularly valuable to at-risk students, who may associate education with difficulties and stress, compounded by learning deadlines imposed by arbitrary calendars or institutional hours.
- **Rigorous curriculum and appropriate course management technology** to enable effective learning through a supportive medium for interaction with the teacher(s), the content, and peers while also providing exposure to computers and technology.
- **Systematic assessments** including diagnostic testing to demonstrate prior subject knowledge, continuous checks for understanding, and opportunities to demonstrate mastery before moving to new content.
- **Continuous and multiple pathways to accumulate course credits** provide both motivation and feedback to engage, retain, and complete the program using innovative instructional and assessment design in course management technology.
- **Credits for accumulated experience,** such as work or community service, allow students to be engaged in valuable diverse learning activities while also making this experience count toward graduation.
- **A significant face-to face component** provides expanded reengagement support through evening, night, or weekend classes as at-risk out-of-school students are non-traditional and need additional nudges and incentives for educational participation and continuation.

Notably, online platforms are particularly scalable and able to expand more easily than programs based entirely on brick-and-mortar classrooms. Yet the flexibility and open nature of distance education is not only an asset but also a risk and, therefore, has to be carefully managed. The technology-mediated setting limits youths' social interactions and hence also their opportunities for protective and promotive engagement through the PSS essential for vulnerable youth. Further, an online and distance learning modality is less likely to be suitable for concepts and subject areas that require demonstrations and practice of physical skills and heavy social interactions, such as the performing arts, fine arts, and vocational skills.

Simpson (2013) found that there is a 'distance education deficit' with many distance institutions having less than one-quarter of the graduation rates of conventional institutions. One reason identified for the deficit is a confusion between teaching and learning. Online / distance education programs have traditionally focused excessively on the provision of teaching materials and have overlooked student motivation to learn. There is accumulating evidence that a blended approach (distance and face-to-face) can support motivation to complete studies, reduce dropout rates, and offer flexible options for those who have already left. Arguably, for at-risk out-of-school students the need for motivation and social interactions is significantly higher, hence they are more likely to engage in a blended- learning environment.

A strong and growing evidence base supports the effectiveness of the blended-learning approach to strengthen both distance education/online learning and classroom instruction. Blended learning can be defined as "the combination of instruction from two separate models of teaching and learning: traditional face-to-face learning systems and distributed learning systems" (Graham 2005). While open/distance education offers students varying levels of flexibility of time, place, path, and pace, the face-to-face interactions with peers and instructors strengthen self-efficacy and performance expectations (Wu, Tennyson and Hsia 2010).

A meta-analysis (Means et al. 2013) of blended learning programs found that students in these learning conditions significantly outperform fully face-to-face classroom-based instruction where no blending occurred (ES = 0.35). Students in both collaborative interactive learning and teacher-directed expository instructional conditions significantly outperformed those engaged only in active self-study. Learners in undergraduate courses seemed to benefit more from blended learning than graduate students. Further, more time in online instruction (as compared to time spent face-to-face) produced a relatively higher weighted average effect size on outcomes, and longer-duration blended learning treatments were more effective than shorter ones.

Another meta-analysis (Bernard et al. 2014), covering 96 blended programs from 1990 to 2000, defined blending as 50 percent of student time spent on classroom-based instruction and 50 percent spent on online learning. That analysis produced a random weighted average effect size of 0.334, similar to the findings by Means et al. (2013). It concluded that improvements in achievement related to blended learning are significantly greater than zero but are limited by confounding effects, as the other meta-analysis also showed.

Qualitative studies suggest that the blended learning environment helps students find value in goal-setting, strategic planning, self-reflection and self-regulation, in addition to remedial academic content and self-learning skills. While there is stronger emerging evidence on the benefits and effectiveness of blended learning environments, there is also ongoing research on how such environments need to be set up and what features they should incorporate for the target group under consideration.

Although based on a small sample, another study assessing the potential of e-learning to support reengagement among 16–18-year-old young people whose status was 'not in education, employment or training' (NEET) provides evidence that the following may be effective (Passey, Williams and Rogers 2008):

- Facilities using mobile technologies to support contact with personal advisers, not just for arranging meetings but also for providing key information;
- Websites that provide ideas, information and guidance on available opportunities, along with examples of other young people's experiences and successes, in visual, auditory, and textual formats for inclusive access; and
- Wide use of ICT to cover aspects such as online testing, interactive digital resources or games focusing on specific skills, research, data recording and numeracy work, portfolio work, presentations, report writing, written work and literacy work, creating CVs and application letters, evidence gathering, and recording practice using digital cameras and video, and in creative media workshops.

WHY THESE INTERVENTIONS WORK: ACCUMULATED EVIDENCE FROM MULTIPLE DISCIPLINES

Substantive evidence from different fields of science help us infer *why* the above interventions and processes work to generate positive outcomes in at-risk youth. This section provides a summary of the fields of study that help understand the science behind the underlying mechanisms of mentoring and psychosocial and financial support, as well as outreach and referral services, for student, family, and community engagement.

Mentoring and resilience

The mentoring approach is rooted in a resilience-oriented framework. *Resilience* is the capacity of youth to recover from, continue to function during, and make positive change through adversity (Ungar 2008). From the resilience perspective, the mentoring relationship is thought to provide a protective influence by helping youth overcome the risk factors to achieve successful outcomes (Randolph and Johnson 2008). In Turkey, a study revealed that high expectations from home, caring relationships and high expectations at school, and peer caring relationships were the prominent external protective factors that predicted academic resilience (Gizir and Aydin 2009). Another instance is evidence from random controlled trials of the Advancing Adolescents program, which shows that those with higher trauma exposure benefited most from program participation and that participation had beneficial impacts both on symptoms of insecurity and distress and on emotional and behavioral difficulties (Panter-Brick et al. 2018).

Psychosocial support and neuroscience

PSS-based interventions are substantiated by studies related to cognitive, affective, and behavioral competencies. PSS programs have a significantly positive effect on the development of the cognitive skills necessary for learning through the development of relevant social and emotional competencies, namely self-awareness, self-management, social awareness, relationship skills, and responsible decision-making (INEE 2016). The field of cognitive neuroscience clarifies how PSS-based interventions work. The malleability/plasticity of the brain between early childhood and adolescence provides an important second window of opportunity for a young person to develop the full range of sophisticated social and emotional skills required to manage their student and adult life (Blakemore and Mills 2014; Casey 2015; Crone and Dahl 2012). Since these are competencies, rather than character traits, these can be learnt and developed through explicit teaching and opportunities for practice and reflection (Main and Whatman 2016). There is extensive evidence from a wide range of promotion, prevention and treatment interventions that youth can be taught personal and social skills (Collaborative for Academic, Social, and Emotional Learning 2005; Commission on Positive Youth Development 2005; Durlak and Weissberg 2007; Greenberg et al. 2003).

Community mobilization, youth outreach, and clinical psychology

The youth outreach process often uses the Stages of Change Model (also called the Transtheoretical Model) from the field of psychotherapy and clinical psychology. It can be described as an integrative, biopsychosocial model to conceptualize the process of intentional behavior change (Knoll 2012; Prochaska, Redding and Evers 2002; Prochaska 2013). It assumes that change in behavior, especially habitual behavior, occurs continuously through a cyclical and intentional process. The progress cycle involves five stages of change: (1) precontemplation (denial and lack of intention to make changes in the foreseeable future due to lack of information or multiple unsuccessful attempts), (2) contemplation (increased awareness of the pros and cons of making changes, experiences of profound ambivalence and procrastination), (3) preparation/determination (a developed intention to take action in the immediate future), (4) action (observable and overt modifications made), and (5) maintenance (reduced temptations for relapse and develop confidence in the modified experiences). The outreach worker's role is to kick-start the process of intentional change by providing the information, nudges, and pushes to move the at-risk youth from precontemplation to action. After the first step, interventions such as focused mentoring, PSS, and financial support can kick in.

Financial support and behavioral economics

Financial assistance conditions an intervention to encourage and induce a range of behaviors, such as school enrolment and attendance, accessing basic health services, and active seeking of employment. Financial support is not a silver bullet. It must contribute to other interventions to encourage and support the successful participation of disadvantaged students in education (Reed and Hurd 2016). There is an ample and growing body of knowledge from the psychology of incentives and behavioral economics on the effect of financial incentives on human behavior, although the evidence of what works and how is not yet conclusive in the context of education. The traditional view is that incentives and effort are positively correlated and that in general, a rational decision maker would prefer more options. But based on contextual inferences in education, there are anomalies in this traditionalist view of the impact of incentives, such as paying too much or too little or providing too many options. These anomalies can be driven by many factors, such as loss aversion, cognitive dissonance, a prompt for implementation intention, self-prophecy effect, adverse effects of stress induced by unusually high stakes, the sunk cost fallacy, etc.[11] It is also important to consider the impact of a financial incentive on extrinsic and intrinsic motivational factors[12] as young people progress from reengagement towards completion.

Learning environments and social cognitive theory

The choice of a learning platform has a direct effect on the learning environment that is experienced by a learner. The rationale underpinning the choice of a learning platform (such as online, face-to-face, or blended) lies in social cognitive theory, which posits that environments influence an individual's self-efficacy and performance expectations. Self-efficacy can be defined as self-belief and confidence in one's capability, leading to higher performance expectations and higher resilience and perseverance in confronting obstacles (Bandura 1986). Various studies of blended learning environments indicate an overall positive relationship between student perceptions of their satisfaction levels and their achievement, social presence, and collaborative learning experiences (Owston, York and Murtha 2013; So and Brush 2008; Wu, Tennyson and Hsia 2010).

Protective and promotive supports and resilience

Different fields of study (in psychology, sociology, institutions, etc.) can contribute to explain the need for a set of diverse interventions for youth facing extreme life adversities. The empirical studies of Ungar and Liebenberg (2005, 2009) with at-risk youth in more than 12 countries linked resilience outcomes of youth—their the capacity to recover, continue to perform and positively change in the face of adversity—to their capacity to navigate their way to diverse resources that sustain well-being: protection, education, guidance, health services, and employment opportunities. Programs that provide access to such a diverse set of services and involve multiple actors and resources, including mentors, individualized plans, partnerships, and referrals, are complex. Also, laying a long-term sustainable foundation involves generating the skills for self-care and empowerment of youth.

Resilience evidence also points to both protective and promotive services. Protection is considered the first level of policy intervention to minimize exposure to risks, for example, through income assistance, child protection, or other services to satisfy the minimum needs of a child/youth. Yet resilience research also suggests that interventions must be promotive as well, by increasing a people's capacity to deter risk, to build relationships, and to utilize their assets to reduce vulnerability. Building both protective and promotive factors associated with resilience into the interventions would build a pathway towards well-being from a situation of adversity (Khanlou and Wray 2014).

LOCATING THE COMPLEX EVIDENCE: WHAT, HOW, WHY, FOR WHOM, AND IN WHAT CONTEXTS?

Our methodological framework (see figure 3.1 in chapter 3) guided the review of the available evidence for supporting at-risk adolescents and youth to re-engage in educational and other protective and promotive activities and has yielded a range of interventions. We conclude our findings from the literature by integrating the evidence on what works, how, why, for whom and in what context. Figure 4.3 presents our synthesis. This framework allows us to move from the initial results concerning what interventions had positive effect sizes (mentoring and PSS) and build more complex causal and associative links between the interventions and the education reengagement outcomes.

FIGURE 4.3

Methodological framework: Reengaging at-risk and out-of-school adolescents and youth

① Embrace complex explanations of phenomena

③ Build causal, correlational, and associative links to identify the mechanisms and processes of change

⑤ Test the theory of change

	What interventions work	How they work	Why they work	For whom	In what contexts
	What does the empirical evidence suggest?	What are the main drivers, underlying mechanisms and features?	Are there scientific bodies of knowledge underpinning the interventions?	What individual factors and characteristics moderate the outcomes?	What contextual factors moderate the outcomes?
	Mentoring	Outreach	Resilience	Demographic	Family and household
	Psychosocial support	Individualized case management and referrals	Neuroscience	Geographic	School
			Psychology	Emotional	Community
			Behavioral economics	Cognitive	Macro-level factors
		Integrated support services	Social sciences	Social/ behavioral	
		Financial incentives			

What interventions work — How they work — Why — For whom — In what contexts

- Quantitative evaluations—meta-analysis and systematic reviews, RCTs, quasi-experimental studies
- Qualitative studies—Realist evaluations, white papers, reports, program-specific case studies, websites, policy analysis
- Multi-disciplinary research across relevant fields of study

② Use multidisciplinary, mixed methods approach

(1) Conduct iterative, small-scale, evidence-based experiments to determine how the program elements can be tweaked to improve the design for effectively 'scaling up' implementation and create significant impact

(2) Refine the design choice of the operational elements of the program such as the terms of reference of an outreach worker, location of the facilitating unit, framing of a financial incentive

④ Identify the theory of change

The above apparatus helped cull out a theory of change that
1. Identifies mentoring and psychosocial support as the core interventions and others as enabling ones
2. Provides a framework for profiling risk characteristics and identifying broader systemic interventions
3. Helps identify the generalizable underlying mechanisms of the reengagement process to guide design
4. Supports policy dialogue and program design by guiding the choice of inputs and activities

⑥ Conduct program-level impact evaluation

Program outcomes

Socioemotional skills: positive change in social and emotional indicators

Education participation: awareness, reenrolment, persistent engagement, and completion

Protection: availability, access, and quality of financial, health and social welfare services

Academic performance: academic outcomes and attainment level

Source: World Bank analysis.

In the next chapter, we use this completed framework to draw together the interconnections and interdependencies between the various aspects of the complex development phenomena of reengagement and begin to propose theories of change that can inform policy, program design and implementation.

NOTES

1. Effect size (ES) is a standardized, scale-free measure of the relative size of the effect of an intervention and is useful to quantify effects measured on unfamiliar or arbitrary scales and for comparing the relative sizes of effects from different studies (Coe 2002).
2. Cohen offered a rule of thumb, namely that effect sizes less than 0.2 are "small" while those greater than 0.8 are considered "large" (1992). Researchers argue that Cohen's scale is not applicable for positive youth development interventions.
3. The analysis excluded interventions such as peer tutoring and mentoring by mental health professionals.
4. This study focused on homeless youth receiving mandated services such as child welfare, mental health, probation, or services where there was no alternative residential care for homeless youth, that is, focusing on at-risk young people. Even when the engagement process begins voluntarily, the nature of the relationship that at-risk youth seek complements

the findings by Pawson (2006). Hence, we use these findings as an extension to define different types of mentor skills.
5. Young people like to influence decisions that affect them (Barnes 2007; McLeod 2010) and negotiate professional boundaries. This could be simple decisions such as the location and timing of meetings (Ungar et al. 2012) or be more far-reaching decisions such as planning their credit recovery (Deci et al. 1994). For example, students can have graduation plans outlining the exact number of courses they need along with options for accelerated credit recovery that teachers could recommend supporting students' individual needs, abilities, and interest to meet graduation requirements. Providing such flexible options to support the development of students' interest, ability, and perceived control over their learning outcomes helps build at-risk students' autonomy and increases their engagement (Deci et al. 1994).
6. For example, financial incentives such as scholarships and bursaries, conditional cash transfers and vouchers have all been used and tested for effectiveness. Scholarships are traditionally associated with competitive financial awards made to high-performing student applicants (based on a predetermined metric). Bursaries are non-competitive financial provisions made to students who are in financial need and get applied automatically. Conditional cash transfers are financial support provided to the family of the beneficiary on the condition that certain agreed-upon conditions are met. Vouchers are government issued funding certificates provided to the beneficiary students and his/her family which can be redeemed at a school of his/her choice to incentivize competition and improve service provision in the education marketplace.
7. Flexible and permeable education systems enable learners to move within and across education, training and employment. *Flexibility* means that young people can adapt their learning pathway as they go along, to suit their interests and abilities. *Permeability* means that young people can progress to programs at higher levels and take forward their long-term career, avoiding requirements to restart and repeat, regardless of the pathway they have chosen. Flexibility in the delivery and timing of learning opportunities means that young people who have other demands on their time can return to learning and continue to work toward their chosen qualification (CEDEFOP 2017).
8. Sites included Sheshatshiu, an aboriginal community in Northern Canada; Hong Kong, SAR, China; East Jerusalem and Gaza, Palestine; Tel Aviv, Israel; Medellín, Colombia; Moscow, Russian Federation; Imphal, India; Tampa, Florida; the Gambia; Njoro, Tanzania; Capetown, South Africa; Halifax, Canada; and Winnipeg, Canada (two sites, one with urban aboriginal youth, the other with non-aboriginal youth in residential care) (Ungar 2006).
9. Terms used to describe programs that enable individuals to access and re-engage in learning outside of mainstream education include *second chance* education programs, *alternative* education programs, *reengagement* programs, and *flexible learning* programs (te Riele 2014).
10. Distance education and/or online learning can be conducted either synchronously (group-based instruction where students in different locations connect via some form of technology and are directed by a teacher simultaneously) or asynchronously (individual-based instruction where students in different locations independently and receive support from the teacher with some delay, also called correspondence education).
11. *Loss aversion* refers to the tendency to prefer avoiding losses relative to acquiring equivalent gains (Kahneman and Tversky 1984). *Dynamic inconsistency* refers to a situation in which a decision-maker's preference changes over time in such a way that a preference can become inconsistent at another point in time (Loewenstein and Prelec 1992). *Cognitive dissonance* (Brehm 1956; Festinger 1962) suggests that if a person chooses an alternative from a given choice set, this act of choice causes a subsequent preference for the previously chosen alternative. *Sunk cost fallacy* (Kahneman and Tversky 1979; Thaler 1980) implies that paying more for some good increases the subsequent desire to use that good. *Self-prophecy effect* (Greenwald et al. 1987) suggests that explicitly asking people whether they expect they will perform a socially desirable action (e.g., vote) causes them to subsequently do so. *Implementation intention* involves prompting subjects to state a plan up front on how and when they will undertake a behavior that makes them more likely to act.
12. The main lesson from the psychology literature on intrinsic motivation is that it is a bad idea to temporarily pay people for an inherently interesting task. Also, extrinsic incentives to induce prosocial behavior can backfire (Deci, Koestner, and Ryan 1999; Kamenica 2012).

REFERENCES

Ager, A., B. Akesson, L. Stark, E. Flouri, B. Okot, F. McCollister, and N. Boothby. 2011. "The Impact of the School-Based Psychosocial Structured Activities (PSSA) Program on Conflict-Affected Children in northern Uganda." *Journal of Child Psychology and Psychiatry* 52 (11): 1124–33.

Akhter, U.A., M. Adato, A. Kudat, D. Gilligan, T. Roopnaraine and R. Colasan. 2007. *Impact Evaluation of the Conditional Cash Transfer Program in Turkey: Final Report*. Washington, DC: IFPRI (in collaboration with the AGRIN Co. Ltd, Ankara).

Allen, J. P., G. Kuperminc, S. Philliber, and K. Herre. 1994. "Programmatic Prevention of Adolescent Problem Behaviors: The Role of Autonomy, Relatedness, and Volunteer Service in the Teen Outreach Program." *American Journal of Community Psychology* 22 (5): 595–615.

Alves, V. 2016. "Background Paper on Psychosocial Support and Social and Emotional Learning for Children and Youth in Emergency Settings." INEE Education Policy Working Group (EPWG) and INEE Standards and Practice Working Group (SPWG). New York, NY: Inter-Agency Network for Education in Emergencies (INEE).

Andersson, B. 2013. "Finding Ways to the Hard to Reach—Considerations on the Content and Concept of Outreach Work." *European Journal of Social Work* 16 (2): 171–86.

Angell, B. and C. Mahoney. 2007. "Reconceptualizing the Case Management Relationship in Intensive Treatment: A Study of Staff Perceptions and Experiences." *Administration and Policy in Mental Health and Mental Health Services Research* 34 (2): 172–88.

Annunziata, D., A. Hogue, L. Faw, and H. A. Liddle. 2006. "Family Functioning and School Success in At-Risk, Inner-City Adolescents." *Journal of Youth and Adolescence* 35 (1): 100–08.

Ayala Consulting. 2003. *Workshop on Conditional Cash Transfer Programs: Operational Experiences*. World Bank Social Protection Network. Washington, DC: World Bank.

Bandura, A. 1977. "Self-Efficacy: Toward a Unifying Theory of Behavioral Change." *Psychological Review* 84 (2): 191–215.

Bandura, A. 1986. *Social Foundations of Thought and Action: A Social Cognitive Theory*. Englewood Cliffs, NJ: Prentice-Hall, Inc.

Barnes, V. 2007. "Young People's Views of Children's Rights and Advocacy Services: A Case for 'Caring' Advocacy?" *Child Abuse Review* 16 (3): 140–152.

Bayer, A., J. B. Grossman, and D. L. DuBois. 2013. *School-Based Mentoring Programs: Using Volunteers to Improve the Academic Outcomes of Underserved Students*. MDRC.

Bedell, J. R., N. L. Cohen, and A. Sullivan. 2000. "Case Management: The Current Best Practices and the Next Generation of Innovation." *Community Mental Health Journal* 36 (2): 179–94.

Beresford, P., S. Croft, and L. Adshead. 2007. "'We don't See Her As a Social Worker': A Service User Case Study of the Importance of the Social Worker's Relationship and Humanity." *British Journal of Social Work*—Advanced Access (May 24).

Bernard, R. M., E. Borokhovski, R. F. Schmid, R. M. Tamim, and P. C. Abrami. 2014. "A Meta-Analysis of Blended Learning and Technology Use in Higher Education: From the General to the Applied." *Journal of Computing in Higher Education* 26 (1): 87–122.

Blakemore, S. J., and K. L. Mills. 2014. "Is Adolescence a Sensitive Period for Sociocultural Processing?" *Annual Review of Psychology* 65, 187–207.

Blinn-Pike, L. 2007. "The Benefits Associated with Youth Mentoring Relationships." In *Blackwell Handbook of Mentoring*, edited by T. D. Allen and L. T. Eby. Oxford: Blackwell.

Börkan, B., Ö. Ünlühisarcıklı, H. A. Caner, and Z. H. Sart. 2015. "The Catch-Up Education Programme in Turkey: Opportunities and Challenges." *International Review of Education* 61 (1): 21–41.

Brehm, J. 1956. "Post-Decision Changes in Desirability of Alternatives." *Journal of Abnormal and Social Psychology* 52 (3): 384–89.

Carneiro, P., and J. Heckman. 2003. "Human Capital Policy." In *Inequality in America: What Role for Human Capital Policies?*, edited by J. Heckman, A. Krueger and B. Freidman. Cambridge, Mass.: MIT Press.

Cartwright, N. 2007. *Causal Powers: What Are They? Why Do We Need Them? What Can Be Done with Them and What Cannot*. Technical Report no. 04, 7. Centre for Philosophy of Natural and Social Science, Contingency and Dissent in Science Project, London School of Economics and Political Science.

Cartwright, N., and J. Hardie. 2012. *Evidence-Based Policy: A Practical Guide to Doing it Better*. Oxford University Press.

Casey, B. J. 2015. "Beyond Simple Models of Self-Control to Circuit-Based Accounts of Adolescent Behavior." *Annual Review of Psychology* 66, 295–319.

CEDEFOP. 2017. *VET Toolkit for Tackling Early Leaving*. http://www.cedefop.europa.eu/en/toolkits/vet-toolkit-tackling-early-leaving/intervene/intervention-approaches

Center for Promise. 2015. *Don't Quit on Me: What Young People Who Left School Say about the Power of Relationships*. Washington, DC: America's Promise Alliance.

Chalker, C. S., and K. Stelsel. 2009. "A Fresh Approach to Alternative Education: Using Malls to Reach At-Risk Youth." *Kappa Delta Pi Record* 45 (2): 74–77.

Chan, C., and M. J. Holosko. 2017. "The Utilization of Social Media for Youth Outreach Engagement: A Case Study." *Qualitative Social Work* 16 (5): 680–97.

Chui, W. H., and H. C. O. Chan. 2012. "Outreach Social Workers for At-Risk Youth: A Test of Their Attitudes towards Crime and Young Offenders in Hong Kong."*Children and Youth Services Review* 34 (12): 2273–79.

Cicchetti, D., J. Rappaport, I. Sandler, and R. P. Weissberg, eds. 2000. *The Promotion of Wellness in Children and Adolescents*. Washington, DC: Child Welfare League of America.

Clayton, B., R. Lewanski, G. Pancini, and S. Schutt. 2010. *Enhancing the Retention of Young People to Year 12, Especially through Vocational Skills*. Australian College of Educators, Department of Education, Employment and Workplace Relations, and TAFE Directors Australia. http://www.tda.edu.au/resources/Enhancing percent20Retention%20Final%20Report%20inc%20cov.pdf.

Coe, R. 2002. "It's the Effect Size, Stupid—What Effect Size Is and Why It Is Important." Presented at the Annual Conference of the British Educational Research Association, and published in the British Education Index Education-Line. https://www.leeds.ac.uk/educol/documents/00002182.htm.

Cohen, J. 1992. "A Power Primer." *Psychological Bulletin* 112 (1): 155.

Coldwell, C. M. and W. S. Bender. 2007. "The Effectiveness of Assertive Community Treatment for Homeless Populations with Severe Mental Illness: A Meta-Analysis." *American Journal of Psychiatry* 164 (3): 393–99.

Collaborative for Academic, Social, and Emotional Learning. 2005. *Safe and Sound: An Educational Leader's Guide to Evidence-Based Social and Emotional Learning (SEL) Programs*. Chicago, IL: Collaborative for Academic, Social, and Emotional Learning.

Commission on Positive Youth Development. 2005. "The Positive Perspective on Youth Development." In *Treating and Preventing Adolescent Mental Health Disorders: What We Know and What We Don't Know*, edited by D. W. Evans, E. B. Foa, R. E. Gur, H. Hendin, C. P. O'Brien, M. E. P. Seligman, and B. T. Walsh, 497–527. New York: Oxford University Press.

Connolly, J. A., and L. E. Joly. 2012. "Outreach with Street-Involved Youth: A Quantitative And Qualitative Review of the Literature." *Clinical Psychology Review* 32 (6): 524–34.

Converse, N., and B. Kraft. 2009. "Evaluation of a School-Based Mentoring Program for At-Risk Middle School Youth." *Remedial and Special Education* 30 (1): 33–46. Hammill Institute on Disabilities. DOI: 10.1177/0741932507314023.

Crone, E. A., and R. E. Dahl. 2012. "Understanding Adolescence as a Period of Social–Affective Engagement and Goal Flexibility." *Nature Reviews Neuroscience* 13 (9): 636.

Cunha, F., J. Heckman, L. Lochner, and D. Masterov. 2006. "Interpreting the Evidence on Life Cycle Skill Formation." In *Handbook of the Economics of Education*, edited by E. Hanushek and F. Welch vol. 1, pp 697–812. Elsevier B.V.

Cunningham, W., L. M. Cohan, S. Naudeau, and L. McGinnis. 2008a. *Supporting Youth at Risk: A Policy Toolkit for Middle Income Countries*. Washington, DC: World Bank.

Cunningham, W., L. McGinnis, R. G. Verdú, C. Tesliuc, and D. Verner. 2008b. *Youth at Risk in Latin America and the Caribbean: Understanding the Causes, Realizing the Potential.* Washington, DC: World Bank.

de Hoyos, R., A. Popova, and H. Rogers. 2016a. *Out of School and Out of Work: A Diagnostic of Ninis in Latin America.* Washington, DC: World Bank.

de Hoyos, R., H. Rogers, and M. Székely. 2016b. *Out of School and Out of Work: Risk and Opportunities for Latin America's Ninis.* Washington, DC: World Bank.

Deci, E., H. Eghrari, B. Patrick, and D. Leone. 1994. "Facilitating Internalization: The Self-Determination Theory Perspective." *Journal of Personality* 62 (1): 119–42.

Deci, E. L., R. Koestner, and R. M. Ryan. 1999. "A Meta-Analytic Review of Experiments Examining the Effects of Extrinsic Rewards on Intrinsic Motivation." *Psychological Bulletin* 125 (6): 627.

Dekelver, J., W. Van den Bosch, and J. Engelen. 2011. "Supporting Social Inclusion of Youth at Risk Using Social Software: Impact, Sustainability and Evaluation, One Year after Pilot Testing." *Housing, Care and Support* 14 (2): 61–66.

Dickson-Gomez, J., M. Convey, H. Hilario, A. M. Corbett, and M. Weeks. 2007. "Unofficial Policy: Access to Housing, Housing Information and Social Services among Homeless Drug Users in Hartford, Connecticut." *Substance Abuse Treatment, Prevention, and Policy* 2 (8). http://www.substanceabusepolicy.com/content/2/1/8.

Dorsey, L. E., and C. M. Baker. 2004. "Mentoring Undergraduate Nursing Students." *Nurse Educator* 29: 260–65.

DuBois, D. L., B. E. Holloway, J. C. Valentine, and H. Cooper. 2002. "Effectiveness of Mentoring Programs for Youth: A Meta-Analytic Review." *American Journal of Community Psychology* 30: 157–97.

DuBois, D. L., N. Portillo, J. E. Rhodes, N. Silverthorn, and J. C. Valentine. 2011. "How Effective Are Mentoring Programs for Youth? A Systematic Assessment of the Evidence." *Psychological Science in the Public Interest* 12 (2): 57–91.

DuBois, D. L., and N. Silverthorn. 2005. "Natural Mentoring Relationships and Adolescent Health: Evidence from a National Study." *American Journal of Public Health* 95: 518–24.

Durlak, J. A., and R. P. Weissberg. 2007. *The Impact of After-School Programs that Promote Personal and Social Skills.* Chicago, IL: Collaborative for Academic, Social, and Emotional Learning.

Durlak, J. A., R. P. Weissberg, A. B. Dymnicki, R. D. Taylor, and K. B. Schellinger. 2011. "The Impact of Enhancing Students' Social and Emotional Learning: A Meta-Analysis of School-Based Universal Interventions." *Child Development* 82 (1): 405–32.

Durlak, J. A., R. P. Weissberg, and M. Pachan. 2010. "A Meta-Analysis of After-School Programs that Seek to Promote Personal and Social Skills in Children And Adolescents." *American Journal of Community Psychology* 45 (3–4): 294–309.

Eby, L. T., T. D. Allen, S. C. Evans, T. Ng, and D. DuBois. 2008. "Does Mentoring Matter? A Multidisciplinary Meta-Analysis Comparing Mentored and Non-Mentored Individuals." *Journal of Vocational Behavior* 72 (2): 254–67.

Eccles, J., T. Adler, S. Goff, C. Kaczala, J. Meece, and C. Midgley. 1983. In *Motives: Psychological and Sociological Approaches*, edited by J. Spencer, 75–146. San Francisco, CA: W. H. Freeman and Company.

Eddy, J. M., C. R. Martinez, J. B. Grossman, J. J. Cearley, D. Herrera, A. C. Wheeler, and T. W. Harachi. 2017. "A Randomized Controlled Trial of a Long-Term Professional Mentoring Program for Children at Risk: Outcomes across the First 5 Years." *Prevention Science* 18 (8): 899–910.

Festinger, L. 1962. "Cognitive Dissonance." *Scientific American* 207 (4): 93–107.

Fredricks, J. A., P. C. Blumenfeld, and A. H. Paris. 2004. "School Engagement: Potential of the Concept, State of the Evidence." *Review of Educational Research* 74 (1): 59–109.

Gizir, C., and G. Aydin. 2009. "Protective Factors Contributing to the Academic Resilience of Students Living in Poverty in Turkey." *Professional School Counseling* 13 (1): 38–49.

Gneezy, U., S. Meier, and P. Rey-Biel. 2011. "When and Why Incentives (Don't) Work to Modify Behavior." *Journal of Economic Perspectives* 25 (4): 191–210.

Graham, C. R. 2005. "Blended Learning Systems." In *The Handbook of Blended Learning: Global Perspectives, Local Designs*, edited by C. J. Bonk and C. R. Graham. Chichester: Wiley (originally Pfeiffer).

Greenberg, M. T., R. P. Weissberg, M. U. O'Brien, J. E. Zins, L. Fredericks, H. Resnik, and M. J. Elias. 2003. "Enhancing School-Based Prevention and Youth Development through Coordinated Social, Emotional, and Academic Learning." *American Psychologist* 58: 466–74.

Greenwald, A. G., C. G. Carnot, R. Beach, and B. Young. 1987. "Increasing Voting Behavior by Asking People if they Expect to Vote." *Journal of Applied Psychology* 72 (2): 315.

Gregory, A., C. A. Hafen, E. Ruzek, A. Y. Mikami, J. P. Allen, and R. C. Pianta. 2016. "Closing the Racial Discipline Gap in Classrooms by Changing Teacher Practice." *School Psychology Review* 45 (2): 171–91.

Gronda, H. 2009. *What Makes Case Management Work for People Experiencing Homelessness? Evidence for Practice*. Australian Housing and Urban Research Institute, AHURI Final Report No. 127, Melbourne. https://www.ahuri.edu.au/research/final-reports/127.

Gutherson, P., H. Davies, and T. Daszkiewicz. 2011. *Achieving Successful Outcomes through Alternative Education Provision: An International Literature Review*. Reading: CfBT Education Trust.

Harrison, N., A. Baxter, and S. Hatt. 2007. "From Opportunity to OFFA: The Implementation of Discretionary Bursaries and Their Impact on Student Finance, Academic Success and Institutional Attachment." *Journal of Access Policy and Practice* 5 (1): 3–21.

Hatt, S., A. Hannan, A. Baxter, and N. Harrison. 2005. "Opportunity Knocks? The Impact of Bursary Schemes on Students from Low-Income Backgrounds." *Studies in Higher Education* 30 (4): 373–88.

Heckman, J. J. 2000. "Policies to Foster Human Capital." *Research in Economics* 54 (1): 3–56.

Heckman, J., A. Krueger, and B. Freidman, eds. 2003. *Inequality in America: What Role for Human Capital Policies?* Cambridge, MA: MIT Press.

Heckman, J. J., J. Stixrud, and S. Urzua. 2006. "The Effects of Cognitive and Noncognitive Abilities on Labor Market Outcomes and Social Behavior." *Journal of Labor economics* 24 (3): 411–82.

Heller, S. B., H. A. Pollack, R. Ander, and J. Ludwig. 2013. "Preventing Youth Violence and Dropout: A Randomized Field Experiment." NBER Working Paper 19014. Cambridge, MA: NPER.

Herrera, C., J. B. Grossman, T. J. Kauh, and J. McMaken. 2011. "Mentoring in Schools: An Impact Study of Big Brothers Big Sisters School-Based Mentoring. *Child Development* 82 (1): 346–61.

Hill, C. J., H. S. Bloom, A. R. Black, and M. W. Lipsey. 2008. "Empirical Benchmarks for Interpreting Effect Sizes in Research." *Child Development Perspectives* 2 (3): 172–77.

Inbar, D., and R. Sever. 1989. "The Importance of Making Promises: An Analysis of Second-Chance Policies." *Comparative Education Review* 33 (2): 232–42.

Inoue, K., E. Di Gropello, Y. S. Taylor, and J. Gresham. 2015. *Out-of-School Youth in Sub-Saharan Africa: A Policy Perspective*. Washington, DC: World Bank.

Jones, S. M., and S. M. Bouffard. 2012. "Social and Emotional Learning in Schools: From Programs to Strategies." *Social Policy Report* 26 (4) (Society for Research in Child Development).

Kahneman, D. and A. Tversky. 1979. "Prospect Theory: An Analysis of Decisions Under Risk." *Econometrica* 47 (2): 263–91.

Kahneman, D., and Tversky, A. 1984. "Choices, Values, and Frames." *American Psychologist* 39 (4): 341–50.

Kamenica, E. 2012. "Behavioral Economics and Psychology of Incentives." *Annual Review of Economics* 4 (1): 427–52.

Keegan, D. 1996. *Foundations of Distance Education*. 3rd ed. London: Routledge.

Kerka, S. 2006. *What Works: Evidence-Based Strategies for Youth Practitioners, Out-Of-School Youth*. Columbus, kOH: Learning Works Connection, The Ohio State University.

Khanlou, N., and R. Wray. 2014. "A Whole Community Approach toward Child and Youth Resilience Promotion: A Review of Resilience Literature." *International Journal of Mental Health and Addiction* 12 (1): 64–79.

Kia-Keating, M., E. Dowdy, M. L. Morgan, and G. G. Noam. 2011. "Protecting and Promoting: An Integrative Conceptual Model for Healthy Development of Adolescents." *Journal of Adolescent Health* 48 (3): 220–28.

Knoll, G. M. 2012. *Stages of Change Training for Youth Outreach Workers: Bridging Research, Theory, and Practice*. York University.

Komosa-Hawkins, K. 2012. "The Impact of School-Based Mentoring on Adolescents' Social-Emotional Health." *Mentoring* and *Tutoring: Partnership in Learning* 20 (3): 393–408.

Kryda, A. D., and M. T. Compton. 2009. "Mistrust of Outreach Workers and Lack of Confidence in Available Services among Individuals who Are Chronically Street Homeless." *Community Mental Health Journal* 45 (2): 148–49.

Kuperminc, G. P. 2016. *Group Mentoring—National Mentoring Resource Center Model Review*. http://nationalmentoringresourcecenter.org/images/PDF/GroupMentoring Review.pdf.

Kuperminc, G. P., J. G. Emshoff, M. M. Reiner, L. A. Secrest, P. H. Niolon, and J. D. Foster. 2005. "Integration of Mentoring with Other Programs and Services." In *Handbook of Youth Mentoring*, edited by D.L. DuBois & M.J. Karcher (2): 314–333.

Kuperminc, G.P., & Thomason, J.D. 2013. Group mentoring. In D.L DuBois & M.J. Karcher (Eds.), Handbook of Youth Mentoring (273–289). Los Angeles: Sage.

Lakind, D., J. M. Eddy, and A. Zell. 2014. "Mentoring Youth at High Risk: The Perspectives of Professional Mentors." *Child* and *Youth Care Forum* 43 (6): 705–27.

Larson, R. W., and S. Verma. 1999. How Children and Adolescents Spend Time across the World: Work, Play, and Developmental Opportunities." *Psychological Bulletin* 125 (6): 701–36.

Liebenberg, L., and M. Ungar, eds. 2008. *Resilience in Action*. Toronto: University of Toronto Press.

Loewenstein, G. and D. Prelec. 1992. "Anomalies in Intertemporal Choice: Evidence and an Interpretation." *Quarterly Journal of Economics* 107 (2): 573–97.

Luthar. S. S., ed. 2003. *Resilience and Vulnerability: Adaptation in the Context of Childhood Adversities*. New York: Cambridge University Press.

Main, K., and S. Whatman. 2016. "Building Social and Emotional Efficacy to (Re) Engage Young Adolescents: Capitalising on the 'Window of Opportunity'." *International Journal of Inclusive Education* 20 (10): 1054–69.

Martin, R. A. 2012. "Social and Emotional Learning Research: Intervention studies for Supporting Adolescents in Turkey." *Procedia—Social and Behavioral Sciences* 69: 1469–76.

Masten, A. S. 2001. "Ordinary Magic: Resilience Processes in Development." *American Psychologist* 56 (3): 227.

Masten, A. S., and J. D. Coatsworth. 1998. "The Development of Competence in Favorable and Unfavorable Environments: Lessons from Research on Successful Children." *American Psychologist* 53 (2): 205.

Masten, A. S., and J. L. Powell. 2003. "A Resilience Framework for Research, Policy, and Practice." In *Resilience and Vulnerability: Adaptation in the Context of Childhood Adversities*, edited by S. S. Luthar, 1–28. New York, NY: Cambridge University Press.

Mauro, J. A. and M. Sophie. 2015. *Understanding Out-of-Work and Out-of-School Youth in Europe and Central Asia* (English). Washington, DC: World Bank Group. http://documents.worldbank.org/curated/en/103971468187482224/Understanding-out-of-work-and-out-of-school-youth-in-Europe-and-Central-Asia.

McCaig, C., N. Harrison, A. Mountford-Zimdars, D. Moore, U. Maylor, J. Stevenson, H. Ertl, and H. Carasso. 2016. *Understanding the Impact of Institutional Financial Support on Student Success: Phase One Report*. Shefflied Institute of Education, Office for Fair Access.

McLeod, A. 2010. "'A Friend and An Equal': Do Young People in Care Seek the Impossible from Their Social Workers." *British Journal of Social Work* 40 (3): 772–88.

Means, B., Y. Toyama, R. Murphy, and M. Baki. 2013. "The Effectiveness of Online and Blended Learning: A Meta-Analysis of the Empirical Literature." *Teachers College Record* 115 (3): 1–47.

Melaville, A. I., and M. J. Blank. 1991. *What It Takes: Structuring Interagency Partnerships to Connect Children and Families with Comprehensive Services*. Washington, DC: Education and Human Services Consortium.

Meyer, K. C., and H. A. Bouchey. 2010. "Daring to DREAM: Results from a Mentoring Programme for At-Risk Youth." *International Journal of Evidence Based Coaching & Mentoring* 8 (1).

Mikkonen, M. I. K. A., J. Kauppinen, M. Huovinen, and E. Aalto. 2007. *Outreach Work among Marginalised Populations in Europe: Guidelines on Providing Integrated Outreach Services.* Amsterdam: Foundation Regenboog AMOC.

Miller, B. M. 2003. *Critical Hours: After-School Programs and Educational Success.* New York: Nellie Mae Education Foundation.

Morley, E., and S. B. Rossman. 1997. *Helping At-Risk Youth: Lessons from Community-Based Initiatives.* Washington, DC: The Urban Institute.

Morris, P. A., J. L. Aber, S. Wolf, and J. Berg. 2017. "Impacts of Family Rewards on Adolescents' Mental Health and Problem Behavior: Understanding the Full Range of Effects of a Conditional Cash Transfer Program." *Prevention Science* 18 (3): 326–36.

Morse, G. 1999. "A Review of Case Management for People who Are Homeless: Implications for Practice, Policy, and Research." In *Practical Lessons: The 1998 National Symposium on Homelessness Research*, edited by L. B. Fosburg and D. L. Dennis. U.S. Department of Housing and Urban Development and the U.S. Department of Health and Human Services.

Myconos, G. 2014. *Lessons from a Flexible Learning Program: The Brotherhood of St Laurence Community VCAL Education Program for Young People 2010–2013.* Victoria, Australia: The Brotherhood of St Laurence.

National Research Council and Institute of Medicine. 2002. *Community Programs to Promote Youth Development.* Washington, DC: National Academy Press.

OFFA (Office for Fair Access). 2014. *Do Bursaries Have an Effect on Retention Rates?* U.K. Office for Fair Access. www.offa.org.uk/guidance-notes/new-research-from-offa-an-interim-report-do-bursaries-have-an-effect-on-retention-rates/.

Okonofua, J. A., D. Paunesku, and G. M. Walton. 2016. "Brief Intervention to Encourage Empathic Discipline Cuts Suspension Rates in Half among Adolescents." *Proceedings of the National Academy of Sciences* 113 (19): 5221–26.

Owston, R., D. York, and S. Murtha. 2013. "Student Perceptions and Achievement in a University Blended Learning Strategic Initiative." *The Internet and Higher Education* 18: 38–46.

Panter-Brick, C., R. Dajani, M. Eggerman, S. Hermosilla, A. Sancilio, and A. Ager. 2018. "Insecurity, Distress and Mental Health: Experimental and Randomized Controlled Trials of a Psychosocial Intervention for Youth Affected by the Syrian Crisis." *Journal of Child Psychology and Psychiatry* 59 (5): 523–41.

Passey, D., S. Williams, and C. Rogers. 2008. *Assessing the Potential of e-Learning to Support Re-Engagement amongst Young People with Not in Education, Employment or Training (NEET) Status.* Lancaster: Lancaster University.

Pawson, R. 2006. "Reviewing Inner Mechanisms: Youth Mentoring." In *Evidence-Based Policy: A Realist Perspective*, edited by R. Pawson, Chapter 6, 122–150. London: Sage.

Polidano, C., D. Tabasso, and Y. P. Tseng. 2015. "A Second Chance at Education for Early School Leavers." *Education Economics* 23 (3): 358–75.

Pollack, K. M., S. Frattaroli, J. M. Whitehill, and K. Strother. 2011. "Youth Perspectives on Street Outreach Workers: Results from a Community-Based Survey." *Journal of Community Health* 36 (3): 469–76.

Prochaska, J. O. 2013 "Trans-Theoretical Model of Behavior Change." In *Encyclopedia of Behavioral Medicine*, edited by M. D. Gellman and J. R. Turner. New York, NY: Springer.

Prochaska, J. O., C. A. Redding, and K. E. Evers. 2002. "The Transtheoretical Model and Stages of Change." In *Health Behavior and Health Education: Theory, Research, and Practice*, edited by K. Glanz, F. M. Lewis, and B. Rimer, 99–120. San Francisco, CA: Jossey Bass Publishers.

Randolph, K. A., and J. L. Johnson. 2008. "School-Based Mentoring Programs: A Review of the Research." *Children & Schools* 30 (3): 177–85.

Reed, R. J., and B. Hurd. 2016. "A Value beyond Money? Assessing the Impact of Equity Scholarships: From Access to Success." *Studies in Higher Education* 41 (7): 1236–50.

Rekkedal, T., S. Qvist-Eriksen, D. Keegan, G. O. Súilleabháin, R. Coughlan, and H. Fritsch. 2003. *Internet Based e-Learning, Pedagogy and Support Systems.* Norway: NKI Distance Education.

Rhodes, J. E. 1994. "Older and Wiser: Mentoring Relationships in Childhood and Adolescence." *Journal of Primary Prevention* 14: 187–96.

Rhodes, J. E. 2002. *Stand by Me: The Risks and Rewards of Mentoring Today's Youth*. Cambridge, MA: Harvard University Press.

Ross, S., and J. Gray. 2005. "Transitions and Re-Engagement through Second Chance Education." *The Australian Educational Researcher* 32 (3): 103–40.

Rumberger, R. W., and S. P. Lamb. 2003. "The Early Employment and Further Education Experiences of High School Dropouts: A Comparative Study of the United States and Australia." *Economics of Education Review* 22 (4): 353–66.

Rutter, M. 1987. "Psychosocial Resilience and Protective Mechanisms." *American Journal of Orthopsychiatry* 57 (3): 316.

Sambunjak, D., S. E. Straus, and A. Marusic. 2006. "Mentoring in Academic Medicine." *Journal of the American Medical Association* 296: 1103–15.

Sameroff, A., L. M. Gutman, and S. C. Peck. 2003. "Adaptation among Youth Facing Multiple Risks: Prospective Research Findings." In *Resilience and Vulnerability: Adaptation in the Context of Childhood Adversities*, edited by S. S. Luthar, 364–92. New York: Cambridge University Press.

Seidman, E., and S. Pedersen. 2003. "Holistic Contextual Perspectives on Risk, Protection, and Competence among Low-Income Urban Adolescents." In *Resilience and Vulnerability: Adaptation in the Context of Childhood Adversities*, edited by S. S. Luthar, 318–42. New York, NY, US: Cambridge University Press.

Shonkoff, J., P. Levitt, S. Bunge, J. Cameron, G. Duncan, P. Fisher, and N. Fox. 2015. *Supportive Relationships and Active Skill-Building Strengthen the Foundations of Resilience*. (PDF). National Scientific Council on the Developing Child.

Simpson, O. 2013. "Student Retention in Distance Education: Are We Failing Our Students?" *Open Learning: The Journal of Open, Distance and e-Learning* 28 (2): 105–19.

So, H. J., and T. A. Brush. 2008. "Student Perceptions of Collaborative Learning, Social Presence and Satisfaction in a Blended Learning Environment: Relationships and Critical Factors." *Computers & Education* 51 (1): 318–36.

Sparrow, R. 2007. "Protecting Education for the Poor in Times of Crisis: An Evaluation of a Scholarship Programme in Indonesia." *Oxford Bulletin of Economics and Statistics* 69 (1): 99–122.

Sumbera, B. G. 2017. *Model Continuation High Schools: Social-Cognitive Promotive Factors that Contribute to Re-Engaging At-Risk Students Emotionally, Behaviorally, and Cognitively towards Graduation*. Pepperdine University.

Taylor, A. S., L. LoSciuto, M. Fox, S. M. Hilbert, and M. Sonkowsky. 1999. "The Mentoring Factor: Evaluation of the across Ages' Intergenerational Approach to Drug Abuse Prevention." *Child & Youth Services* 20 (1–2): 77–99.

Taylor, R. D., E. Oberle, J. A. Durlak, and R. P. Weissberg. 2017. "Promoting Positive Youth Development through School-Based Social and Emotional Learning Interventions: A Meta-Analysis of Follow-Up Effects." *Child Development* 88 (4): 1156–71.

Te Riele, K. 2014. *Putting the Jigsaw Together: Flexible Learning Programs in Australia*. Final report. Melbourne: The Victoria Institute for Education, Diversity and Lifelong Learning.

Thaler, R. 1980. "Toward a Positive Theory of Consumer Choice." *Journal of Economic Behavior & Organization* 1 (1): 39–60.

Tolan, P. H., D. B. Henry, M. S. Schoeny, P. Lovegrove, and E. Nichols. 2014. "Mentoring Programs to Affect Delinquency and Associated Outcomes of Youth at Risk: A Comprehensive Meta-Analytic Review." *Journal of Experimental Criminology* 10 (2): 179–206.

Underhill, C. M. 2006. "The Effectiveness of Mentoring Programs in Corporate Settings: A Meta-Analytical Review of the Literature." *Journal of Vocational Behavior* 68: 292–307.

Ungar, M. 2006. "Nurturing Hidden Resilience in At-Risk Youth in Different Cultures." *Journal of the Canadian Academy of Child and Adolescent Psychiatry* 15 (2): 53.

Ungar, M. 2008. "Putting Resilience Theory into Action: Five Principles for Intervention." In *Resilience in Action*, edited by Liebenberg, L. and Ungar, M., 17–38. Toronto: University of Toronto Press.

Ungar, M., and J. Ikeda. 2017. "Rules or No Rules? Three Strategies for Engagement with Young People in Mandated Services." *Child and Adolescent Social Work Journal* 34 (3): 259–67.

Ungar, M., and L. Liebenberg. 2005. "Resilience across Cultures: The Mixed Methods Approach of the International Resilience Project." In *Handbook for Working with Children and Youth Pathways to Resilience across Cultures and Contexts*, edited by Ungar, M., 211–26. Thousand Oaks, CA: Sage.

Ungar, M., and L. Liebenberg. 2009. Cross-cultural consultation leading to the development of a valid measure of youth resilience: The International Resilience Project. Studia Psychologica, 51(2-3), 259–268.

Ungar, M., L. Liebenberg, N. Landry, and J. Ikeda. 2012. "Caregivers, Young People with Complex Needs, and Multiple Service Providers: A Study of Triangulated Relationships and Their Impact on Resilience." *Family Process* 51 (2): 193–206.

van Harmelen, Anne-Laura, Jenny L. Gibson, Michelle C. St Clair, Matt Owens, Jeannette Brodbeck, Valerie Dunn, Gemma Lewis, Tim Croudace, Peter B. Jones, Rogier A. Kievit, Ian M. Goodyer. 2016. "Friendships and Family Support Reduce Subsequent Depressive Symptoms in At-Risk Adolescents." *PLoS One* 11 (5): e0153715.

Voelkl, K. 1997. "Identification with School." *American Journal of Education* 105 (3): 204–319.

Watson, J., and B. Gemin. 2008. "Using Online Learning for At-Risk Students and Credit Recovery." In *Promising Practices in Online Learning*, 1–18. Vienna, VA: North American Council for Online Learning.

Weiner, B. 2007. "Examining Emotional Diversity in the Classroom: An Attribution Theory of Achievement Motivation and Emotions." In *Emotion in Education*, edited by P. A. Schutz and R. Pekrun, 73–88. San Diego, CA: Academic.

West, A., A. Hind, C. Pennell, C. Emmerson, C. Frayne, S. McNally, and O. Silva. 2006. *Evaluation of Aimhigher: Excellence Challenge synthesis report: Surveys of opportunity bursary applicants and economic evaluation*. UK Department of Education and Skills Research Report RR709. Slough: National Foundation for Education Research.

Wigelsworth, M., A. Lendrum, J. Oldfield, A. Scott, I. ten Bokkel, K. Tate, and C. Emery. 2016. "The Impact of Trial Stage, Developer Involvement and International Transferability on Universal Social and Emotional Learning Programme Outcomes: A Meta-Analysis." *Cambridge Journal of Education* 46 (3): 347–76.

Wolf, P. J., B. Kisida, B. Gutmann, M. Puma, N. Eissa, and L. Rizzo. 2013. "School Vouchers and Student Outcomes: Experimental Evidence from Washington, DC." *Journal of Policy Analysis and Management* 32 (2): 246–70.

Wolff, N., T. W. Helminiak, G. A. Morse, R. J. Calsyn, W. D. Klinkenberg, and M. L. Trusty. 1997. "Cost-Effectiveness Evaluation of Three Approaches to Case Management for Homeless Mentally Ill Clients." *American Journal of Psychiatry* 154: 341–48.

Wu, J. H., R. D. Tennyson, and T. L. Hsia. 2010. "A Study of Student Satisfaction in a Blended e-Learning System Environment." *Computers & Education* 55 (1): 155–64.

Yang, P. 2011. "The Impact of Financial Aid on Learning, Career Decisions, and Employment: Evidence from Recent Chinese College Students." *Chinese Education and Society* 44 (1): 27–57.

Yazzie-Mintz, E. 2007. *Students Are Bored, Many Skip School, Lack Adult Support: High School Students from 110 Schools in 26 States Participate in IU Study*. Bloomington, IN: Center for Evaluation and Education Policy, University of Indiana.

Yeager, D. S. 2017. "Social and Emotional Learning Programs for Adolescents." *The Future of Children* 27(1), 73–94.

Zins, J. E., R. P. Weissberg, M. C. Wang, and H. J. Walberg, eds. 2004. *Building Academic Success on Social and Emotional Learning: What Does the Research Say?* New York: Teachers College Press.

Zulkhibri, M. 2016. "The Relevance of Conditional Cash Transfers in Developing Economy: The Case of Muslim Countries." *International Journal of Social Economics* 43 (12): 1513–38.

5 Understanding the Complex Process of Reengagement

This chapter has two parts. The first part presents the best practices and evidence from multicomponent reengagement programs in different contexts. It embraces the inherent complexity of the reengagement process with its multiple interacting components and stakeholders, acknowledges contradictions, and highlights the need for contextually relevant empirical evidence. The second part attempts to manage this complexity to guide program design.

The reviewed literature offers salient evidence on what, how, and why some interventions help at-risk youth to reach educational, behavioral, and social outcomes as well as for whom and in what contexts these are relevant. We found that 're-engaging and retaining at-risk youth in the education process' requires multiple interventions that address protective and promotive outcomes across affective, cognitive, and behavioral domains. The range of literature showed complexity in both outcomes and interventions. Such a perspective requires attention to multiple influences on youth development, ranging from individual competencies and the characteristics of the many social settings individuals participate in to flexibility in the systemic avenues available for education engagement. Embracing this complexity will help guide the policy and design of programs that seek to respond to the complex needs of at-risk and out-of-school youth.

REENGAGEMENT PROGRAMS WITH MULTIPLE INTERVENTIONS: THE EVIDENCE

What works: Best practices from different regional contexts

This study has identified the core interventions of mentoring and psychosocial support as well as enabling interventions of outreach, case management, integrated support services, and financial incentives, along with blended learning platforms and flexible educational pathways. Other regional studies (CEDEFOP 2017; Cunningham et al. 2008; Inoue et al. 2015; Kerka 2006; Te Riele 2014) that have focused on identifying what works for re-engaging out-of-school youth in the United States, Australia, and other OECD contexts as well as regions of Latin America and the Caribbean and Sub-Saharan Africa corroborate these findings. The best practices for working with at-risk out-of-school youth from different regional contexts may be summarized as follows:

- **Caring connections and one-to-one support for young people through coaching or mentoring** in the form of mentors and other positive relationships to build trust and to motivate and encourage young people to re-discover their interest in learning, reinforce high expectations and self-belief, and destigmatize the seeking of professional counseling or other supports to address barriers to learning.
- **Motivating young people to rediscover their interest in learning and foster retention,** such as active, hands-on learning, relevant application to real-world problems, variety of activities outside formal learning environments, clear communication of outcomes and behaviors, high expectations, and scaffolded and challenging milestones.
- **Financial incentives to youth to change risky behaviors and fulfill basic needs,** including options such as scholarships, bursaries, conditional cash transfers (CCTs), individual learning accounts, and deferred grants for pursuing higher education.
- **Proactive outreach and recruitment** using print and broadcast media, incentives, intake procedures, and credible partnerships that are youth-friendly, authentic, and respectful.
- **Comprehensive support services for young people with complex needs** (case management) carried out by engaged and knowledgeable staff, including teachers, youth workers, and mental health workers, as well as supports to address a range of needs such as transportation, housing, and medical care.
- **Alternative ways to complete education or access second-chance measures,** such as transitional programs, bridge programs for earning both high school and college credits, and mixed-age programs that allow 16–18-year-old youth to join adult basic education programs.
- **Provision of work-based learning or a close-to-real simulation** to offer opportunities where youth can earn while they learn, develop on-the-job skills, gain work experience, and meet immediate monetary needs.
- **Flexible learning pathways tailored to youth's interests and learning styles** to move both across and within education, as well as flexibility in the delivery and timing of learning opportunities such as the option to defer, to attend on a part-time basis, or to attend in an online or blended format.
- **Follow-along supports based on an exit assessment** of each youth's capacity to navigate and negotiate his or her way to access relevant resources, including a development plan and follow-up strategy as well as a network of relationships and supports outside the program.

Based on the context, the intervention mix would need to vary, focusing on some areas more than others. Evidence indicates that for rural youth facing severe poverty and access constraints, financial incentives in the form of CCT, scholarships, and microlending as well as flexible qualification and certification programs may be very relevant. For poor urban youth, the prevalence and incidence of specific risks such as violent crime, HIV, TB, and other communicable diseases must be considered through outreach and case management for delivering appropriate social and health support services. For youth who hold financial responsibilities and may be playing the role of head-of-household, specific trainings and guidance on prudent financial management are appropriate, whereas for youth supported financially by parents but facing other vulnerabilities affecting their mental health, careful redressal mechanisms through psychosocial therapy are appropriate.

Given the complex contexts young people live in and their exposure to multiple risks (from community, peers, family, school, work, etc.), programs with a complex mix of interventions are likely necessary to address the different needs. In the next section, we review some of the evidence from such complex, multicomponent programs.

Evidence on what works from complex, multi-component intervention programs

Quantitative methods of measuring outcomes have difficulty assessing the impact of multiple interventions.[1] Nonetheless, a recent systematic review and meta-analysis (Mawn et al. 2017) attempted to identify the quantifiable impact of programs with multiple components and interventions for at-risk populations with a variety of needs. It synthesizes the literature on the effectiveness of a complex set of reengagement interventions targeting young people not in employment, education, or training (NEET).[2] The interventions included social skills, vocational or educational classroom-based training, counseling, financial incentives, internships, occupational training, case management, and individualized support. In all, 18 studies were included, nine of them experimental and nine quasi-experimental, of which 13 were multi-component interventions with intensities greater than 6 months. The primary effectiveness outcome was employment, while the secondary outcomes included earnings, welfare receipt, education, health and other behaviors.

The meta-analysis demonstrated a small but statistically significant 4 percent increase (CI: 0.0–0.7) in employment among the target group. Programs with significant positive effects had commonalities relating to (1) *deprivation* indicators (such as serving people below the poverty line or in the lowest decile of household income), (2) use of *multi-component interventions* (such as classroom, jobs-based, and skills) for cognitive, affective, and behavioral support, and (3) a minimum of 6 months of *high intensity contact*.

Two studies with multicomponent interventions featuring skills training and work-based learning demonstrated significant effects on the receipt of public assistance, with reductions of $84.29/year and $460 across a 4-year follow-up period, respectively. And two studies with the most minimal intervention of a change in case management procedures showed no significant effects on welfare receipt. Concerning the outcome of educational attainment, no meta-analysis could be conducted due to the inadequacy of high quality data. Nevertheless, three studies reported significant increases in educational attainment, with one showing a 7 percent increase compared to the control group.

In an evaluation of an education program for young people disengaged from secondary school education, Myconos (2014) found that an integrated program combining teaching, well-being, and supportive pathways led to positive outcomes, including increased school completion rates and school attendance and improvements in engagement and well-being, with many students reporting improvements in their attitudes to schooling and their relationships. Students attributed this to a welcoming environment that was tailored to their needs; a holistic learning approach which emphasized social and emotional learning; pathways such as enhanced career guidance; onsite vocational training; and enabling former students to remain engaged with the program and connected to staff who provided them with ongoing assistance (Savelsberg, Pignata, and Weckert 2017). A literature review by Gutherson, Davies, and Daszkiewicz (2011) of alternative education programs covering Australia, Canada, the United Kingdom, the United States, and New Zealand reiterate the effectiveness of interventions in a multicomponent program setting.

How do diverse interventions interact in complex programs for at-risk youth?

The findings of the meta-analysis of multicomponent programs discussed above encourage us to develop a better understanding of the mechanisms of success, such as how to target deprived groups; how to integrate across multiple cognitive, affective, and behavioral support components; and how to maintain high-contact across mentors and mentees. There are examples of how to infer these mechanisms. For instance, the impact evaluation of the Toronto-based Pathways to Education program—an intervention program for re-engaging youth—quantifies size effects and explains how its complex set of interventions work (Oreopoulos, Brown and Lavecchia 2017).

The evaluation of this comprehensive low-income youth support program for those entering high school (grade 9 and above) indicates statistically significant positive results in enrollments and in 5-year graduation rates (Oreopoulos, Brown, and Lavecchia 2017). The mechanisms underlying the Pathways to Education Program are inclusive, with voluntary participation and high expectations. The program includes a slew of services: (1) proactive case workers called Student-Parent Support Workers, who are full-time employees of the program assigned to mentor a limited number of individual students and also work with the parents, (2) immediate monetary support for students, such as bus tickets to cover the daily commute to school in addition to long-term financial incentives, (3) free weekly tutoring and group activities, and (4) career counseling and college transition assistance. The main features of this complex set of interventions for at-risk youth reengagement were identified as follows:

- **High expectations.** Having high expectations from students acts as the primary fuel across interventions.
- **Case planning to address complex student needs.** Mentors understand the complex needs of students and help learners set a personal development goal and milestones through a proactive case approach.
- **Clear educational purpose.** The mentee recognizes that financial incentives, tutoring, and longer-term planning (college/work) are there to support them reach their educational goals.
- **Interlinked and cohesive incentive structure.** Long-term financial incentives are linked to minimum stipulated weekly participation in tutoring. Similarly, bus tickets for the school commute are collected weekly and

in-person by the student from the mentor, providing an opportunity for a weekly interaction.
- **Integrated and adaptive monitoring.** As an example, weekly mentor-mentee meetings can enable regular and consistent monitoring of student participation, grades, and absenteeism while also providing students with incentives to meet, such as collecting funds for commuting.
- **Relevant evaluations methods.** Evaluation methods need to unpack the dynamic and complex relationships between the youth, the ecosystem of interventions, and the broader social context to determine the effectiveness of certain processes/ mechanisms[3] and then use statistically robust and nimble evaluations to quantify their effectiveness.

Need for more empirical research evidence on reengagement

The above summary of interventions from different regions as well as programmatic evidence on what works and how interventions interact supports the findings of this study. Yet it is important to note the lack of rigorous empirical evidence on the impact of several large programs[4] for at-risk out-of-school youth in the lower-middle and low-income contexts. Well-designed impact evaluations of existing interventions and systematic evaluations can inform complex multi-component program designs in high-risk contexts. It is also important to note here that rigorous empirical evidence to predict factors affecting reengagement is very limited, as is evidence to establish the relationship between risk factors and potential interventions for reengagement (rather than prevention, including in the United States). This area needs considerably more research focus, and given the complex nature of the reengagement process, it needs to use mixed-methods approaches (Ungar and Liebenberg 2005).

Some questions of interest identified by field researchers include: What mechanisms make youth facing severe risks re-engage and demonstrate strength-based competencies? Is it because they have more opportunities to get involved in a relationship with a caring, supportive adult? Are they engaged in more structured and/or supervised activities? (Mahoney and Stattin 2000). To answer these questions, researchers suggest (1) treating as the unit of analysis the individual-in-context and using multivariate investigations where risk is treated as both additive and interactive; (2) using intensive within-group studies of at-risk populations to avoid broad generalizations; (3) explicitly incorporating both positive and negative outcomes; and (4) using an aggregation approach of comprehensive cumulative risk for better overall prediction of outcomes, but using pattern-based[5] data analytic strategies to examine phenomena involving complex interactions.

Reconciling critical and inconsistent evidence through complexity

Recognizing the complexity of outcomes and interventions needed for at-risk youth, when we found critical and inconsistent evidence, it was a signal to reflect deeper on this evidence. Mainly we found two topics that need deeper analytical engagement: (1) lack of subsequent opportunities for youth beyond the program; and (2) the mixed impact of mentoring interventions.

(1) **Lack of opportunities for at-risk youth beyond the program.** Some researchers have expressed concern about the goals and options open to youth after they re-engage in education services--especially for those at the higher end of the age spectrum. For example, Smyth, McInerney, and Fish (2013) point to limitations in vocational opportunities after school completion and existing exclusions and social injustice that may continue to marginalize youth from certain backgrounds (depending on the socio-economic exclusion in each context). To reconcile this problem, school engagement programs must explicitly address longer-term school and employment opportunities and equip learners with critical thinking to address exclusion and discrimination (Ungar 2008). points to the importance of the social justice and inclusion agenda in interventions for at-risk youth. Among the ways to navigate this real concern are the following:

- **Refer and mentor youth** to develop their knowledge of the range of services available to them, how to access them, and how to negotiate and choose meaningful and relevant services catering to their specific needs.
- **Provide services across sectors through systematized referrals** so that learners can access different service providers (one program or agency alone will not suffice).
- **Incorporate a collaborative and nonpunitive voluntary intake process** supported by rigorous student and parent orientation that clarifies expectations, opportunities, incentives, and attendance requirements. Limiting involuntary transfers can avoid having the program become a dumping ground for students and educators seen as disruptive and ineffective (Sumbera 2017, p. 49, 119).
- **Systematize follow-along supports during the transitional phase** where the youth can access relevant resources, review their development plan and staff time for follow-ups, and access additional networking supports outside the program.
- **Strengthen the pathways to multiple, flexible, and recognized educational credentials** so that youth have options to change, switch gears, defer, and personalize their learning.

(2) **Mixed results of mentoring interventions.** One-on-one support and case management interventions are noted across the literature as critical for children and youth engagement and reengagement in education. However, research finds mixed results across contexts. For example, Rodriguez-Planas (2010) points to some potential pitfalls of some types of mentoring. For example, overprotecting youth who may get in trouble with the law may reduce accountability and encourage rather than deter risky behavior. Also, if parents are not involved, mentors may substitute parental roles rather than complementing them. Researchers such as Pawson (2006) recommend ways to mitigate some of the potential pitfalls, including the below:

- **Providing access to multiple mentoring roles:** This means systematically ensuring, with necessary checks and balances, that multiple mentors—offering befriending, direction-setting, and accountability skills—are accessible to a vulnerable youth.
- **Using team skills.** Mentors need multiple skills that cannot be possessed by one individual. Some mentors are better at offering academic support, others at psychosocial support, and yet others at working with parents. Pawson recommends that mentoring should be the work not of one adult but of a team that contributes a range of different skills to a mentee.

- **Providing diverse types of mentors.** In certain circumstances, peer mentors—rather than adult mentors—may be more effective. For example, in an intervention to modify the sexual behavior and attitudes of youngsters, it was found that peer leaders were more successful in establishing conservative attitudes related to sexual behavior ("if I can do it, you can do it") while adults were more successful in warning and creating accountability on issues of pregnancy and sexually transmitted diseases.

In the following section, the preceding complex evidence is synthesized to provide a parsimonious framework of generalizable mechanisms to guide program design.

A SYNTHESIS OF THE COMPLEX PROCESS OF REENGAGEMENT: THE INTERRELATION OF CORE AND ENABLING INTERVENTIONS

In the education reengagement process—from lack of engagement to enrolment to retention and finally completion—the core interventions of mentoring and psychosocial support are enabled by interventions such as outreach, case management, and referrals.[6] In addition to protective and academic support, this process requires: (1) *befriending* to develop mutual trust and confidence; (2) *direction-setting* to promote self-reflection; (3) *coaching* to drive actions and behaviors for acquiring skills and credentials; and (4) *advocating and networking* on behalf of the mentee.

These four activities can be initially referred to as underlying mechanisms.[7] Each of these appears to closely map to the characteristics of the four enabling interventions (see box 5.1): awareness raising and outreach, case management and referrals, followed by mentorship and guidance and finally, accessing academic and nonacademic opportunities. Hence, it can be inferred that the *core interventions* form the bedrock on which the *enabling interventions* operate. In other words, *each enabling intervention for re-engaging youth in education is associated with the mechanisms of befriending, direction setting, coaching, and sponsoring. The enabling interventions seem to operationalize the core interventions.*

Notably, some of the reviewed scientific evidence also supports this association and provides additional clues to the underlying interrelationships. For example, the Stages of Change model from clinical psychology alludes to the intentional process a person needs to go through to be able to fully adapt to a new set of behaviors, from precontemplation to contemplation, determination, action, and finally maintenance. Further, the effectiveness of these interventions is a function of the relationship quality between the mentee and various mentors and other supports he/she receives across all the stages, moderated by mentee characteristics and contextual factors. Thus, the internal transformation of youth rests, to a significant degree, on the extent and nature of the psychosocial and mentoring support the mentees receive through various relationships and the way(s) they learn to navigate, negotiate, and access resources relevant to their individual needs. The four mentor stages are elaborated below (see next page, box.5.1).

Uncovering these underlying mentoring mechanisms, that seem to support the change in at-risk youth, helps us trace a generalizable process and identify interventions that can be adapted to different contexts, as needed. For example, drawing from the mentoring literature (see chapter 4), we can identify the characteristics of the supports that work effectively at different stages. During the befriending stage of awareness raising and outreach, informal

> **BOX 5.1**
>
> ## The reengagement mechanism: Stages of the mentor-mentee relationship
>
> **Befriending—Awareness building and outreach.** It is essential to create awareness of the potential opportunities for program engagement, clearly articulating them in local languages and through accessible media. In parallel, it is essential to identify the target beneficiaries, make contact, and begin an engagement process in a manner that is amenable to the psychosocial frame of reference of at-risk learners with the goal of enrolling them in the program. Outreach can take various forms: calling, texting, making home visits, accompanying during chores, engaging social workers and caseworkers, playing a sport, sharing a hobby, and other ways of communicating with adolescents and youth in comfortable spaces. In this stage, the outreach worker plays the mentoring role of an *informal supporter* and needs to demonstrate the ability to manage resistance, befriend and build trust, network with the support services and referral system, and be comfortable in the targeted youth's environment. The incentives of the outreach worker must not be tied to the number of youth he/she engages with.
>
> **Direction setting—Case management, integrated support services, and referrals.** At-risk learners face multiple risks that translate into multiple needs, which in turn condition education access, learning, and completion. This requires individualized assessments, referrals to relevant educational pathways, and connecting to need-based services. Effective case management by highly skilled and colocated staff, along with comprehensive, practical, on-site support services (including referral services), can act as the bridge between the multitude of challenges and possible solutions. In this stage, the goal is to assess the specific needs the student has and his/her readiness levels, from both academic and nonacademic standpoints. Based on this analysis, a near-term action plan should be devised to get the student immediately back on track. This can mean offering support services, involving the youth with a coach/counsellor, and introducing him/her to various academic pathways and learning platforms (in class, online, or blended). Regular follow-ups and progress tracking are critical to ensure that the person is well-supported to complete the agreed actions, including any steps for course correction. In this stage, the case manager/case team play the mentoring role as *administrators* in this stage and need to demonstrate relevant skills such as enabling direction setting and reflection for purpose clarification and strengthening their linkages to integrated service provision.
>
> **Coaching–Mentoring.** The youth at this stage would be enrolled and under the supervision of a case manager or case team. A highly skilled and experienced coach plays the role of a *caregiver*. He or she is required to understand the youth's interests and talents and provide relevant inputs and guidance for him/her to begin formulating a concrete individualized action plan that is regularly monitored and course-corrected through trial and error. The goal here is to identify the nature of specific skills and credentials that will set the youth on a path to success and make referrals based on a best-fit match between the young person and available options. At this stage, youth demonstrate significant resilience in facing and recovering from adversities, develop a strong sense of possibility for their future, and through these positive experiences, reconnect and formally re-engage in education.
>
> **Sponsoring—Multiple and flexible educational pathways, blended learning platforms, and financial support.** This is the stage where concrete goals are set and specific skills are actively being learned by the youth. They are involved in classes for gaining credits in new courses, recovering lost credits, gaining opportunities to display their talents in front of adults and peers, and engaging with potential employment, apprenticeship, and internship opportunities. They can engage through a flexible online modality as well as face-to-face classrooms where their teacher-mentors advocate and network on their behalf, provide encouragement, and teach targeted social-emotional skills. While this is a promotion-focused stage, it is important to note that a sudden adverse situation can reverse the gains made over several months. Hence, *protective supports* need to be systematically built into the program such as the provision of scholarships, conditional cash transfer programs, and social protection services.

FIGURE 5.1

Interlinkages between education reengagement mechanisms, interventions, and supporters

Mentoring mechanisms		Interventions		Supporters
Befriending	◄----►	Awareness building and outreach	◄----►	Informal supporters
Direction setting	◄----►	Case management and integrated support services	◄----►	Administrators
Coaching	◄----►	Mentoring	◄----►	Caregivers
Sponsoring	◄----►	Multiple and flexible educational pathways, blended learning, financial support	◄----►	Several options, online and face-to-face, SEL curriculum, CCT, scholarship, etc.

Source: World Bank analysis.
Note: CCT = conditional cash transfers; SEL = social-emotional learning.

supports are required for building trust and providing quick response to any urgent and critical vulnerabilities. In the next, direction setting stage, a formal support is required in the form of case managers and case team that assess the individual and contextual risks, understand aspirations and goals, and offer potential avenues for immediate relief and medium to long-term engagement solutions. In the coaching stage, a balance of accountability and friendliness is required, akin to family and parent-like support, to mentor the young person. Mentors can advocate for and sponsor youth to access multiple reengagement pathways and financial supports to strengthen their social-emotional and academic skills. Focusing on the underlying process rather than specific interventions can provide more flexible guidance for designing programs in different contexts. The inter-linkages inferred between the mechanisms, interventions, and supporters can be visualized as in figure 5.1.

INITIAL THOUGHTS ON GENERALIZABLE CAUSAL MECHANISMS TO GUIDE DESIGN

Through the complex evidence reviewed through the literature, we have inferred the mechanisms underlying the core interventions: mentoring and psychosocial support. This provides a more parsimonious guidance to program designers, because what is shared is not a specific intervention but generalizable mechanisms that any intervention approach on mentorship and psychosocial support needs to engage with when supporting youth to return to education. Generalizing mechanisms that contribute to the desired outcome allow us to ask context-specific questions: What interventions will work 'here' to establish these mechanisms to achieve similar outcomes of interest?

A discussion of 'causal or generative' mechanisms is not the intention of this study, as we cannot do justice to the important emerging theoretical and methodological literature on applications to policy and programing (Cartwright 2007; Cartwright and Hardie 2012; Pawson 2006). However, we believe that a collection and analysis of the evidence on reengagement of at-risk youth across questions of what, how, why, for whom and in what contexts contributes to a more in-depth analysis. We were able to move from core interventions—mentoring and psychosocial support—assessed as relevant through their effect sizes, to the enabling interventions that began to open the black box of change: outreach, case management, integrated support services (including referrals) and financial incentives.

To assess underlying causal processes will require further analysis. For example, one would need to answer the question of how these interventions work by clarifying three aspects for each enabling intervention: (1) Who drives the reengagement that propels the young person forward (such as the staff, leadership, networks and available study options); (2) What aspects of the underlying mechanisms in the mentor-mentee relationship (i.e., in each mentoring stage) are important; and (3) What features of the intervention can be activated based on the beneficiaries and their context. Answering these more in-depth questions can provide an even better understanding of the design elements to build a theory of change for re-engaging and retaining at-risk learners in an educational program. An example is summarized in figure 5.2. More detailed guidance is provided by Pawson (2004, 2006).

What we can conclude from our review of the literature, so far, is that no single factor can explain why some learners are able to overcome adversity and develop and maintain positive psychosocial skills and behavior, leading to positive

FIGURE 5.2

Reengagement program design elements

	What works		How		Why
Core interventions	Enabling interventions	Engagement drivers	Underlying mechanisms	Features	Why it works
Mentoring Psychosocial support	Awareness raising and outreach	Targeting data and analysis; outreach worker	**Befriending:** Managing resistance; building trust	Tailored to the local context, culturally sensitive, in the environment of the youth, targeted through caring, networked, adaptive staff, staff incentives decoupled from numbers contacted	(1) Protective and promotive supports increase capacity of youth to recover, function, and make positive change through adversity (resilience) (2) Brain malleability allows development of sophisticated social and emotional skills and competencies which in turn impact learning (cognitive science) (3) Community mobilization and outreach enable the intentional change of habitual behavior (stages of change in psychology) (4) Learning environments influence an individual's self-efficacy and performance expectations (social cognition) (5) Financial incentives affect human behavior but many anomalies in education hence, careful design needed informed by behavioral economics and psychology
	Case management	Case team / case worker	**Direction-setting:** Identifying academic and nonacademic needs; promoting self-reflection and goal-setting; leveraging other social support	• Segmentation analysis and targeting using data • Use of relevant diagnostic instruments • Centralized intake and individualized services • Formal institutional collaboratives and partnerships with decision-making parity, knowledge exchange • Caring, skilled, multidisciplinary, colocated staff • Appropriately managed caseloads (smaller loads per staff if greater client needs) • Adaptive monitoring and regular followups • Wide network offering integrated support services	
	Reconnect to educational services (assessments and referrals)	Cognitive and psychometric assessments; referral network			
	Integrated Support Services (ISS)	Dynamic ISS network (health, transport, finances, food, childcare etc.)			
	Financial incentives	Funding support and grants	**Protecting:** To fulfill basic needs and promote positive psychological effects	Clarify for who, for what behaviors and actions, how much (quantum), which instrument (scholarship, bursaries, CCT, UCT, voucher, other), in what form (framing, priming, default choice, etc.)	
	Engaged mentoring and SEL	Highly skilled and matched mentor, counsellor and advocacy support	**Coaching and sponsoring:** Driving actions for skill and credential acquisition; advocate, network and leverage other social supports on behalf of individual	• Mentor as an authoritative parent-like caregiver with permeable but enforceable boundaries and well-articulated expectations • Cognitive and noncognitive development opportunities (individual learning plan, integrated or standalone SEL, earn academic credentials, remedial and language classes) • Blended learning (self-paced, flexible timing, location agnostic, peer exchange, anonymity)	
	Multiple educational pathways; choice of learning platform	Availability of quality options; online, face-to-face or blended format			

Source: World Bank analysis.
Note: CCT = conditional cash transfers; SEL = social-emotional learning; ISS = integrated support services; UCT = Unconditional cash transfers.

educational and other social outcomes. Resilience is not an individual process but requires a strength-based conception of youth development in school- and community-based programs as well as through relevant education policies. Given the central role of mentors—be it outreach workers, case managers, coaches/counselors, or social workers—all mentoring stages require advanced skillsets and cover a range of abilities: meeting the youth in their environment, effectively managing stone-walling and pushbacks, establishing connections and networks in the local community and with a range of service providers, and providing targeted coaching and counseling. Both protective and promotive interventions represent important pillars of support for developing resilience and must work in harmony with contextual forces, which can either facilitate or inhibit results.

NOTES

1. Quantitative analysis provides rigorous evidence of the effect sizes of variables on an outcome of interest for at-risk youth from an intervention. To do so, it controls complexity, rather than engaging with it. By isolating size effects, RCTs provide a rigorous way to infer the contributions of each intervention needed to support the education reengagement of at-risk youth. However, policy makers and program designers also require evidence on how to implement an intervention and why a strategy works or does not work in a context.
2. The review included studies that targeted NEET-category youth ages 16–24 in four regions: North America (USA), South America (Argentina, Colombia, and Dominican Republic), Australia, and the United Kingdom. It included the full range of interventions with no restrictions on their type and intensity.
3. Realist evaluation methods help to unpack "how" programs work, in addition to identifying the size effects of interventions. They synthesize the available evidence on what works, for whom and under what conditions (Pawson & Tilley 1997; Sayer 2000). In this program example, the set of interventions works when the resources on offer (material, cognitive, social, emotional) strike a chord with program subjects. Realist evaluation research is thus fundamentally about unearthing and inspecting vital program mechanisms: the how, why and under what conditions an intervention or set of interventions work. The other crucial explanatory ingredient is the program *context*, recognizing and directly addressing the fact that the same intervention never gets implemented identically and never has the same impact because of differences in setting, process, stakeholders and outcomes (Pawson 2003).
4. Such as USIKO in South Africa, COBET in Tanzania, and ASAMA in Madagascar, to name a few.
5. Pattern-based methods are tools that allow us to examine co-occurrence (or complex interactions) more easily and make it possible to search for and identify multiple holistic expressions of socially embedded risk, protection, and competence (Bergman 2000; Cairns 2000).
6. In complex systems, such processes are non-linear and would have significant variance within and across cohorts based on the nature and extent of disadvantage faced by the youth.
7. Although we refer to these processes noted in the literature for mentoring and psychosocial support as underlying mechanisms, we acknowledge that analysis of the "causal mechanisms" will require much more than this initial identification across the interventions we have assessed (Cartwright 2007; Cartwright & Hardie 2012; Pawson 2006).

REFERENCES

Bergman, L. R. 2000. The Application of a Person-Oriented Approach: Types and Clusters. In L. R. Bergman, R. B. Cairns, L.-G. Nilsson, & L. Nystedt (Eds.), Developmental Science and the Holistic Approach, 137–154. Mahwah, NJ, US: Lawrence Erlbaum Associates Publishers.

Cairns, R. B. 2000. Developmental Science: Three Audacious Implications. In L. R. Bergman, R. B. Cairns, L.-G. Nilsson, & L. Nystedt (Eds.), Developmental Science and the Holistic Approach, 49–62. Mahwah, NJ, US: Lawrence Erlbaum Associates Publishers.

Cartwright, N. 2007. *Causal Powers: What Are They? Why Do We Need Them? What Can Be Done with Them and What Cannot*. Technical Report 04, 7, Centre for Philosophy of Natural and Social Science Contingency and Dissent in Science.

Cartwright, N., and J. Hardie. 2012. *Evidence-Based Policy: A Practical Guide to Doing it Better*. Oxford University Press.

CEDEFOP. 2017. *VET Toolkit for Tackling Early Leaving*. http://www.cedefop.europa.eu/en/toolkits/vet-toolkit-tackling-early-leaving/intervene/intervention-approaches.

Cunningham, W., L. McGinnis, R. G. Verdú, C. Tesliuc, and D. Verner. 2008. *Youth at Risk in Latin America and the Caribbean: Understanding the Causes, Realizing the Potential*. Washington, DC: The World Bank.

Gutherson, P., H. Davies, and T. Daszkiewicz. 2011. *Achieving Successful Outcomes through Alternative Education Provision: An International Literature Review*. Reading: CfBT Education Trust.

Inoue, K., E. Di Gropello, Y. S. Taylor, and J. Gresham. 2015. *Out-of-School Youth in Sub-Saharan Africa: A Policy Perspective*. The World Bank.

Kerka, S. 2006. *What Works: Evidence-Based Strategies for Youth Practitioners, Out-of-School Youth*. Columbus, OH: Learning Works Connection, The Ohio State University.

Mahoney, J. L. and H. Stattin. 2000. "Leisure Activities and Adolescent Antisocial Behavior: The Role of Structure and Social Context." *Journal of Adolescence* 23: 113–27.

Mawn, L., E. J. Oliver, N. Akhter, C. L. Bambra, C. Torgerson, C. Bridle, and H. J. Stain. 2017. "Are We Failing Young People Not in Employment, Education or Training (NEETs)? A Systematic Review and Meta-Analysis of Re-Engagement Interventions." *Systematic Reviews* 6 (1).

Myconos, G. 2014. *Lessons from a Flexible Learning Program: The Brotherhood of St Laurence Community VCAL Education Program for Young People 2010–2013*. Victoria, Australia: The Brotherhood of St Laurence.

Oreopoulos, P., R. S. Brown, and A. M. Lavecchia. 2017. "Pathways to Education: An Integrated Approach to Helping At-Risk High School Students." *Journal of Political Economy* 125 (4): 947–84.

Pawson, R. 2003. "Nothing as Practical as a Good Theory." *Evaluation* 9 (4): 471–90.

Pawson, R. 2004. *Mentoring Relationships: An Explanatory Review*. ESRC UK Centre for Evidence Based Policy.

Pawson, R. 2006. *Evidence-Based Policy: A Realist Perspective*. Sage.

Pawson, R., and N. Tilley. 1997. *Realistic Evaluation*. Sage.

Rodriguez-Planas, N. 2010. "Mentoring, Educational Services, and Economic Incentives: Longer-Term Evidence on Risky Behaviors from a Randomized Trial." IZA Discussion Papers 4968, Institute for the Study of Labor (IZA).

Savelsberg, H., S. Pignata, and P. Weckert. 2017. "Second Chance Education: Barriers, Supports and Engagement Strategies." *Australian Journal of Adult Learning* 57 (1): 36–57.

Sayer, A. 2000. *Realism and Social Science*. Sage.

Smyth, J., P. McInerney, and T. Fish. 2013. "Re-Engagement to Where? Low SES Students in Alternative-Education Programmes on the Path to Low-Status Destinations?" *Research in Post-Compulsory Education* 18 (1–2): 194–207.

Sumbera, B. G. 2017. "Model Continuation High Schools: Social-Cognitive Promotive Factors that Contribute to Re-Engaging At-Risk Students Emotionally, Behaviorally, and Cognitively towards Graduation." PhD dissertation, Pepperdine University, 174–93.

Te Riele, K. 2014. *Putting the Jigsaw Together: Flexible Learning Programs in Australia*. Final Report. Melbourne: The Victoria Institute for Education, Diversity and Lifelong Learning.

Ungar, M. 2006. "Nurturing Hidden Resilience in At-Risk Youth in Different Cultures." *Journal of the Canadian Academy of Child and Adolescent Psychiatry* 15 (2): 53.

Ungar, M. 2008. "Putting Resilience Theory into Action: Five Principles for Intervention." In *Resilience in Action*, edited by Liebenberg, L. and Ungar, M. 17–38.

Ungar, M., and Liebenberg, L. 2005. Resilience Across Cultures: The Mixed Methods Approach of the International Resilience Project. In M. Ungar (Ed.), *Handbook for Working with Children and Youth Pathways to Resilience Across Cultures and Contexts*, 211–226. Thousand Oaks, CA: Sage Publications.

6 Implications for Program Design and Implementation

This chapter discusses three areas where the analysis of the evidence on education engagement may be applied to policy and program design: in building theories of change using the generalizable mechanisms, in programming principles and guidance, and in policy questions for reflection and action.

This study has, thus far, clarified the global challenge of out-of-school and at-risk adolescents and youth, the various risk factors young people face, and the need for resilience- and strength-based conceptions of youth development for actively re-engaging them. The more complex analysis of the evidence on education engagement and reengagement of at-risk youth led us to better understand what interventions work, how they work, and why. *Core interventions of mentoring and psychosocial support* showed relevant effect sizes, but these needed to be better understood through other *enabling interventions,* such as *outreach, case management, and integrated support services, including referrals and financial incentives*. Differences across at-risk youth, including the type, level, and variety of risks they face, also called for multiple education pathways and platforms of engagement.

In this chapter, the intent is to translate the evidence into helpful guidance and reflections for policy makers and program designers so that they can plan and implement interventions effectively. To this end, the generalizable mechanisms of *befriending, direction setting, coaching,* and *sponsoring,* which seem to cut across the range of interventions reviewed, can serve as guideposts when designing education (re-) engagement policies and programs. These mechanisms underline the nature of successful mentor-mentee relationships and psychosocial programs intended to deliver educational outcomes.

Here, we discuss three areas of application for policy and program design: building a theory of change, programing principles and guidance, and policy questions.

A THEORY OF CHANGE FOR EDUCATION REENGAGEMENT OF AT-RISK AND OUT-OF-SCHOOL ADOLESCENTS AND YOUTH

Since our aim is to inform policy makers and program designers of the program characteristics that can impact desired education reengagement outcomes, one way of better understanding the associations between inputs and outcomes is to develop a theory of change.[1] We provide here a theory of change that can guide more context-specific theories for education reengagement of at-risk youth.

First, we describe each element of this evolving theory of change. The starting point is the four desired outcomes of an education reengagement process followed by the inputs, products, and services required to deliver these outcomes. Then, using the design elements (figure 5.2), an expanded view of the theory of change is presented, where the findings on what works, how, and why are located at the intersection of the inputs and activities. Finally, a proposal for a general theory of change for reengagement programs emerges.

Education reengagement outcomes

Specific reengagement outcomes for at-risk and out-of-school youth and adolescents have not been clearly and consensually identified in the literature. Typically, reengagement programs are multi-component, offering a variety of services that contribute to the success of the youth and the program. Also, as a relatively nascent field of work and with many empirical studies based on the U.S. context, there are limited empirical evaluations and literature available on reengagement programs from the developing world. Furthermore, among the evaluations of these interventions there is a wide variation in outcomes, in terms of both what is being measured and how it is being measured. Based on the outcomes theoretically analyzed as well as those measured in the reviewed literature, we can categorize the outcomes into four domains: (1) socio-emotional skills; (2) education participation; (3) protection; and (4) academic performance (see figure 2.1 in chapter 2).

Socio-emotional skills
These skills encompass emotional, cognitive and behavioral competencies covering five domains: self-awareness, self-management, social awareness, relationship skills, and responsible decision making. An extensive literature base (discussed in chapter 4) offers a range of outcome determinants, such as social behaviors, attitudes toward self, others and school, conduct problems, emotional distress, substance use, and crime offenses.

Education participation
This outcome domain refers to the awareness of, re-enrolment in, persistent engagement with and completion of an education program. Re-enrolment refers to the re-enrolling of a student into a program that provides a recognized degree or diploma. Persistent engagement is typically determined using indicators such as attendance, participation in activities, sense of belongingness and program continuity after 1 year.

Protection
This refers to the availability of, access to, and quality of protective factors that enable the young person to successfully re-engage with education. This includes outcome indicators on financial, health and social welfare services such as nutrition, healthcare, transportation, employment, and childcare, when applicable.

Stability in these outcomes mainly works to counteract the risks in the youth's environment (both individual and contextual risk factors).

Academic performance

This refers to the academic outcomes of the reengagement process. This will include indicators as measured by grades that demonstrate cognitive skills and the educational attainment level the person reaches. These outcomes are associated with individual and contextual characteristics as well as their mechanisms of interaction, such as the pathways of engagement available (e.g., courses of study, quality and relevance of the credential in the labor market, ease and flexibility of access to the courses).

Program Inputs, Products, and Services

The inputs, products, and services offered by reengagement programs would be part of the structural arrangement through which interventions are implemented, and hence would play an important role in delivering outcomes (figure 6.1). This includes: (1) *facilitating units* that organize outreach workers, case managers, mentors and other qualified facilitators; (2) *collaborative partnerships* with different agencies—government, private sector, community organizations and research centers; (3) a select *mix of interventions* based on the needs of beneficiaries in their context; (4) *multiple and varied pathways of educational engagement* to develop a vibrant ecosystem to deliver the core and enabling interventions; and (5) *flexible learning platforms* that allow vulnerable young people to engage at their pace, time and convenience (Center for Promise 2014, 2015).

Facilitating units

The main purpose of a facilitating unit is to implement the interventions and deliver planned outcomes. The resources and skillsets required for the intervention program would be potentially housed and organized here, with the role of aggregating and integrating the different services required to re-engage

FIGURE 6.1

Inputs, products, and services for reengagement

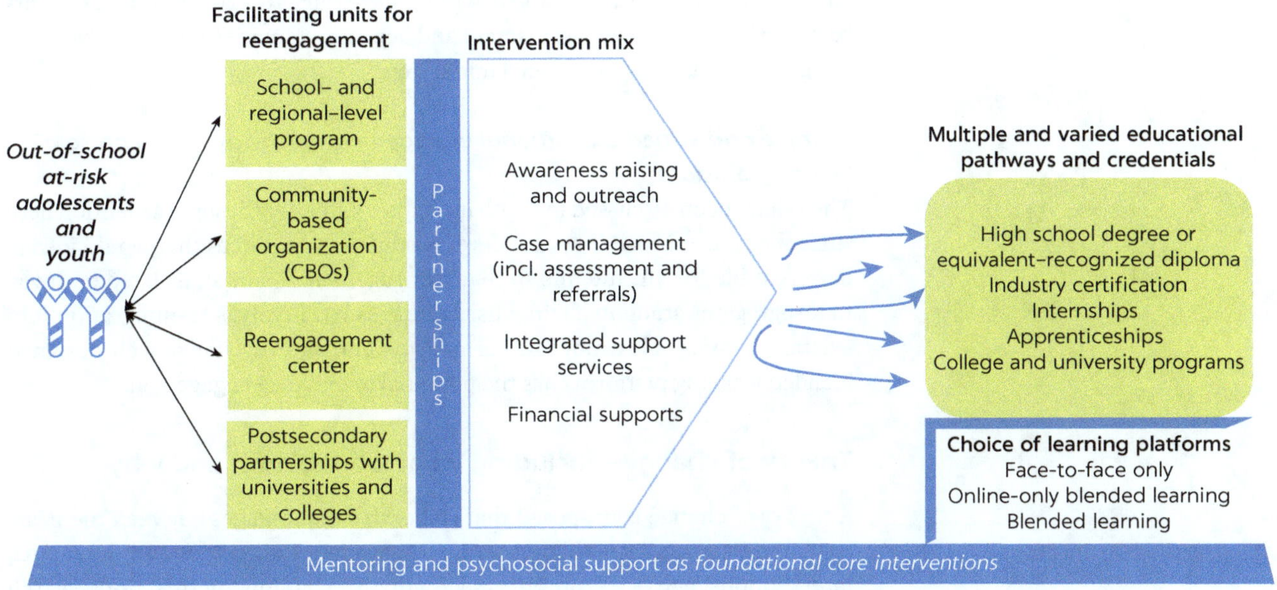

Source: World Bank compilaton.

young people in education. Existing programs (Center for Promise, 2014, 2015) suggest different models,[2] (figure 6.1)) such as school and regional level units, community-based organizations (CBOs), standalone reengagement centers and post-secondary partnerships with universities and colleges). Some important considerations relate to ease of access, level of autonomy, capacity, information access and flow, efficiency, and cost effectiveness. It is also to be noted that such facilitating units are not discrete stand-alone entities but have to work through innovative partnerships to support young people.

Partnerships

To identify, reach out, and engage with out-of-school at-risk youth requires strong, sustained and strategic partnerships across programs, national, and sub-national governments and related agencies, private businesses and philanthropic donors, affiliated support service providers, CBOs, and workforce development organizations. To target youth who are facing multiple and varied risks, both individual and contextual, requires collaborative implementation partnerships for data-sharing, funding, services, and facilities. It also requires having knowledge partners, including research agencies and policy making committees and councils. These partnerships can be organized in many forms, such as through contracts, MoUs, and cooperative agreements, depending on the purpose of the partnership. In any case, it is necessary to have early and frequent communication to ensure common direction and to sustain efforts.

Intervention mix

Data and evidence from comparable impact evaluations, whenever available, need to inform the intervention mix based on the risk profile (individual and contextual) of the out-of-school youth. Given the complex nature of reengagement interventions, it is important to consider multicomponent designs whenever feasible. In the context of extreme poverty, immediate and targeted financial support may be most beneficial. However, for youth facing significant risks due to, say, experiences of school segregation and community violence, intervention programs that strengthen psychosocial skills would be more appropriate. Given constraints on program funds, it will be necessary to prioritize investments based on thorough needs assessment and hence, systematize data collection and integration processes as a crucial initial step.

Multiple and varied educational engagement pathways and choice of learning platform

These have been discussed in depth in chapter 4, yet they deserve a mention here since they cover broader system-level products and services that would ideally be accessible for all students so that reengagement is not an isolated pathway that segregates students facing disadvantages but involves re-integration into existing systems of learning and earning credentials. Provision of well-designed blended learning platforms has the potential to enhance engagement.

Theory of change—including what works, how, and why

A theory of change is proposed that elaborates the linkages between the near-term and intermediate- to long-term reengagement outcomes and the inputs, interventions, activities, outputs (see figure 6.2). Following this, the research findings synthesized from this study of what works, how, and why (see figure 5.2

FIGURE 6.2

A theory of change for reengaging at-risk and out-of-school adolescents and youth

Target population	Inputs	Interventions	Activities	Outputs	Intended outcomes
12–17-year-old at-risk and out-of-school adolescents and youth Heterogenous group following different trajectories Variation by individual and contextual characteristics	Facilitating unit such as a school or district level program, a reengagement center, a CBO or a postsecondary preparation setup, or another contextually-relevant and feasible format	Awareness raising and outreach	Run ads in local media, distribute flyers, web presence, direct contact (texting, calling, home visits, activity-based interactions)	Increased awareness of program; targeted youngsters contacted	*Near-term* • Increased awareness amongst youngsters, family, and community • No. of youth contacted via outreach • No. of youth assessed and a case file built • No. of youth enrolled in an education service • No. of youth matched to an identified mentor • No. of youth who remained reengaged for 1 year • No. of youth earned an education credential/met goals in ILP in 1 year • No. of established collaborative and data sharing partnerships • No. and quality of alternative educational pathways available
		Case management	Build the case file, interview the young person and family and community members, analyze findings, conduct appropriate cognitive and socioemotional assessments, identify specific needs, matchmaking to a mentor, reconnect to suitable academic pathway through referral, connect to other ISS and financial support as required	Needs assessments completed and data analyzed	
		Reconnect to educational services (assessments and referrals)		Based on needs, enrolment in education service, and matched to mentor	
Challenges	Partnerships for data, funding, services, and facilities across programs, govt. agencies, private businesses, and philanthropy and CBOs	Integrated Support Services (ISS)		Need-based connection with a comprehensive set of services	
Facing multiple disadvantages Disconnected from formal system and no clear mechanism for reconnection and accountability Social and economic burden on society Low number and quality of educational options		Financial incentives	Identify the need for financial support; build incentive structure based on need; timely payments and regular follow-ups	Provided the requisite financial support to fulfill basic needs	*Intermediate to long-term* • *Socioemotional skills:* Positive change in social and emotional indicators • *Protection:* Availability, access, and quality of financial health and social welfare services • *Education participation:* Awareness, reenrolment, persistent engagement, and completion • *Academic performance:* Increase in academic outcomes and attainment levels
		Engaged mentoring and coaching	Regular and prescheduled contact times; clear mentoring objectives and plan; follow-up on individual learning plan; can be delivery point of financial/nonfinancial incentives	Regular sessions held; student and mentor feedback and follow-up	
	Knowledge partners, research agencies and policy-making committees, and councils	Multiple educational pathways; choice of learning platform	Expand alternative education options and platforms for learning; build awareness through media	Creation of more options; better cross agency collaboration and data sharing	

Source: World Bank analysis.
Note: CCT = conditional cash transfers; CBO = community-based organizations; SEL = social-emotional learning; ILP = Individual learning plan; UCT = Unconditional cash transfer.

in chapter 5) are located within this theory of change with the intent to help the reader visualize the interconnections across all levels of the results chain to guide program design, implementation, and monitoring (see figure 6.3). Using this, one can begin to see the linkages between the inputs, interventions (the *what*), engagement drivers, underlying mechanisms and features (the *how*), and why these work, followed by the associated activities, outputs, and outcomes. This is useful because:

(1) It contributes to better our understanding of what the underlying elements are that make interventions work;
(2) It helps open the black box between the inputs and the outputs to tinker with the so-called plumbing to improve outcomes; and
(3) It can help design and implement such complex multi-component programs better by foreseeing the interlinkages and interdependencies.

PRINCIPLES FOR PROGRAM DEVELOPMENT

This study examined the evidence and sought to answer three questions on re-engaging at-risk and out-of-school adolescents and youth: *What interventions work? How to provide relevant services? Why these work and for whom and in what contexts?* Building on the proposed theory of change for re-engaging at-risk, out-of-school youth described previously, this section offers practical

FIGURE 6.3

A proposed theory of change—including what works, how, and why

		'What works'			'How'		'Why'				
Target population	Inputs	Core interventions	Enabling interventions	Engagement drivers	Underlying mechanisms	Features	Why it works	Activities	Outputs	Intended outcomes	
12–17-year old at-risk and out-of-school adolescents and youth; Heterogenous group following different trajectories; Variation by individual and contextual characteristics	Facilitating unit such as a school or district level program, a reengagement center, a CBO or a post-secondary preparation setup, or another contextually-relevant and feasible format	Mentoring; Psycho-social support	Awareness raising and outreach	Targeting data and analysis; outreach worker	**Befriending:** Managing resistance, building trust	Tailored to the local context, culturally sensitive, in the environment of the youth, targeted through caring, networked, adaptive staff, staff incentives decoupled from numbers contacted	(1) Protective promotive support increases capacity of youth to recover, function, and make positive change through adversity (resilience)	Run ads in local media, distribute flyers, web presence, direct contact (texting, calling, home visits, activity-based interactions)	Increased awareness of program; targeted youngsters contacted	**Near-Term** • Increased awareness amongst youngsters, family, and community • No. of youth contacted via outreach	
			Case management	Case team/ caseworker	**Direction-setting:** Identifying academic and nonacademic needs, promoting self-reflection and goal-setting, leveraging other social supports	• Segmentation analysis and targeting using data • Use of relevant diagnostic instruments • Centralized intake and individualized services • Formal institutional collaboratives and partnerships with decision-making parity, knowledge exchange • Caring, skilled, multidisciplinary, colocated staff • Appropriately managed caseloads (smaller loads per staff if greater client needs)	(2) Brain malleability allows development of sophisticated social and emotional skills and competencies which in turn impact learning (cognitive science)	Build the case file, interview the young person and family and community members, analyze findings, conduct appropriate cognitive and socioemotional assessments, identify specific needs, matchmaking to a mentor, reconnect to suitable academic pathway through referral, connect to other ISS and financial support as required	Needs assessments completed and data analyzed	• No. of youth assessed and a case file built • No. of youth enrolled in an education service • No. of youth matched to an identified mentor • No. of youth who remained reengaged for 1 year • No. of youth earned an education credential/ met goals in ILP in 1 year • No. of established collaborative and data sharing partnerships • No. and quality of alternative educational pathways available	
	Partnerships for data, funding, services and facilities across programs, govt. agencies, private businesses and philanthropy, and CBOs		Reconnect to educational services (assessments and referrals)	Cognitive and psychometric assessments; referral network					Based on needs, enrolment in education service and matched to mentor		
			Integrated Support Services (ISS)	Dynamic ISS network (health, transport, finances, food, childcare, etc.)		• Adaptive monitoring and regular follow-ups achieve outcomes • Wide network offering integrated support services	(3) Community mobilization and outreach enable the intentional change of habitual behavior (stages of change in psychology)	Identify the need for financial support; build incentive structure based on need; timely payments and regular follow-ups	Need-based connection with a comprehensive set of services	**Intermediate to Long-Term** • **Socioemotional skills:** Positive change in social and emotional indicators	
			Financial incentives	Funding support and grants	**Protecting:** To fulfill basic needs and promoting positive psychological effects	Clarify for who, for what behaviors and actions, how much (quantum), which instrument (scholarship, bursaries, CCT, UCT, voucher, other), in what form (framing, priming, default choice, etc.)	(4) Learning environments influence an individual's self-efficacy and performance expectations (social cognition)		Provided the requisite financial support to fulfill basic needs	• **Protection:** Availability, access, and quality of financial health and social welfare services	
	Knowledge partners, research agencies, and policy-making committees and councils		Engaged mentoring and coaching	Highly skilled and matched mentor, counsellor, and advocacy support		• Mentor as an authoritative parent-like caregiver with permeable but enforceable boundaries and well-articulated expectations • Cognitive and noncognitive development opportunities (individual learning plan, integrated or standalone SEL, earn academic credentials, remedial and language classes)	(5) Financial incentives affect human behavior but many anomalies in education hence careful design needed informed by behavioral economics and psychology	Regular and prescheduled contact times; clear mentoring objectives and plan; follow-up on individual learning plan; can be delivery point of financial nonfinancial incentives	Regular sessions held; student and mentor feedback and follow-up	• **Education participation:** Awareness, reenrolment, persistent engagement, and completion	
			Multiple educational pathways; choice of learning platform	Availability of quality options; online, face-to-face, or blended format	**Coaching and sponsoring:** Driving actions for skill and credential acquisition, advocate, network and leverage other social supports on behalf of individual	• Blended learning (self-paced, flexible timing, location agnostic, peer exchange, anonymity)		Expand alternative education options and platforms for learning; build awareness through media	Creation of more options; better cross agency collaboration and data sharing	• **Academic performance:** Increase in academic outcomes and attainment levels	

Challenges
Facing multiple disadvantages; Disconnected from formal system and no clear mechanism for reconnection and accountability; Social and economic burden on society; Low number and quality of educational options

Source: World Bank analysis.
Note: CCT = conditional cash transfers; SEL = social-emotional learning; CBO = community-based organizations; ILP = Individual Learning Plan; UCT = Unconditional cash transfer.

insights on program design and implementation and can inform the dialogue around available options.

Programmatic approach

Research overwhelmingly favors adopting a positive youth development (PYD) approach as opposed to a deficit focused one. Based on developmental systems theory, this perspective offers a strength-based conception of adolescence and youth. Any program design focused on re-engaging young people at-risk would benefit by basing itself on the PYD conceptualization of the five Cs—competence, confidence, connection, character, and caring (Lerner et al. 2005; 2011).

Program design needs to be informed by data. A common approach is to build a dynamic profile database of young people and use segmentation analysis to identify the relevant beneficiaries to target as well as determine any patterns of disengagement, such as by gender, ethnicity, and socioeconomic indicators. Such a database should provide information on which students to focus and help prioritize issues that need to be addressed. Such information is useful for policy and program design when aggregated at the system level and for goal setting and progress tracking at the student level. Similarly, it is also useful to build a database of the existing ecosystem of programs in a region (covering program details including quality, cost, and impact). It is beneficial and cost-effective to use existing data systems, merge data from multiple sources, and share data across different entities through partnership agreements. In sum, strategically and carefully thinking about data and its treatment upfront is important for better design.

Programs should offer a menu of relevant interventions. This study highlights that multicomponent programs, although complex, are characteristic of reengagement programs and address the many challenges young people face. Core and enabling interventions are part of an ecosystem of services that provide support on all dimensions—emotional, behavioral, cognitive, and developmental. That said, stand-alone interventions are also undertaken based on the youth's individual and contextual factors. For example, if physical access due to financial constraints is found to be the biggest factor for disengagement, then support in the form of transportation passes may be able to deliver outcomes.

Operational considerations for programming

Operational considerations include institutional designs, context, and partnerships. These also need to be aligned to the dynamic and complex process of engaging and re-engaging at-risk youth in an educational program. We list some relevant considerations here.

Programs with multiple options for engagement work best. Key considerations in program design are questions such as these: where should the program housed? Should it be run independently, as an extension of the formal education system, or as a combination? What should be the role of the central ministry, the subnational ministries and other non-state entities? Based on the programs reviewed for this study and their contexts, there is limited but optimistic evidence that a vibrant ecosystem with multiple options works best. However, there is a paucity of rigorous empirical evidence on the effectiveness of different program structures. Clarifying program goals and setting time-bound targets, preferably grounded in research and carefully considering issues of feasibility, accountability and capacity for a specific context, can guide the design choices.

The people delivering the interventions should be well-qualified, empathic individuals institutionally linked to and supported by a community of partners. A wide network of actors is typically involved, including outreach specialists, experienced teachers, mental health professionals, case managers, trained coaches and counselors, and experts in cognitive and psychosocial assessments. These adults must be well qualified, empathic, caring individuals and be institutionally linked to, and supported by, a community of partners who take collective responsibility for disengaged youth and coordinate action to provide them with a pathway to education.

Service-delivery locations must be selected carefully with attention to youths' needs and mindset. Determining the location of the facilitating unit for service delivery is critical. Since many young people may have actively exited the formal school system due to various reasons, including negative past experiences, distrust, academic or social emotional issues, or other issues such as transportation and safety, it is important to determine and be aware of the attitude and mindset of youngsters in a given context and determine the location accordingly.

Partnerships require a shared vision, strategically relevant resources, and an established system for communication. The evidence in this study reflects the need for upstream, downstream, and lateral partnerships for multiple purposes such as data sharing, joint donor fundraising, knowledge exchange, capacity development, centralized intake mechanisms, and advocacy. It is strategic to pool capacity and resources based on a best-fit approach to deliver different aspects of the program. The sustainability of such partnerships is more assured when there is a shared vision, an offer of strategically relevant skillsets and resources, formalization in the form of contracts, MoUs and cooperative agreements, and an established system for clear and frequent communication and reporting.

To sustain program effects, follow-up services and post-program resources are valuable. Program effects tend to decay over time due to the difficulty young people face in maintaining momentum after leaving a structured and supportive program environment to confront a competitive market with limited opportunities. To address this, programs can offer post-program resources and alumni support, building links to higher education and keeping channels open till the young person wants or needs to maintain contact.

Considerations for monitoring and evaluation of complex programs

The monitoring and evaluation of designs and methods need to pay attention to the nature of complex problems and interventions. A paucity of conclusive empirical evidence makes it difficult to direct resources effectively and magnifies the need for new programs and initiatives to incorporate rigorous evaluations of impacts. This may mean that some traditional approaches to evaluation, such as randomized control trials (RCTs), which either do not explain or under-explain the mechanisms of change (so-called black boxes) need to be complemented with mixed-methods approaches (Luthar 2003; Pawson 2006).

For complex multicomponent programs, there is a well-recognized need for diverse research methodologies to understand what components (or combination of components) make a reengagement program effective. Program design must not only be evaluated at the end for results but also monitored and adapted based on contextual feedback—from learners, mentors, schools, and community. Ongoing and periodic small-scale targeted evaluations to assess the progress of program improvement efforts or testing the incremental impact of program enhancements based on implementation experience are useful to inform the design of program elements (Bloom 2010; Duflo 2017).

Additional research is required to build on our current understanding of how reengagement programs work, as well as how they can best be developed, executed, and improved. Programs can support this process by collecting data on the moderators—program, youth and contextual characteristics—to create a rich data source for researcher use. Other areas that require further research are: the link between short-term effects and long-term economic outcomes in different contexts and for different target group and contextual characteristics; the design of multiple educational pathways; and labor market payoffs of different educational credentials targeted by reengagement programs and their link to other socio-economic outcomes.

Finally, given the wide variations among individuals with frequent start-stop-restart patterns of engagement, determining at what point a reengagement process for a cohort can be considered to have delivered the desired program outcomes is important. While this can be done at multiple points of entry and engagement along the results chain until the adolescent or youth completes his/her educational goal, it would be useful to know more about the tipping point, if there is one, in the near-term that would indicate a higher likelihood of sustenance.

Inputs: staffing and costing

Human and financial resources are core inputs into any program or project. The management and staff capacity required to implement a reengagement program requires a combination of hard and soft skills. The findings in this study concerning how interventions work (see in chapter 4) summarizes the wide range of staff expertise and skillsets required for delivering outcomes. Capacity development of staff at different program levels and for different interventions requires a well-planned curriculum, training, and continuous support.

Broadly, the curriculum coverage should include trainings on the use and application of specific assessment tools; outreach and case management work; different mentoring styles matched to needs; instructional and engagement strategies at different mentoring stages; knowledge sharing on PYD and equity-based approaches and practices; issues specific to the targeted group of adolescents and youth using data analysis; information on different educational pathways and networks for advocacy; information on network of resources for providing integrated support services; legal requirements, remedies and recourse such as the means and processes for reporting on issues such as abuse; de-escalation strategies and conflict management; and communication techniques.

Capacity building can be delivered as one-off, on-the-job coaching and regular follow-ups offered by a mix of carefully identified and experienced experts from relevant fields. Leveraging partnerships between national and subnational governments and the private sector and CBOs can lead to useful synergies and potential cost savings.

Financial resources for education (re-)engagement programs involve questions on (1) sources of funds and (2) use of funds. On the sources of funds, it is important to note that secondary education provision by the state is relatively more expensive. Alternative education options face tough competition from formal education and other welfare and social support schemes promoted by governments and donor agencies. One way to get around this is through an early and active leveraging of partnerships for donor coordination to generate additional funds. While we know that the per-pupil cost of reengagement varies widely as it is a function of many variables, the data and evidence on multi-component program costs for different contexts and sub-groups is meagre.

On the use of funds, the costs of a facilitating unit would, at a minimum, cover staff, administration and oversight, facility management, materials, financial incentives, and scholarships. It is critical to note that a comprehensive approach, including personalization and contextualization, is likely to be expensive, although these are also more likely to deliver results. Given the glaring lack of empirical evidence, especially in the context of low- and lower-middle-income countries, it is important to prioritize funds for such evaluations to inform future program design. As a final note on the use of funds, constraints around available capacity and resources limit the number and scale of alternative options, whether it is about making a choice from the menu of interventions, delivery platforms, educational pathways or the extent and nature of financial incentives. Thus, in practical terms, careful design is required that can balance the prevailing socio-economic-political factors and resource availability with sectoral priorities and goals.

POLICY QUESTIONS

Any design process to support the systematic (re)engagement of at-risk youth starts with a decision by policy makers to address the problem. This entails a range of policy questions for which complex evidence needs to be collected, both in terms of causes and solutions. We end this chapter with a list of questions that exemplify the range of policy concerns and evidence needed and designate these to the core stakeholders: policy makers, partners, and local education set-ups. This is not a comprehensive set of questions but is intended to draw attention to some practical issues during the process of dialogue and design.

For policy makers

- Is the reengagement of young people into education a policy priority? What are the vision, policy goals and targets for education reengagement? Is the government willing to make fiscal commitments to address this issue and to what extent?

BOX 6.1

Lessons learned from the design and implementation of the project: Reengaging at-risk and out-of-school youth in education in Turkey

Turkey aims to re-engage and retain at-risk and out-of-school youth by strengthening its open distance education program. The Life Long Learning Department, within the Ministry of National Education (MoNE), aims to design interventions specifically to reengage at-risk and out-of-school youth in their Open Education Program. This is a self-paced, mostly distance-based education program offering grades 5–12 for school-age students ages 14 through 17 (it also provides access to adults). In Turkey, despite ample school-based and open education offers, many vulnerable youths do not continue their studies and could benefit from complementary services to reengage them in a relevant education program.

Some preliminary country-based studies and assessments exist. The categories of the needs of Turkish learners on these studies include attitudes toward self and others, positive social behaviors, and social skills. For example, in the case of PSS/SEL, a review of 52 articles on the social-emotional learning needs of Turkish adolescents, published from 2000 to 2012, showed how educational programs could address them (Martin 2012; Martin and Alacaci 2015). Using a three-level framework borrowed from Eccles and Roeser (2011), the researchers reviewed (1) teachers, tasks, and classrooms; (2) school environments; and (3) national policies and practices. Among their findings:

- Teachers and instruction. At the level of teachers, the preservice education of teachers presents an opportunity to introduce SEL skills, including courses in educational psychology and guidance counseling.
- School climate and culture. At the school level, issues of school climate, safety, and interpersonal relations are to be addressed, including some of the highest rates of bullying in OECD countries (Craig et al. 2009; Harel-Fisch et al. 2011). In terms of socioeconomic differences, Turkey has begun to close the performance gap between schools (TIMSS, PIRLS and PISA).
- Education policies. For national education policies, issues such as the grade structure, school sizes, tracking, and extracurricular offerings also have implications for SEL.

For these interventions at the teacher-, school-, and policy-level to function and be effective for youth reentering education through open education, the instruction, culture, and policies need to align with reengagement services to effectively address the multiple needs and learning goals of at-risk youth. With this in mind, Turkey could improve its open education programs with some of the interventions noted in this study and those integrated into the emerging theory of change (figures 6.2 and 6.3) as well as the concrete program design elements identified in figure 5.2.

- What is known about the youth and contextual characteristics that can inform program design? What are the cultural and linguistic sensitivities that must be kept in mind at the outset?
- What systems and mechanisms exist (such as existing social identification systems) to leverage data collection and analysis of out-of-school and at-risk youth that can inform evidence-based policy making and programing?
- What do policy makers know about existing programs of interest for re-engaging youth run by state and nonstate actors—concerning approach, evaluations, study design, rigor, and effectiveness? How can this information be best collected, evaluated, and leveraged to support the policy intent?
- How can the proposed program be located within systemic, ongoing national or district level planning, programing, and evaluation?
- How flexible and open is the government's approach toward recognizing and offering legitimacy to different educational pathways and a larger menu of educational qualifications? Do these include occupationally oriented options

such as industry certifications and not only those focused on secondary diplomas, higher secondary, and college education?
- To make substantive impact, are policy makers willing and able to offer financial incentives to promising and innovative programs to participate in rigorous evaluations with the intent to expand those with positive results?
- Is it feasible to offer different funding streams including competitive grant options to encourage small scale experimentation and rigorous evaluation as a requirement for the receipt of grant funds?
- What combination of options from the institutional arrangements (as described in the previous section) is feasible for implementation with the given constraints?

For partners

- Is there a partnership network focused on reengagement? How active is it? Who are the players in terms of donors, grassroots implementers, agencies focused on service delivery, capacity building, evaluation, advocacy and donor engagement?
- How can these be leveraged systematically to create a learning and advocacy network and develop a diversified funding pool? How can a partnership between national and sub-national governments, CBOs and private enterprises be forged and goals aligned to deliver reengagement outcomes?
- Which of these partners have access and/or capacity to develop data systems, conduct rigorous data analysis and track progress?
- Can innovative delivery platforms be developed and tested especially for blended learning?
- How can the referrals and other social support systems for health, transport, clothing, childcare etc. be strengthened through this network of partners?

For education leaders and staff in school districts and facilitation units

- How can frontline leaders and staff use data for better planning and targeting?
- What program structure in their context allows them to leverage the ministry level actors as well as other partners to deliver outcomes?
- Are innovative and flexible re-enrolment and delivery options being implemented? If yes, how can these be evaluated and scaled?
- What policy supports do they need to develop partnerships—upstream, downstream, and laterally—to deliver the services? Conversely, how can these partnerships better support research and be more responsive to rigorous program evaluations?
- What specific capacity building[3] efforts are required to develop a pool of skilled staff that can create a consistently caring, supportive and welcoming environment and deliver a wide range of services?
- What mechanisms can education leaders and staff use to build greater awareness and connect with youth through outreach work—in person, through social media, using other technology solutions, or in community groups?

- What strategies can they use to identify and set up the location of a facilitating unit that encourages disconnected young people to re-engage?
- What insights and practices, based on local context, cultures and youth issues, is required to be kept in mind when hiring staff for delivering the selected set of interventions?
- What are the program costs per youth? What are the fixed and variable costs? How can these costs be systematically collected and analyzed to inform funding requirements and leverage partnerships for donor funding?

NOTES

1. A solid theory of change is the foundation of strong program design and a sound monitoring and evaluation strategy (Innovations for Poverty Action 2016).
2. Includes models that have been tried with success and documented in case studies in the U.S. context (e.g., Boston Reengagement Centre, Gateway to College, Learning Works Charter School).
3. *Capacity Building* requires decisions on training modules and approaches, time required, relevant participants, pre-requisites, opportunities for practice, feedback, development of implementation plans, post training consultations, observations, feedback and facilitation modalities such as peer coaching, forums for celebrating successes and sharing challenges, etc.

REFERENCES

Bloom, D. 2010. "Programs and Policies to Assist High School Dropouts in the Transition to Adulthood." *The Future of Children* 20(1), 89–108.

Center for Promise. 2014. *Back to School: Exploring Promising Practices for Re-engaging Young People in Secondary Education.* Washington, DC: America's Promise Alliance.

Center for Promise. 2015. *Don't Quit on Me: What Young People who Left School Say about the Power of Relationships.* Washington, DC: America's Promise Alliance.

Craig W, Harel-Fisch Y, Fogel-Grinvald H, Dostaler S, Hetland J, Simons-Morton B, Molcho M, de Mato MG, Overpeck M, Due P, Pickett W. 2009. "A Cross-National Profile of Bullying and Victimization among Adolescents in 40 Countries." *International Journal of Public Health* 54 (2): 216–24.

Duflo, E. 2017. "The Economist as Plumber—Richard T. Ely Lecture." *American Economic Review* 107 (5): 1–26.

Eccles, J. S., and R. W. Roeser. 2011. "Schools as Developmental Contexts during Adolescence." *Journal of Research on Adolescence* 21 (1): 225–41.

Harel-Fisch, Walsh S. D., Fogel-Grinvald H, Amitai G, Pickett W, Molcho M, Due P, de Matos MG, Craig W; Members of the HBSC Violence and Injury Prevention Focus Group. 2011. "Negative School Perceptions and Involvement in School Bullying: A Universal Relationship across 40 Countries." *Journal of Adolescence* 34 (4): 639–52.

Innovations for Poverty Action. 2016. *Theory of Change and Program Design.* Goldilocks Resource.

Lerner, R. M., J. B. Almerigi, C. Theokas, and J. V. Lerner. 2005. Positive Youth Development a View of the Issues." *The Journal of Early Adolescence* 25 (1): 10–16.

Lerner, R. M., J. V. Lerner, and J. B. Benson. 2011. "Positive Youth Development: Research and Applications for Promoting Thriving in Adolescence." *Advances in Child Development and Behavior* 41: 1–17.

Luthar, S. S., ed. 2003. *Resilience and Vulnerability: Adaptation in the Context of Childhood Adversities.* Cambridge University Press.

Martin, R. A. 2012. *Social and Emotional Learning Research: Intervention Studies for Supporting Adolescents in Turkey*. Istanbul, Turkey: International Conference on Education and Educational Psychology.

Martin, R. A., and Alacaci, C. 2015. Positive youth development in Turkey: A critical review of research on the social and emotional learning needs of Turkish adolescents, 2000–2012. *Research Papers in Education* 30 (3): 327–46.

Pawson, R. 2006. *Evidence-based policy: A realist perspective*. Sage.

7 Conclusion

Overall, this study suggests that a range of interventions that address cognitive, affective, social cohesion, and behavioral needs and skills can create an enabling environment for re-engaging out-of-school and vulnerable youth. These range from effective outreach and enrolment processes, mentoring and individualized support, and psychosocial interventions to financial support and referral schemes. However, these are not 'off-the-shelf' interventions; they must be contextualized, constantly adapted, and inter-connected.

This is especially so for interventions more directly associated with human interactions, such as mentoring, psychosocial counseling, and family support services. Culture and context-sensitive design, planning and capacity building are crucial. The evidence also shows that while some interventions such as financial incentives and scholarships can show a positive impact by rewarding certain behaviors, in most cases they do not act alone, especially for sustainable long-term change.

Finally, much of the evidence base of the interventions is rooted in theoretical principles from scientific fields such as resilience studies, psychology, behavioral sciences, sociology, neuroscience, and education. There are other conceptual and theoretical frameworks, such as the psychosocial development theory and social capital theory, that can further our understanding in the future. Overall, a multidisciplinary analysis enables a clearer and deeper understanding of how and why the interventions elaborated above work.

Mentoring and psychosocial support can be fundamentally extracted from postulates in resilience theories and neuroscience that allude to the capacity of individuals to face, recover from, continue to function during, and make positive change through adversity. This ability to persevere and strengthen one's social, emotional, and cognitive skills in the face of difficulties can be linked to the malleability of the brain to learn and experience positive change[1] when knowledge and skills are taught explicitly through focused, sequenced, and active forms of learning.

This study shows that the above theoretical knowledge from diverse fields can be grounded in concrete guidance, processes, and interventions for policy and programing. The theory of change that emerges can support the design of multicomponent programs that work as complements to one another to help at-risk and out-of-school youth successfully re-engage in education.

NOTE

1. Also called the growth mindset (Dweck 2006).

REFERENCE

Dweck, C. S. 2006. *Mindset: The New Psychology of Success*. New York: Penguin Random House LLC.

Appendix A
Risk Factors

INDIVIDUAL RISK FACTORS	CONTEXTUAL RISK FACTORS			RISKY BEHAVIORS	NEGATIVE OUTCOMES
	FAMILY/HH RISK FACTORS	SCHOOL-RELATED RISK FACTORS	COMMUNITY RISK FACTORS	MACRO-LEVEL RISK FACTORS		
Demographic factors (Gender, age, income group, marital status, language, race, ethnicity, minority group affiliations, disability)	**Family membership** Number and gender of adults and children below age 12, 12–18, >18 years in a household	**School climate** Segregation, safety, discrimination, sexual abuse, corporal punishment, bullying, delinquent peer affiliations and influence	**Access to quality schools** Access to and availability of quality schools, especially in lower- and upper-secondary levels, Safety	**Economic and political aspects** Including corruption, inflation and interest rate, ease of accessing credit, labor market conditions, political unrest and instability, conflict, migration and internal displacement	Grade retention, age inappropriate credentials (overage), chronic absenteeism	Early school leaving/NEET; poorer labor market outcomes; unemployment; exploitative work environments
					Early labor force entry	
Geographic factors (Urban/rural, country and region, LIC/LMIC/MIC/HIC, conflict/non conflict)	**Family structure** Gender, marital status, education level, occupational field of the head-of-household	**Education quality** Including curriculum, pedagogy, language of instruction, teacher absenteeism, learning standards, teacher qualification, overcrowding	**Social and cultural norms** Practices and prejudices of communities and neighborhoods related to age, gender, disability etc.		Early marriage	Early pregnancy; poor pregnancy outcomes; Inability to support child care; early immature motherhood responsibilities; unsafe abortion; sexually transmitted diseases and HIV/AIDS
	Socioeconomic status Household income and household earning capacity (proxied by the number of working adults)				Early and risky sexual activity	
Cognitive factors (Education attainment level; academic performance; IQ scores, attentional skills, executive functioning skills)		**Infrastructure** Safe buildings, access to toilets, availability of learning material, non-conducive physical spaces for learning and physical activities	**Social and health support services** Appropriate, accessible and approachable services to deal with issues such as teenage pregnancy, parental unemployment, death or illness	**Law enforcement** Safety, police presence and effectiveness, access to weapons	Drug and alcohol abuse	Addiction to drugs and alcohol, social exclusion, depression
	Parental availability (death, illness, divorce, discord), **attitudes towards education** (time, level of involvement), and **behaviors** (youth victimization such as abuse, violence, corporal punishment)	**School policies and practices** Class size, school size, program diversity, tracking and learning options, type of school (public/private, selective/non-selective, free/subsidized)		**Social and cultural norms** Practices and prejudices of communities and neighborhoods related to age, gender, disability etc.	Violent and delinquent behavior	Criminal activities; gang membership; incarceration; militant activities
Emotional factors Self-efficacy, self-regulation skills, hopefulness, perceived value of returns to education, relatedness (sense of belonging, interest, satisfaction)				**National and regional education policies and practices** related to quality and access	Victims of violent behaviors, conflict, forced migration	Post traumatic stress disorder; depression; social withdrawal; unwanted pregnancy
Social/Behavioral factors (Close relationships with competent adults, connections to prosocial and rule-abiding peers, adaptability, sociability, effort, attention, persistence						

Source: World Bank analysis.
Note: HIC = high income countries; LIC = low income countries; LMIC = low- and middle-income countries; MIC = middle income countries; NEET = not in education, employment or training.

Appendix B
Evidence Summary of What Works

INTERVENTION TYPE	STUDY	NUMBER OF STUDIES & PERIOD	OUTCOME DOMAINS AND EFFECTS	EFFECT SIZES (ES)	NOTABLE FINDINGS
Mentoring	Meta-analytic study (DuBois et al., 2002)	55 evaluations of youth mentoring programs over the period 1970 to 1998	Youth benefited significantly in five outcome domains: emotional/ psychological, high-risk behavior, social competence, academic and employment	Mean weighted ES of 0.18 at 95% CI when collapsed across all outcome domains; ES ranging from 0.10 to 0.22 for specific outcome domains	Mentoring as an intervention strategy has the capacity to serve both promotion and prevention. Research points to importance of developing 'close' mentor-mentee relationships
Mentoring	Meta-analytic study (Eby et. Al., 2007)	40 quantitative studies of youth mentoring programs over period 1985 to 2006 with mentoring as sole intervention	Mentoring found to be significantly and positively correlated with behavioral, attitudinal, health-related, interpersonal, motivational, and career outcomes, albeit at different levels	Absolute ES across all outcome domains ranged from 0.03 to 0.14; significant & positive correlations with behavioral, attitudinal, health-related, interpersonal, motivational, and career outcomes	Largest effect was found between mentoring and the mentee's behavioral and attitudinal changes: helping others, school attitudes and career attitudes
Mentoring	Meta-analytic study (DuBois et al., 2011)	73 independent evaluations of youth mentoring programs over the period 1999 to 2010	Youth benefited significantly in each of outcome domains: emotional, behavior, social, and academic	Mean weighted ES of 0.21 at 95% CI when collapsed across all outcome domains and Mean ES ranging from 0.18 to 0.24 for specific outcome domains	Modest gains on outcome score between mentored vs. non-mentored youth (difference of 9 percentile points) More effective for youth with pre-existing difficulties or been exposed to significant level of risk

continued

INTERVENTION TYPE	STUDY	NUMBER OF STUDIES & PERIOD	OUTCOME DOMAINS AND EFFECTS	EFFECT SIZES (ES)	NOTABLE FINDINGS
Mentoring	Meta-analytic study (Tolan et al., 2014)	46 evalutaions of youth mentoring interventions over the period 1970-2011 in the United States	Significant effects on delinquency and three associated outcomes (aggression, drug use, and academic functioning) for at-risk youth	Mean ES significant and positive for each outcome category (0.11 for academic achievement, 0.16 for drug use, 0.21 for delinquency, 0.29 for aggression)	Stronger effects when the mentor's motivation was his/her professional development and advancement (vs personal motivation or civic duty)
					Greater effects when when advocacy and emotional support were emphasized
PSS (Social and Emotional Learning)	Meta-analytic study (Taylor et al. 2017)	82 school-based, universal SEL interventions (i.e. involving classroom, school and parents) at follow-up over the period 1981-2014	Statistically significant positive effects for each of seven outcome categories (social and emotional skills; attitudes toward self, others, and school; positive social behaviors; academic performance; conduct problems; emotional distress; and substance use)	Mean ES ranged from 0.13 to 0.33 and positive impact across ethnic, socio-economic and geographic backgrounds, but with no significant differences across them	Postintervention social-emotional skill development was the strongest predictor of well-being at follow-up
					Eighty-nine percent of the interventions were rated as having sequenced, active, focused, and explicit (SAFE) practices (Durlak et al., 2011)
PSS (Social and Emotional Learning)	Meta-analytic study (Durlak et al. 2011)	213 school-based, universal social and emotional learning (SEL) programs over the period 1970-2007	Statistically significant positive effects on all six outcomes variables: (a) social and emotional skills, (b) attitudes toward self and others, (c) positive social behaviors, (d) conduct problems, (e) emotional distress, and (f) academic performance	Overall mean ES of 0.31 (95% CI, [0.26,0.36]) for the targeted socio-emotional skills. All six means significantly greater than zero (range = 0.22 to 0.57). A mean ES of 0.27 on academic acheivement or 11-percentile gain relative to control group	Two variables were found to moderate student outcomes: the use of recommended training practices (SAFE) for developing skills and adequate program implementation.
PSS (Social and Emotional Learning)	Meta-analytic study (Durlak and Weissberg 2007)	73 after-school programs in the United States	Statistically significant positive impact in three areas: feelings and attitudes (self-perceptions and bonding), behavioral adjustment (increases in positive social behaviors and decreases in problem behaviors and drug use), and school performance (grades and level of academic achievement)	Overall mean ES of +0.22 (95% CI, [0.16,0.29])	Most effective programs utilized evidence-based skills-development training activities that were sequential, active, focused, and explicit (SAFE)

continued

INTERVENTION TYPE	STUDY	NUMBER OF STUDIES & PERIOD	OUTCOME DOMAINS AND EFFECTS	EFFECT SIZES (ES)	NOTABLE FINDINGS
PSS (Social and Emotional Learning)	Meta-analytic study (Wigelsworth et al. 2016)	89 studies on school-based, universal SEL programs conducted between 1995 and 2013	Statistically significant impact on all seven outcome variables related to the five SEL competency domains of self-awareness, self-management, social awareness, relationship skills, and responsible decision making	Largest effect for measures of social-emotional competence (0.53), and the smallest in attitudes towards self (0.17)	Studies implemented within the same country in which they were developed showed greater and significant effects than those transported abroad for four of seven outcome variables. Six of seven outcome variables showed greater size effects for efficacy than for effectiveness

Source: World Bank analysis.

Appendix C
Additional Reading

EXECUTIVE SUMMARY

Eurostat. 2017. "Early Leavers from Education and Training." In *Statistics Explained*. Eurostat. Retrieved from: https://ec.europa.eu/eurostat/statistics-explained/index.php/Early_leavers_from_education_and_training.

Pan, J., Zaff, J. F., and Donlan, A. E. 2017. "Social Support and Academic Engagement among Reconnected Youth: Adverse Life Experiences as a Moderator." *Journal of Research on Adolescence* 27 (4): 890–906.

Ungar, M. 2011. "The Social Ecology of Resilience: Addressing Contextual and Cultural Ambiguity of a Nascent Construct." *American Journal of Orthopsychiatry* 81 (1): 1.

Ungar, M. 2013. "Resilience, Trauma, Context, and Culture." *Trauma, Violence, & Abuse* 14 (3): 255–66.

UNICEF. 2015. *Middle East and North Africa Region Out-of-School Children Report*. http://www.oosci-mena.org/.

Wigelsworth, M., A. Lendrum, J. Oldfield, A. Scott, I. ten Bokkel, K. Tate, and C. Emery, C. 2016. "The Impact of Trial Stage, Developer Involvement and International Transferability on Universal Social and Emotional Learning Programme Outcomes: A Meta-Analysis." *Cambridge Journal of Education* 46 (3): 347–76.

World Bank. 2015. *World Development Report 2015: Mind, Society, and Behavior*. Washington, DC.

CHAPTER 1

Center for Promise. 2014a. *Don't Call Them Dropouts: Understanding the Experiences of Young People Who Leave High School Before Graduation*. Washington, DC: America's Promise Alliance.

Garmezy, N. 1991. "Resiliency and Vulnerability to Adverse Developmental Outcomes Associated with Poverty." *American Behavioral Scientist* 34 (4): 416–30.

Gutman, L. M., Sameroff, A. J., and Cole, R. 2003. "Academic Growth Curve Trajectories from 1st Grade to 12th Grade: Effects of Multiple Social Risk Factors and Preschool Child Factors." *Developmental Psychology* 39 (4): 777.

Liebenberg, L. and Ungar, M., eds. *Resilience in Action*. pp. 17–38. Toronto: University of Toronto Press.

Pepin, E. N., and V. L. Banyard. 2006. "Social Support: A Mediator between Child Maltreatment and Developmental Outcomes." *Journal of Youth and Adolescence* 35 (4): 612–25.

Rumberger, R. W., and S. A. Lim. 2008. "Why Students Drop Out of School: A Review of 25 Years of Research." *California Dropout Research Project* 15: 1–3.

Rutter, M. 1987. "Psychosocial Resilience and Protective Mechanisms." *American Journal of Orthopsychiatry* 57 (3): 316–31.

Rutter, M. 1990. "Psychosocial Resilience and Protective Mechanisms." In *Risk and Protective Factors in the Development of Psychopathology*, edited by J. Rolf, A. S. Masten, D. Cicchetti, K. H. Nuechterlein, and S. Weintraub, 181–214. New York: Cambridge University Press.

Thurman, T. R., Snider, L. A., Boris, N. W., Kalisa, E., Nyirazinyoye, L., and Brown, L. 2008. "Barriers to the Community Support of Orphans and Vulnerable Youth in Rwanda." *Social Science & Medicine* 66 (7): 1557–67.

Wahby, S., Ahmadzadeh, H., Çorabatır, M., Hashem, L., and Husseini, J. 2014. *Ensuring Quality Education for Young Refugees from Syria (12–25 years): A Mapping Exercise*. Refugee Studies Centre, Oxford Department of International Development, University of Oxford.

CHAPTER 2

Armstrong, M. I., S. Birnie-Lefcovitch, and M. T. Ungar. 2005. "Pathways between Social Support, Family Well-Being, Quality of Parenting, and Child Resilience: What We Know." *Journal of Child and Family Studies* 14 (2): 269–81.

Bridgeland, J. M., J. J. DiIulio, and K. B. Morison. 2006. *The Silent Epidemic: Perspectives of High School Dropouts*. Washington, DC: Civic Enterprises, LLC.

Catalano, R. F., Haggerty, K. P., Oesterle, S., et al. 2004. "The Importance of Bonding to School for Healthy Development: Findings from the Social Development Research Group." *Journal of School Health* 74: 252–61.

Cohen, M. 1998. "The Monetary Value of Saving a High-Risk Youth." *Journal of Quantitative Criminology* 14 (1): 5–33.

MacGillivary, Heather L. 2014. "Who Comes Back? Exploring Reengagement within the School Year." Graduate Thesis 46. School of Education, University of Colorado. http://scholar.colorado.edu/educ_gradetds/46.

Reyes, J. 2019. "The Transformative Resilience Framework: Using Critical Realism and Resilience to Explain Complex Problems in Education in Emergencies." Unpublished doctoral thesis in progress. Falmer: University of Sussex.

UNESCO. 2018. *One in Five Children, Adolescents and Youth Is Out of School*. UIS Fact Sheet No. 48.

CHAPTER 3

Andrews, M., L. Pritchett, and M. Woolcock. 2010. *An Introduction to Design Thinking Process Guide*. Hasso Plattner Institute of Design, Stanford.

Banerjee, A. V., and Duflo, E. 2009. "The Experimental Approach to Development Economics." *Annual Review of Economics* 1 (1): 151–78.

Breuer, E., Lee, L., De Silva, M., and Lund, C. 2015. "Using Theory of Change to Design and Evaluate Public Health Interventions: A Systematic Review." *Implementation Science* 11 (1): 63.

Karlan, Dean. 2017. *Nimble RCTs—A Powerful Methodology in the Program Design Toolbox*. Washington, DC: World Bank. http://pubdocs.worldbank.org/en/626921495727495321/Nimble-RCTs-WorldBankMay2017-v4.pdf.

Ludwig, J., J. R. Kling, and S. Mullainathan. 2011. "Mechanism Experiments and Policy Evaluations." *Journal of Economic Perspectives* 25 (3): 17–38.

Pawson, R. 2003. "Nothing as Practical as a Good Theory." *Evaluation* 9 (4): 471–90.

Pawson, R. 2006. *Evidence-Based Policy: A Realist Perspective*. Sage.

Pawson, R., T. Greenhalgh, G. Harvey, and K. Walshe. 2005. "Realist Review—A New Method of Systematic Review Designed for Complex Policy Interventions." *Journal of Health Services Research & Policy* 10 (1_suppl): 21–34.

Pawson, R., and N. Tilley. 1997. *Realistic Evaluation*. Sage.

CHAPTER 4

Ager, A., B. Akesson, L. Stark, E. Flouri, B. Okot, F. McCollister, and N. Boothby. 2011. The Impact of the School-Based Psychosocial Structured Activities (PSSA) Program on Conflict-Affected Children in Northern Uganda." *Journal of Child Psychology and Psychiatry* 52 (11): 1124–33.

Allen, T. D., L. T. Eby, M. L. Poteet, E. Lentz, and L. Lima. 2004. "Outcomes Associated with Mentoring Proteges: A Meta-Analysis." *Journal of Applied Psychology* 89: 127–36.

Bernard, R.M., Abrami, P.C., Lou, Y., Borokhovski, E., Wade, A., Wozney, L., Wallet, P.A., Fiset, M. and Huang, B. 2004. "How Does Distance Education Compare with Classroom Instruction? A Meta-Analysis of the Empirical Literature." *Review of Educational Research* 74 (3): 379–439.

Busseri, M. A., and L. Rose-Krasnor. 2009. "Breadth and Intensity: Salient, Separable, and Developmentally Significant Dimensions of Structured Youth Activity Involvement." *British Journal of Developmental Psychology* 27 (4): 907–33.

Burt, M. R., Resnick, G., and Matheson, N. 1992. *Comprehensive Service Integration Programs for at Risk Youth*." An Urban Institute report produced for the U.S. Department of Education. https://aspe.hhs.gov/basic-report/comprehensive-service-integration-programs-risk-youth.

Catalano, R. F., Berglund, M. L., Ryan, J. A. M., Lonczak, H. S., and Hawkins, J. D. 2004. "Positive Youth Development in the United States: Research Findings on Evaluation of Positive Youth Development Programs." *The Annals of the American Academy of Political and Social Science* 591 (1): 98–124.

Center for Prevention Research and Development. 2009. *Background Research: Mentoring Programs*. Champaign, IL: Center for Prevention Research and Development, Institute of Government and Public Affairs, University of Illinois.

Cook, Philip J., Kenneth Dodge, George Farkas, Roland G. Fryer Jr., Jonathan Guryan, Jens Ludwig, Susan Mayer, Harold Pollack, and Laurence Steinberg. 2014. "The (Surprising) Efficacy of Academic and Behavioral Intervention with Disadvantaged Youth: Results from a Randomized Experiment in Chicago." NBER Working Paper 19862. Cambridge, MA: NBER.

DuBois, D. L., and M. J. Karcher, eds. *Handbook of Youth Mentoring* (Sage program on Applied Developmental Science). Thousand Oaks, CA: Sage.

Durlak, J. A., and E. P. Dupre. 2008. "Implementation Matters: A Review of Research on the Influence of Implementation on Program Outcomes and the Factors Affecting Implementation." *American Journal of Community Psychology* 41: 327–50.

Freidhoff, J., J. Borup, R. Stimson, and K. DeBruler. 2015. "Documenting and Sharing the Work of Successful On-Site Mentors." *Journal of Online Learning Research* 1 (1): 107–28.

Heckman, J. J., and T. Kautz. 2012. "Hard Evidence on Soft Skills." NBER Working Paper 18121, National Bureau of Economic Research, Cambridge, MA.

House, A. 2008. *Good Practice in Re-Engaging Disaffected and Reluctant Students in Secondary Schools*. London: Ofsted Publication.

Kuperminc, G. P., and Thomason, J. D. 2014. "Group Mentoring." In *Handbook of Youth Mentoring*, edited by DuBois and Karcher, 273–89.

Lakind, D., M. Atkins, and J. M. Eddy. 2015. "Youth Mentoring Relationships in Context: Mentor Perceptions of Youth, Environment, and the Mentor Role." *Children and Youth Services Review* 53: 52–60.

López-Pérez, M. V., M. C. Pérez-López, and L. Rodríguez-Ariza. 2011. "Blended Learning in Higher Education: Students' Perceptions and Their Relation to Outcomes." *Computers and Education* 56 (3): 818–26.

Martin, R. A., and C. Alacaci. 2015. "Positive Youth Development in Turkey: A Critical Review of Research on the Social and Emotional Learning Needs of Turkish Adolescents, 2000–2012." *Research Papers in Education* 30 (3): 327–46.

Mawn, L., Oliver, E. J., Akhter, N., Bambra, C. L., Torgerson, C., Bridle, C., and Stain, H. J. 2017. "Are We Failing Young People Not in Employment, Education or Training (NEETs)? A Systematic Review and Meta-Analysis of Re-Engagement Interventions." *Systematic Reviews* 6 (1).

Nursaw Associates. 2015. *What Do We Know about the Impact of Financial Support on Access and Student Success?* For the U.K. Office for Fair Access (OFFA).

Oler, R. M. 2011. "Feeling Special: A Study of Local, Named, Need-Based Scholarships for Remediated Community College Students." PhD Thesis, Indiana State University.

Pawson, R. 2004. *Mentoring Relationships: An Explanatory Review*. ESRC UK Centre for Evidence Based Policy and Practice.

Pellitteri, J., and Smith, B. 2007. "Building Academic Success on Social and Emotional Learning: What Does the Research Say? A Review of 'Building Academic Success on Social and Emotional Learning: What Does the Research Say?' edited by J. Zins, R. Weissberg, M. Wang, and H. Walberg. "*Reading & Writing Quarterly* 23 (2): 197–202.

Prochaska, J. O., and Velicer, W.F. 1997. "The Trans-theoretical Model of Health Behavior Change." *American Journal of Health Promotion* 12: 38–48.

Pryce, J. M., Kelly, M. S., and Lawinger, M. 2018. "Conversation Club: A Group Mentoring Model for Immigrant Youth." *Youth & Society*, June 8.

Rhodes J. E. 2005. A Model of Youth Mentoring. In: DuBois D. L., Karcher M. J. (Eds.) Handbook of Youth Mentoring 30–43. Thousand Oaks, CA: Sage.

Tversky, A. and D. Kahneman. 1981. "The Framing of Decisions and the Psychology of Choice." *Science* 211 (4481): 453–58.

Wang, M., and Eccles, J. 2013. "School Context, Achievement Motivation, and Academic Engagement: A Longitudinal Study of School Engagement using a Multidimensional Perspective." *Learning and Instruction* 28: 12–23.

Weingarten, E., Chen, Q., McAdams, M., Yi, J., Hepler, J., and Albarracín, D. 2016. From Primed Concepts to Action: A Meta-Analysis of the Behavioral Effects of Incidentally Presented Words." *Psychological Bulletin* 142 (5): 472–97.

Weissberg, R. P., J. A. Durlak, C. E. Domitrovich, and T. P. Gullotta. 2015. "Social and Emotional Learning: Past, Present, and Future. In *Handbook for Social and Emotional Learning: Research and Practice*, edited J. A. Durlak, C. E. Domitrovich, R. P. Weissberg, and T. P. Gullotta, 3–19. New York, NY: Guilford.

Weissberg, R. P., Goren, P., and Domitrovich, C. 2012. *Effective Social and Emotional Learning Programs, CASEL Guide*. Chicago, IL: Collaborative for Academic, Social, and Emotional Learning (CASEL).

Weissberg, R. P., and M. U. O'Brien. 2004. "What Works in School-Based Social and Emotional Learning Programs for Positive Youth Development." *The Annals of the American Academy of Political and Social Science* 591 (1): 86–97.

Wolf, P. J. 2010. "School Vouchers in Washington, DC: Achievement Impacts and Their Implications for Social Justice." *Educational Research and Evaluation* 16 (2): 131–50.

Yildirim, J., S. Ozdemir, and F. Sezgin. 2014. "A Qualitative Evaluation of a Conditional Cash Transfer Program in Turkey: The Beneficiaries' and Key Informants' Perspectives." *Journal of Social Service Research* 40 (1): 62–79.

CHAPTER 5

Bloom, D. 2010. "Programs and Policies to Assist High School Dropouts in the Transition to Adulthood." *The Future of Children* 20(1), 89–108.

Byrne, D. July, 2009. "Working Within a Complexity Frame of Reference–The Potential of Integrated Methods' for Understanding Transformation in a Complex Social System." Paper prepared by the CFSC Consortium for UNAIDS, 1–5. School of Applied Social Sciences, Durham University, UK.

Cartwright, N. 2010. "What Are Randomised Controlled Trials Good For?" *Philosophical Studies* 147 (1): 59.

Duflo, E. 2017. "The Economist as Plumber—Richard T. Ely Lecture." *American Economic Review* 107 (5): 1–26.

Dweck, C. S. 2006. *Mindset: The New Psychology of Success*. New York: Penguin Random House LLC.

Ramalingam, B. 2013. *Aid on the Edge of Chaos: Rethinking International Cooperation in a Complex World*. Oxford University Press.

Ramalingam, B., H. Jones, T. Reba, and J. Young. 2008. *Exploring the Science of Complexity: Ideas and Implications for Development and Humanitarian Efforts*, vol. 285. London: Overseas Development Institute.

Rodríguez-Planas, N. 2012a. "Longer-Term Impacts of Mentoring, Educational Services, and Learning Incentives: Evidence from a Randomized Trial in the United States." *American Economic Journal: Applied Economics* 4 (4): 121–39.

Rodriguez-Planas, N. 2012b. "Mentoring, Educational Services, and Incentives to Learn: What Do We Know about Them?" *Evaluation and Program Planning* 35(4): 481–90.

Rodriguez-Planas, N. 2014. "Do Youth Mentoring Programs Change the Perspectives and Improve the Life Opportunities of At-Risk Youth?" IZA World of Labor, 62.

Ungar, M., and L. Liebenberg. 2005. "Resilience across Cultures: The Mixed Methods Approach of the International Resilience Project." In *Handbook for Working with Children and Youth Pathways to Resilience across Cultures and Contexts*, edited by M. Ungar, 211–26. Thousand Oaks, CA: Sage.

UNICEF. 2012. *Turkey Country Study*. Global Initiative on Out-of-School Children.

CHAPTER 6

Bloom, D., S. L. Thompson, and R. Ivry. 2010. *Building a Learning Agenda around Disconnected Youth*. MDRC.

CEDEFOP. 2017. *VET Toolkit for Tackling Early Leaving*. http://www.cedefop.europa.eu/en/toolkits/vet-toolkit-tackling-early-leaving/intervene/intervention-approaches.

Dweck, C. S. 2006. *Mindset: The New Psychology of Success*. Penguin Random House LLC.

Murphy, K. L. 1989. "Turkey's Open Education Policy." *Educational Technology Research and Development* 37 (2): 122–23.

Rennie Center for Education Research and Policy. 2012. *Forgotten Youth: Re-Engaging Students through Dropout Recovery*." Cambridge, MA: Rennie Center for Education Research and Policy.

Rennie-Hill, L., J. Villano, M. Feist, N. Legters, J. Thomases, and P. Williams. 2014. "Bringing Students Back to the Center: A Resource Guide for Implementing and Enhancing Re-Engagement Centers for Out-of-School Youth." Prepared by The Millennium Group and U.S. Department of Education.

Reyna, R. 2011. *State Policies to Reengage Dropouts*. NGA Center for Best Practices.

Seccombe, K. 2002. "'Beating the Odds' versus 'Changing the Odds': Poverty, Resilience, and Family Policy." *Journal of Marriage and Family* 64 (2): 384–94.

Stayton, C. (n.d.). *Dropout Prevention and Recovery*. Washington, DC: American Youth Policy Forum. http://www.aypf.org/projects/briefs/DropoutPreventionRecovery.htm.

Te Riele, K. 2014. *Putting the Jigsaw Together: Flexible Learning Programs in Australia*. Final report. Melbourne: The Victoria Institute for Education, Diversity and Lifelong Learning.

ADDITIONAL WEB RESOURCES ON SOME REVIEWED PROGRAMS

http://www.projectuturn.net/#resources

http://ccp.jhu.edu/documents/Malawi%20Bridge%20I%20Outreadh%20flyer.pdf

http://www.gatewaytocollege.org

https://www.bostonpublicschools.org/domain/1389

https://www.givengain.com/c/usikostb/about/

https://www.unicef.org/infobycountry/uganda_52304.html

www.ingramcontent.com/pod-product-compliance
Lightning Source LLC
Chambersburg PA
CBHW082211300426
44117CB00016B/2753